CAREERS IN INFORMATION AND COMMUNICATION TECHNOLOGY

MNIKO SIMON MNIKO

ISBN: 9798390128602

DEDICATION

I dedicate this book to all the people who have supported me throughout my writing journey. I am grateful for your encouragement, feedback, and friendship. You have inspired me to pursue my passion and share my ideas with the world. Without you, this book would not have been possible. Thank you for believing in me and for being part of this adventure.

FOREWORD

Dear readers, I am pleased to introduce this comprehensive guide to the world of Information and Communication Technology (ICT) careers. This book is an excellent resource for anyone looking to pursue a career in ICT or transition into a new specialisation of ICT that is rapidly changing.

The Information and Communication Technology industry has proliferated and has become an integral part of our daily lives. The field encompasses a broad range of various, from specialisation and software development to data analysis, network management, and cybersecurity. This book provide an in-depth analysis of the different ICT specializations, the required skills and knowledge, and the career opportunities available in the industry.

One of the biggest challenges faced by students and professionals interested in ICT careers is choosing the right specialization. This book provides a comprehensive overview of the various ICT specializations available in the industry, including software development, cybersecurity, data analysis and networking. It is an essential resource for students looking to make informed decisions about their career paths and professionals seeking to upskill or transition to new roles.

The book's content has carefully curated to provide readers with the most up-to-date and accurate information about the field. Whether you are a student, a recent graduate, or a seasoned professional, this book is an invaluable resource for anyone looking to build a successful career in ICT.

I am confident that this book will provide readers with a comprehensive guide to the world of ICT and equip them with the knowledge and skills necessary to pursue successful careers in the industry. It is an excellent resource for anyone interested in the field of ICT, and I highly recommend it to students, professionals, and educators alike.

Best regards,

MNIKO SIMON

14/02/2023

PREFACE

The proliferation of computer technology has resulted in the emergence of various specializations in the field of Information and Communication Technology (ICT). However, students seeking admission to universities or technical colleges in ICT-related fields face difficulty selecting a specialization due to their limited knowledge and understanding of these fields. Additionally, parents and guardians lack adequate information about the criteria for choosing a profession that aligns with their children's interests and career aspirations.

Higher education institutions' ICT curricula are designed to equip students with broad skills rather than prepare them for specific technological areas. For example, a student studying for a bachelor's degree in computer science can specialize in networking, programming, database, graphics, or other fields depending on their preferred courses of study. However, this lack of clarity on the specialization could result in confusion and a sense of directionlessness among students. This book intends to provide prospective students in the ICT field with a comprehensive understanding of various specializations available in the market. The book explains the required skills and knowledge that a person must possess to become a professional in a particular ICT specialization. By understanding the skills and knowledge necessary for a specific specialization, students and parents can make informed decisions and enable students to focus on courses that align with their career aspirations.

The book is an excellent resource for students, parents, and educators who want to better understand the various ICT specializations available and how to prepare for a career in these fields. It is essential reading for anyone interested in pursuing a career in the ever-evolving field of ICT. Furthermore, the book could guide professionals looking to alter into other ICT specializations, providing them with the necessary knowledge and skills for success in their new roles.

MNIKO SIMON

23/02/2023

CONTENTS

ACKNOWLEDGMENTS

I want to express my most profound appreciation and gratitude to my beloved family, especially my wife Beatrice, my daughter Hellen, and my sons Denzel and Derrick, for their unwavering support, encouragement, and patience throughout the journey of writing this book.

Special thanks to my colleagues at the Informatics department for their invaluable inputs, guidance, and careful review that have helped shape this book into its current form. I would also like to thank my office mates at the Institute of Accountancy Arusha Dar es Salaam for their valuable advice, support, and encouragement during the writing process. Finally, I am thankful to individuals who contributed to this book in various ways, including those who provided inspiration, feedback, and assistance with research.

Lastly, I sincerely thank the Almighty for His blessings and guidance throughout this journey.

01
INTRODUCTION

Information and Communication Technology (ICT) has become an important sector in this era. Every continent, country, international organizations, companies, communities, group, family and individual are now aware of the significant roles played by ICT in our day-to-day life. Living in today's world without essential ICT skills is very difficult as automation keeps growing and technology becomes essential to every task humans perform.

The majority of Higher Learning Academic Institutions and Technical Colleges all over the world have included ICT among the programmes offered. Hence the increasing number of ICT professionals worldwide and this speciality continue to be narrowed to specific specializations which are becoming critical to the markets. This book will give vivid descriptions and knowledge of different ICT specializations and their current categories. It will further explain the knowledge required to attain the said ICT profession and the various jobs that will be performed by these professionals. This book will help ICT students, parents and communities be aware of different ICT professions available and will assist them in making informed decisions once they want to join colleges, higher learning institutions in ICT fields. The basic five ICT programmes which originate all specializations in ICT include Computer Science, Information Technology, Information Systems, Software Engineering and Computer Engineering.

From the above five programmes, various ICT specializations can be obtained; for the case of this book, 15 different professions will be explained.

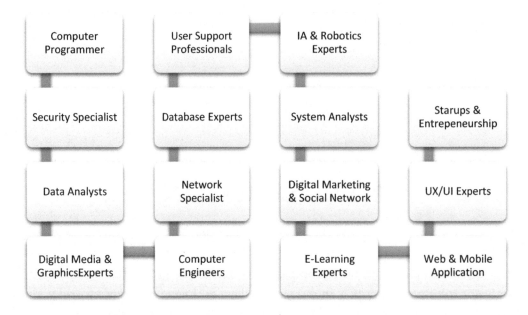

Figure 1 Different ICT Specializations

This book will give a detailed explanation of each specialization above, the required qualifications and expected duties to be performed will be elaborated in chapters.

Evolution of ICT

ICT is an umbrella term that encompasses a wide range of technologies used to process, transmit, and store information. ICT has profoundly impacted virtually every aspect of modern society, from how we communicate and work to how we access and share information.

The evolution of ICT can be traced back to the invention of the telegraph in the 19th century, which allowed for the rapid transmission of information over long distances. This was followed by the telephone, which allowed for real-time voice communication, and the development of radio and television, which allowed the transmission of audio and video signals over long distances.

The invention of the computer in the mid-20th century marked a significant turning point in the evolution of ICT. Computers were initially used primarily for scientific and military applications. However, they quickly became more widespread with the development of personal computers in the 1970s and 1980s. In addition, the internet, developed in the 1960s and 1970s as a way for researchers to share information, quickly became a global phenomenon in the 1990s, transforming how we communicate, access information, and do business.

In recent years, the evolution of ICT has accelerated, driven by rapid technological advancements, such as mobile devices, social media, cloud computing, artificial intelligence, and the Internet of Things (IoT). These technologies transform how we live and work, creating new opportunities and challenges for individuals, businesses, and society.

As the evolution of ICT continues, we will likely see even more profound changes in how we interact with technology and each other. New technologies such as virtual and augmented reality, quantum computing, and blockchain will likely play an increasingly important role in the evolution of ICT, enabling new forms of communication, collaboration, and information processing.

The evolution of ICT has been a fascinating and transformative journey, with many exciting opportunities and challenges along the way. As technology continues to evolve, we must stay up-to-date with the latest trends and developments and explore new ways of harnessing the power of ICT to drive innovation and progress in all aspects of our lives.

Historical overview of the development of ICT

The development of ICT is a story that spans centuries. From the earliest forms of communication and information processing to the advanced technologies of today, the evolution of ICT has revolutionized the way we live, work, and interact with each other.

The history of ICT can be traced back to the invention of the printing press by Johannes Gutenberg in 1440. This invention revolutionized the dissemination of information, enabling the mass production of books and other printed materials for the first time.

Over the next few centuries, various forms of communication technology were developed, including the telegraph, telephone, and radio. The telegraph, invented by Samuel Morse in 1837, allowed for rapidly transmitting messages over long distances using Morse code. The telephone, invented by Alexander Graham Bell in 1876, revolutionized real-time voice communication, while the radio, invented by Guglielmo Marconi in the late 19th century, allowed for the transmission of audio signals over long distances.

The development of electronic computers in the mid-20th century marked a significant turning point in the evolution of ICT. The first electronic computer, ENIAC, was built in 1945 and was used primarily for scientific and military applications. However, with the development of personal computers in the 1970s and 1980s, computers became more widespread and accessible to the general public. In addition, the invention of the internet in the 1960s and 1970s marked another significant milestone in the evolution of ICT. The Internet was developed initially as a way for researchers to share information. However, it quickly became a global phenomenon, transforming how we communicate, access information, and do business.

In the 1990s, the development of the World Wide Web, which allowed for creating and sharing web pages, led to a new era of online communication and commerce. The rise of mobile devices, social media, and cloud computing in the 21st century has further transformed the way we interact with technology and each other. Today, we are on the cusp of a new era of ICT, with emerging technologies such as artificial intelligence, the Internet of Things (IoT), and blockchain poised to revolutionize how we live and work in the coming decades.

The historical overview of the development of ICT is a story of innovation, creativity, and perseverance. From the printing press to the internet and beyond, the evolution of ICT has been driven by the human desire to communicate, share information, and solve problems. As we continue to explore the potential of emerging technologies, we must stay true to this spirit of innovation and continue to push the boundaries of what is possible with ICT.

The Impact of ICT on Society and the Economy

ICT has profoundly impacted society and the economy, transforming how we live, work, and interact with each other. Some of the ways ICT has impacted the community and the economy are that ICT has revolutionized communication, making it faster, easier, and more efficient. People can now communicate with each other from anywhere in the world in real-time through email, instant messaging, social media, and other online platforms. In addition, ICT has enabled people to access a wealth of information on a wide range of topics. For example, with the internet, people can easily access educational resources, news, research, and other information that was once difficult or impossible to obtain.

Also, ICT has made it possible for people to work more efficiently and effectively. With tools like email, instant messaging, and project management software, teams can collaborate from anywhere in the world in real time, increasing productivity and efficiency. Moreover, ICT has created new industries and job opportunities, such as software development, digital marketing, and e-commerce. It has also allowed people to work remotely, opening up new opportunities for freelancers and entrepreneurs.ICT has had a significant impact on healthcare, enabling the development of new treatments and therapies, improving patient outcomes, and enhancing the efficiency of healthcare delivery.ICT has transformed how we shop, with e-commerce accounting for a significant percentage of retail sales. Consumers can now shop online from anywhere worldwide and have products delivered right to their doorstep. While ICT has brought many benefits, it has also created new challenges, such as cybercrime, privacy concerns, and the digital divide between those without access to technology.

The impact of ICT on society and the economy has been significant and far-reaching. As we continue to explore the potential of emerging technologies, it is crucial to consider their social and economic implications and work to address any challenges that arise.

ICT and the Future of Work

ICT has become integral to our daily lives. In the present day, it is not easy to imagine a world without ICT, as it has revolutionized the way we communicate, work, learn, and interact with the world around us. With rapid technological advancements, ICT continues to evolve and shape our society. Here are some of the current trends and technologies in ICT:

1. Artificial Intelligence (AI): AI is the development of computer systems that can perform tasks that typically require human intelligence, such as visual perception, speech recognition, decision-making, and language translation. AI is used in various applications, including chatbots, virtual assistants, fraud detection, and autonomous vehicles.

2. Internet of Things (IoT): IoT is the interconnection of various devices, sensors, and software that allow them to communicate and exchange data. IoT is used in smart homes, healthcare monitoring, industrial automation, and smart cities.

3. Cloud Computing: Cloud computing delivers computing services, including servers, storage, and software, over the internet. It enables organizations to access and use computing resources on demand without physical infrastructure.

4. Blockchain Technology: Blockchain is a decentralized, secure, and transparent digital ledger that records transactions and maintains data in a tamper-proof manner. It is used in various applications, including cryptocurrencies, supply chain management, and identity verification.

5. 5G Technology: 5G is the fifth-generation mobile network that provides faster data transfer rates, lower latency, and increased capacity than its predecessors. It enables faster and more reliable internet connectivity, which is essential for developing new technologies such as autonomous vehicles, smart cities, and augmented reality.

6. Cybersecurity: With the increasing use of ICT, cybersecurity has become a significant concern for individuals, organizations, and governments. Cyber threats such as hacking, malware, and phishing attacks

can result in the loss of valuable data and damage reputation. Therefore, cybersecurity measures such as encryption, firewalls, and multi-factor authentication are crucial in protecting sensitive information.

7. Virtual and Augmented Reality: Virtual Reality (VR) and Augmented Reality (AR) allow users to immerse themselves in a simulated environment or enhance their perception of reality. VR is used in gaming, education, and training, while AR is used in marketing, retail, and navigation.

8. Edge Computing: Edge computing is a distributed computing model that processes data closer to the source rather than sending it to a central server. It is used in applications that require low latency, such as self-driving cars, smart grids, and industrial automation.

9. Big Data Analytics: Big Data analytics analyses large and complex data sets to uncover hidden patterns, insights, and trends. It is used in various applications, including business intelligence, healthcare, and finance.

ICT has transformed how we live and work and continues to evolve rapidly. The above technologies and trends are just a few examples of how ICT changes our world. As we move forward, it is essential to embrace these technologies and leverage them for the betterment of society. However, we must also be mindful of their potential risks and use them responsibly and ethically.

Globalization and ICT

ICT has had a profound impact on the nature of work, which is expected to continue in the future. With the rapid technological advancements, many traditional job roles are being automated or augmented, creating new career opportunities in the ICT sector. Below are some of how ICT is changing job roles and creating new career opportunities:

- Automation: is the use of technology to perform tasks that humans previously did. As a result, many routine and repetitive job roles are being automated, creating a shift towards more creative and complex job roles. This shift creates new opportunities for workers to develop machine learning, artificial intelligence, and robotics skills.

- Remote Work: ICT has enabled remote work, allowing employees to work from anywhere in the world with an internet connection. This shift towards remote work has created opportunities for workers in software development, digital marketing, and customer service.

- Digital Transformation: Digital transformation uses technology to transform business processes and operations. This shift towards digital transformation creates opportunities for workers in data analysis, cybersecurity, and software development.

- Augmented Reality (AR) and Virtual Reality (VR): AR and VR allow users to immerse themselves in a simulated environment or enhance their perception of reality. These technologies create new job roles in gaming, education, and training.

- Data analytics analyses large and complex data sets to uncover hidden patterns, insights, and trends. This shift towards data analytics creates new job roles in data analysis, business intelligence, and artificial intelligence.

- Cybersecurity: With the increasing use of ICT, cybersecurity has become a significant concern for individuals, organizations, and governments. The shift towards cybersecurity creates new job roles such as cybersecurity analyst, penetration tester, and security consultant.

ICT is changing the nature of work and creating new career opportunities. As a result, workers must be prepared to adapt to the changing job market and develop new skills in areas such as automation, digital transformation, data analytics, and cybersecurity. As we move forward, it is essential to embrace these changes and leverage the opportunities created by ICT for the betterment of society.

The intersection of ICT with other emerging technologies

The convergence of ICT with other emerging technologies, such as biotechnology and nanotechnology, creates new possibilities for innovation and growth. Here are some of how ICT is intersecting with these emerging technologies:

- Biotechnology: Biotechnology uses living organisms, cells, and biological processes to create new products and services. ICT's intersection with biotechnology creates new possibilities in personalized medicine, genetic engineering, and bioprocessing. In addition, ICT in biotechnology enables researchers to collect, analyze, and share large amounts of data, accelerating the pace of research and development.
- Nanotechnology: Nanotechnology is manipulating matter at the nanoscale, creating materials with new and unique properties. The intersection of ICT with nanotechnology creates new possibilities in nanoelectronics, nanomedicine, and nanomaterials. ICT in nanotechnology enables researchers to design, simulate, and test materials at the nanoscale, accelerating research and development.
- Robotics: Robotics is using machines to perform tasks that humans previously did. The intersection of ICT with robotics creates new possibilities in areas such as automation, manufacturing, and healthcare. ICT in robotics enables the development of more intelligent and autonomous robots capable of performing complex tasks with greater accuracy and efficiency.
- Artificial Intelligence (AI): AI uses algorithms and machine learning to simulate intelligent behaviour. The intersection of ICT with AI creates new possibilities in areas such as automation, data analytics, and natural language processing. ICT in AI enables the development of more intelligent and autonomous systems capable of making decisions and learning from data.

The intersection of ICT with other emerging technologies creates new possibilities for innovation and growth. As we move forward, it is essential to continue to explore these intersections and leverage the opportunities created by these technologies for the betterment of society. However, we must also be mindful of the potential risks and ensure we use these technologies responsibly and ethically.

The potential risks and benefits of ICT development and adoption.

ICT has transformed the world in once unimaginable ways. ICT has brought numerous benefits to society, from connecting people across the globe to automating tasks and improving productivity. However, with ICT's continued development and adoption, potential risks must also be considered. Some of the potential risks and benefits of continued ICT development and adoption:

Potential Risks:

1. Cybersecurity: The increasing reliance on ICT has made cybersecurity a significant concern for individuals, organizations, and governments. Cyber threats like hacking, phishing, and identity theft can lead to financial loss, reputational damage, and even physical harm.

2. Privacy: The collection, storage, and use of personal data by organizations and governments raise privacy concerns. Misusing personal data can lead to identity theft, discrimination, and other harm.

3. Job Displacement: The automation of tasks through ICT can lead to job displacement, particularly for those in low-skilled and routine-based jobs. This displacement can lead to economic and social inequality.

4. Digital Divide: The uneven distribution of ICT resources across different populations and regions can exacerbate existing social and economic inequalities.

Potential Benefits:

1. Productivity: ICT can improve productivity by automating routine tasks, enabling remote work, and facilitating collaboration.

2. Innovation: ICT can enable new forms of innovation, such as crowdsourcing, open innovation, and collaboration.

3. Access to Information: ICT can provide access to information, education, and healthcare services to people without access.

4. Economic Growth: ICT can contribute to economic growth by creating new industries and jobs and improving the efficiency of existing initiatives.

The ongoing development and adoption of ICT offer opportunities and challenges. To fully exploit the potential benefits and minimize the associated risks, ensuring that ICT is developed and adopted responsibly and ethically is imperative. This entails addressing issues related to cybersecurity and privacy, minimizing the negative impact on employment, bridging the digital divide, and fostering innovation and economic growth.

02
DATABASE EXPERTS

Databases have become the backbone of all computerized systems. For example, all automated systems must have a special place to store data. These data are generated by the operating system, such as log file data and user inputs that occurred through clicks or filled forms. Database Management Systems is special software that supports storing, retrieving, and running various queries on data. The Importance of databases paves the way for different giant companies to invest in database businesses, including Oracle, Microsoft and IBM. This is why the database has become a particular area in ICT that needs specialists.

Specializations in Database

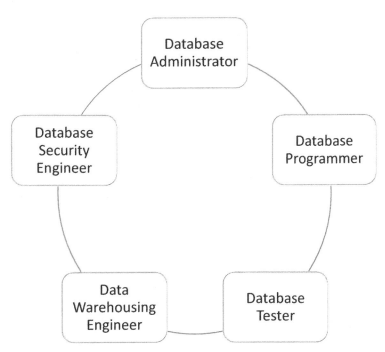

Figure 2:Different Specializations in Database

Database Administrator(DBA)- This is the head of data, controlling and managing database systems, and must have strong knowledge of the database engine used. They pay attention to the day-to-day performance of the database and ensure data is secured and out of threat. They should be conversant in a structured query language and possess strong database maintenance skills. Moreover, DBA is responsible for the installation, configuration, and maintenance of a database system

Database administrators are required in a variety of industries and areas, including:

- IT departments of organizations of all sizes
- Government agencies
- Healthcare organizations
- Financial institutions
- E-commerce and retail companies
- Education and research institutions
- Telecommunications companies
- Media and entertainment companies
- Energy and utility companies

DBAs are responsible for designing, implementing, maintaining, and managing databases, ensuring they are secure, efficient, and reliable.

Database Programmer/Developer- these are database expertise with solid knowledge of methods and languages used to develop databases. They must possess the highest SQL skills and be able to create views, functions or stored procedures to guide other database users. Database programmers must have other data manipulation languages and skills like Python and R. Essentially, these are responsible for designing and implementing database systems, creating and maintaining the database schema, and writing SQL queries.

Database Tester- these are responsible for testing the functionality and performance of a database system to ensure it meets the requirements. Some responsibilities for this position includes install, configuring, tuning, and troubleshooting database systems in both on-premise and cloud deployment. They write test plans with the ability to ensure proper coverage and perform risk-based regression testing.They participate in the business requirements and software development life cycles related to testing activities. They also evaluates, configure or administer DBMS products to match user requirements with system capabilities.

Data Warehousing Engineer – these are responsible for the design and development of data warehousing systems to support data analysis and reporting. A Data Warehousing Engineer is a professional responsible for designing, building, and maintaining data warehousing systems, which are large-scale databases that store and manage large amounts of structured and semi-structured data. This data supports decision-making, analysis, and reporting in organizations. Data Warehousing Engineers typically have a strong background in database management and computer science and experience working with data warehousing technologies and methodologies, such as extract, transform, load (ETL) processes, data modelling, and reporting tools. Certification programs for Data Warehousing Engineers may vary by vendor and technology, but some popular certifications include

- Oracle Certified Professional, Data Warehouse Administrator
- Microsoft Certified: Azure Data Engineer Associate
- Cloudera Certified Data Warehouse Administrator (CCDWA)
- Amazon Web Services (AWS) Certified Data Analytics – Specialty

These certifications demonstrate a professional's expertise in specific data warehousing technologies and tools and can be valuable for individuals seeking to advance their careers in this field.

Database Security Engineers – these are responsible for ensuring the security and privacy of a database system and its data. A Database Security Engineer is a professional responsible for ensuring the safety of an organization's database systems. This includes implementing security measures to protect sensitive data, such as personal, financial, and confidential business information, from unauthorized access and theft. Database Security Engineers possess a robust computer science and database administration foundation and expertise in database security methodologies and industry standards. Their work involves handling different database systems, including relational databases, NoSQL databases, and cloud databases. Their key responsibility is establishing and sustaining security measures such as firewalls, encryption protocols, access controls, and audit trails.

Certification programs for Database Security Engineers may vary by vendor and technology, but some popular certifications include the following:

- Oracle Certified Professional, MySQL 5.6 Database Administrator
- Certified Information Systems Security Professional (CISSP)
- Certified Ethical Hacker (CEH)
- Certified Information Systems Auditor (CISA)

These certifications demonstrate a professional's expertise in specific database security technologies and best practices. As a result, they can be valuable for individuals seeking to advance their careers in this field.

Required Skills for database expert.

Looking at the explained roles above, database experts must have different skill sets to make them fit for database roles. However, the skills required may vary depending on the organization and the nature of the work they are required to perform. The following are some common skills that must be possessed by anyone who specializes in databases. Database experts must have the following:

Strong knowledge of database management systems (e.g. Oracle, MySQL, MS SQL Server and PostgreSQL) with advanced SQL skills, including optimization, data modelling, and database design and normalization principles.He/she must have enough knowledge in data warehousing, data mining, and business intelligence. To be comfortable, one must know programming languages like Java, Python, and C# for database integration and automation, familiarity with database security, backup and recovery, and disaster recovery planning. Due to the advancement of cloud computing, database expert is expected to know about cloud-based databases and their management. Knowledge of big data technologies (e.g. Hadoop, NoSQL databases)and ability to effectively manage large amounts of data and ensure its accuracy, completeness and consistency. Familiarity with data visualization tools such as Tableau, Power BI, and QlikView are among the critical skills for database experts.

Moreover, database experts must have other skills, such as understanding data governance and data management best practices. Experience with data migration and warehousing, a good understanding of database scalability, performance tuning, and optimization techniques.Experience with Agile and DevOps methodologies. With excellent problem-solving and analytical skills.

To work better in the development team, experts in databases are expected to have strong interpersonal, communication and leadership skills to work with cross-functional teams. Good problem-solving and analytical skills also must possess excellent communication skills

Certifications in Database

A database certification is a professional recognition that indicates proficiency in designing, implementing, and managing database systems. Some popular database certifications include

Table 1:Database Certifications

Oracle Certified Professional
An Oracle Certified Professional is skilled in Oracle technologies. This level of certification validates an advanced understanding of Oracle concepts and skills and experience applying these in real-world scenarios. Prepares you for Administrator, Developer, Implementer, Consultant, and Architect roles. Recognizes these skills: Focused on advanced skills with a strong foundation in technology.
Oracle Certified Master
The Oracle Certified Master credential is the pinnacle of Oracle Certifications. It demonstrates the ability to perform hands-on tasks that require advanced problem-solving skills. Reaching this level of certification usually requires multiple certifications and training along the way. This certification validates deep experience with Oracle Technologies and an ability to complete very advanced tasks
MySQL Database Administrator
MySQL is the world's most popular open-source database. Whether you are a beginner or an experienced user, a MySQL database administrator, or An Oracle Certified Professional, MySQL 8.0 Database Administrator credential acknowledges that the candidate has the required knowledge of the MySQL architecture and possesses the skills to install and configure MySQL database. This certification shows that the professional has the needed skills to monitor, maintain, and secure MySQL databases. It also demonstrates the mastery of the professional on how to optimize query performance, implement backup and recovery strategies, and implement high availability techniques. Microsoft Certified: Azure Database Administrator Associate
IBM Certified Database Administrator – Db2
The IBM Certified Database Administrator is the lead database administrator (DBA) for the DB2 product on the z/OS operating system. This individual has significant experience as a DBA and extensive knowledge of DB2, specifically the new features and functionality related to version 11. This person is capable of performing the intermediate to advanced tasks related to database design and implementation, operation and recovery, security and auditing, performance, and installation and migration/upgrades specific to the z/OS operating system.

Free Online Courses on Database

Many free online courses are available for those looking to improve their database skills or learn about the database. The following are a few popular options.

Table 2:Free Online Courses on Database

SN	INSTITUTION	COURSE NAME	LEVEL AND DURATION	LINK
1	University of Michigan	PostgreSQL for Everybody	Intermediate · Specialization · 3-6 Months	https://www.coursera.org/specializations/postgresql-for-everybody
2	Universidad Nacional Autónoma de México	Database systems	Intermediate · Specialization · 3-6 Months	https://www.coursera.org/specializations/database-systems
3	Coursera Project Network	Introduction to Relational Database and SQL	Beginner · Guided Project · Less Than 2 Hours	https://www.coursera.org/projects/introduction-to-relational-database-and-sql
4	IBM Skills Network	IBM Data Analyst	Beginner · Professional Certificate · 3-6 Months	https://www.coursera.org/professional-certificates/ibm-data-analyst
5	Google	Google Data Analytics	Beginner · Professional Certificate · 3-6 Months	https://www.coursera.org/professional-certificates/google-data-analytics
6	University of California, Davis	SQL for Data Science	Beginner · Course · 1-4 Weeks	https://www.coursera.org/learn/sql-for-data-science

Available free resources on the database

There are several free resources available for database experts to enhance their skills and knowledge:

 Online forums and communities-Sites like Stack Overflow, Reddit, and Quora provide a wealth of information and support for database professionals

 Open source databases:-Open source databases like MySQL, PostgreSQL, and MongoDB provide a great opportunity for database professionals to learn about different database technologies and gain hands-on experience with them

 Technical blogs and websites-Websites like DBA StackExchange and Percona provide up-to-date information, tips, and best practices for database professionals.

 Documentation and manuals:-Most database management systems have detailed documentation and manuals that provide in-depth information on their features, usage, and administration

 Webinars and podcasts-Webinars and podcasts provide an opportunity to learn from industry experts and stay up-to-date with the latest developments in the field of databases

 Conferences and events: -Attending database-related conferences and events provides an opportunity for database professionals to network, learn about new developments, and stay up-to-date with the latest trends and technologies.

Figure 3:Resources for Database Experts

These resources can help database professionals to improve their skills, stay informed, and stay current with the latest trends and technologies in the field of databases.

Anticipated Salaries for Database Experts

The expected salary for a database administrator can vary greatly depending on several factors, including:

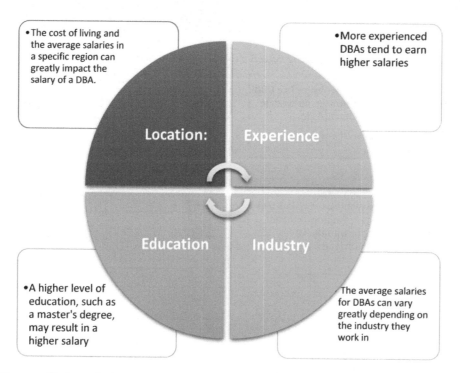

Figure 4:Factors affecting salaries

As of 2021, the average salary for a database administrator in the United States is approximately $87,000 annually. However, this figure can range from $60,000 to $140,000 or more, depending on the abovementioned factors.

The future of database

The demand for database professionals is expected to continue to grow in the future, driven by the increasing amount of data being generated and the need for organizations to store, manage, and analyze this data. The following trends are expected to shape the future of the database career:

◎ **Cloud databases:** The adoption of cloud computing is expected to continue to grow, leading to an increased demand for database professionals with experience in cloud databases.

- ⊙ **Big data:** The increasing amount of data organisations generate is driving the need for big data solutions, creating opportunities for database professionals with expertise in big data technologies.
- ⊙ **NoSQL databases**: The popularity of NoSQL databases is expected to continue to grow as organizations seek more flexible and scalable solutions for storing and managing data.
- ⊙ **Data security:** With the increasing amount of data being stored, the importance of data security is also expected to increase, leading to a growing demand for database professionals with expertise in data security.
- ⊙ **Artificial Intelligence and Machine Learning:** The integration of Artificial Intelligence and Machine Learning with databases is expected to increase, creating new opportunities for database professionals with experience in these areas.

Statistics on Database

Here are some statistics related to database experts:

Demand	Education	Gender
According to the U.S. Bureau of Labor Statistics, the demand for database administrators is expected to grow 11% from 2019 to 2029, faster than the average for all occupations.	A bachelor's degree in computer science, management information systems, or a related field is typically required for a career as a database administrator. Some employers may also require a master's degree or certification.	According to data from the National Center for Women & Information Technology, the field of database administration has a low representation of women, with women making up only 24% of the workforce in this field.

Figure 5:Statistics Related to Database

These statistics provide a general overview of the field of database, and the actual numbers may vary depending on factors such as location, experience, and company size.

03
SPECIALIST IN COMPUTER NETWORKING

Computer networking is important because it allows computers and other devices to communicate and share resources, such as data, printers, and the internet connection. This enables users to access information, collaborate on projects, and share files with others quickly, reliably, and efficiently, regardless of their physical location. Networking also helps improve productivity and increase efficiency by enabling seamless communication between devices and facilitating the sharing of information and resources. Additionally, computer networking plays a crucial role in supporting the growth and development of various industries and organizations

Different Roles in computer networking

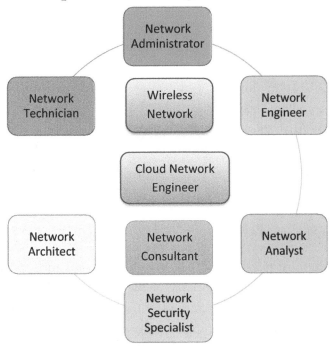

Figure 6:Diffferent Roles in Computer Networking

There are various specializations in computer networking depending on company size or project where a professional is required. However, their responsibilities may be the same sometimes; some professions in computer networking are as follows:

Network Administrator: is responsible for designing, implementing, and maintaining a company's computer network systems. A Network Administrator is responsible for computer network maintenance, configuration, and reliable operation. Their job duties include managing network security, ensuring the high availability of network resources, implementing network policies, and monitoring network performance. In addition, network Administrators work with network hardware, software, and communication protocols to maintain the smooth operation of the network and resolve any issues that arise.

Network Engineer: is responsible for designing and implementing computer networks and performing network troubleshooting and optimization. A Network Engineer is a professional who develops, implements, and maintains an organisation's computer networks. They are responsible for ensuring the stable and secure operation of the network infrastructure, which includes hardware and software components such as routers, switches, firewalls, and servers. Network Engineers use their technical knowledge and experience to plan, design, and implement new network solutions and upgrade existing networks. They also troubleshoot network problems and provide technical support to end users. Network Engineers often work closely with other IT professionals, such as System Administrators, Database Administrators, and Software Developers, to support the overall IT goals of the organization.

Network Analyst: monitors and analyzes network performance and identifies and resolves network issues. A Network Analyst is a professional who analyses, plans and supports an organization's computer network. Their job duties involve monitoring network performance, identifying and resolving network problems, and analyzing network data to make recommendations for improving network efficiency. Network Analysts use specialized software and tools to collect and analyze network performance data. They work with Network Administrators and Network Engineers to implement solutions that enhance network performance. They also assist in planning network upgrades and expansions and work with other IT professionals to ensure that the network infrastructure meets the organisation's needs. Network Analysts play a crucial role in ensuring the stability and security of an organization's network.

Network Security Specialist: is responsible for securing a company's network systems and implementing security measures and technologies. A Network Security Specialist is a professional responsible for protecting an organization's computer network from unauthorized access and potential security threats. Their duties include implementing and maintaining security measures such as firewalls, intrusion detection systems, and encryption technologies to secure the network and its data. Network Security Specialists also monitor network activity for signs of security breaches and respond to security incidents. In addition, they work with Network Administrators and Network Engineers to ensure that security policies and procedures are integrated into the network design and operation. Network Security Specialists stay up-to-date with the latest security technologies and trends. They may be called upon to conduct security assessments, provide security training to end-users, and conduct regular security audits. Their primary goal is to ensure an organisation's critical information assets' confidentiality, integrity, and availability.

Network Architect: is responsible for the overall design and planning of a company's network systems. A Network Architect is a professional who designs and oversees the implementation of an organization's computer network. They work with senior management to align the network architecture with the overall business strategy and to ensure that the network meets the current and future needs of the organization. Network Architects are responsible for creating high-level designs and specifying the hardware, software, and communication protocols required to implement the network. They also oversee the implementation of network projects, ensuring that the network is deployed according to the design and meets quality standards. Network Architects often work with Network Administrators and Network Engineers to troubleshoot complex network problems and to implement network upgrades and expansions. They play a critical role in ensuring that the network infrastructure is scalable, secure, and capable of meeting the organisation's changing needs.

Network Technician: is responsible for installing, configuring and maintaining network systems. A Network Technician is a professional responsible for installing, configuring, and maintaining computer networks. Their duties include installing network hardware and software, configuring network devices such as routers, switches, and firewalls, and providing technical support to end-users. Network Technicians work with Network Administrators and Network Engineers to resolve network issues and upgrade the network infrastructure. They are responsible for ensuring the stability and reliability of the network and for providing first-level support to end-users. Network Technicians may also be involved in installing and configuring network security systems, and they may train end-users on network usage and best practices. They are critical in ensuring the network is available and functioning effectively for the end users.

Network Consultant: provides expert advice and assistance to companies on their network systems and infrastructure. A Network Consultant is a professional who provides expert advice and support to organizations regarding their computer networks. They assess the client's current network infrastructure and provide recommendations for improvement. Network Consultants work with clients to understand their business needs and to develop customized solutions that meet their unique requirements. They also assist with the implementation of network projects and provide ongoing support and maintenance. Network Consultants bring a high level of technical expertise and industry knowledge to the table. They may work with various technologies and vendors to provide the best possible solutions for their clients. They may work independently or as part of a consulting firm and be engaged on a project basis or as a long-term strategic advisor to the client. The ultimate goal of a Network Consultant is to help organizations maximize the value of their network investments and to ensure the stability, security, and efficiency of their networks.

Wireless Network Engineer: specializes in wireless network systems, including Wi-Fi and cellular networks. A Wireless Network Engineer is a professional who designs, implements, and maintains wireless computer networks. They are responsible for ensuring the stable and secure operation of wireless network infrastructure, which includes wireless access points, controllers, and other wireless components. Wireless Network Engineers use their technical knowledge and experience to plan, design, and implement wireless network solutions and to upgrade existing networks. They also troubleshoot wireless network problems and provide technical support to end users. Wireless Network Engineers work closely with other IT professionals, such as Network Administrators, Network Engineers, and System Administrators, to support the overall IT goals of the organization. They must stay up-to-date with the latest wireless technologies and trends and deeply understand wireless network security best practices. The ultimate goal of a Wireless Network Engineer is to ensure the efficient and effective operation of an organization's wireless network.

Cloud Network Engineer: specializes in cloud computing and network systems, responsible for designing and implementing cloud network infrastructure. A Cloud Network Engineer is a professional who designs, implements, and maintains cloud-based computer networks. They are responsible for ensuring the stable and secure operation of cloud network infrastructure, which includes cloud-based virtual network components, firewalls, load balancers, and other network components. Cloud Network Engineers use their technical knowledge and experience to plan, design, and implement cloud network solutions and to upgrade existing networks. They also troubleshoot cloud network problems and provide technical support to end-users. Cloud Network Engineers work closely with other IT professionals, such as Cloud Administrators, Network Administrators, and System Administrators, to support the overall IT goals of the organization. They must stay up-to-date with the latest cloud technologies and trends and deeply understand cloud network security best practices. The ultimate goal of a Cloud Network Engineer is to ensure the efficient and effective operation of an organization's cloud-based network infrastructure.

In all of the roles above, the specific responsibilities and qualifications for each job may vary depending on the organization and industry

Required skills for network experts

A computer network expert typically requires different skills to perform their duties among skills that are vital, including network architecture and design skills. They must understand different network topologies, protocols and technologies. Should have the ability to configure, manage and troubleshoot routers and switches.Proficiency in the Transmission Control Protocol/Internet Protocol and subnetting concepts.Knowledge of security technologies such as firewalls, VPNs, and intrusion detection/prevention systems. Due to the rise of cloud computing, network experts should be familiar with cloud computing platforms and infrastructure and understand virtualization technologies such as VMWare and Hyper-V. Knowledge of different operating systems and their networking components will have an excellent advantage for a network expert. Moreover, they must be able to automate network tasks using scripting languages such as Python and Perl.

Other general skills required include good communication and collaboration skills to work with teams and clients. Strong problem-solving and critical thinking skills to diagnose and resolve network issues

Certifications in Networking.

These are widely recognized certifications in computer networking

Cisco Certified Network Associate (CCNA)

CCNA certification proves you have what it takes to navigate the ever-changing landscape of IT. CCNA exam covers networking fundamentals, IP services, security fundamentals, automation and programmability. Designed for agility and versatility, CCNA validates that you have the skills required to manage and optimize today's most advanced networks. No formal prerequisites, but one or more years of experience implementing and administering Cisco solutions is recommended.

The CCNA training course and exam give you the foundation to advance your career. When you certify with Cisco, you are living proof of the standard and rigour businesses recognize and trust to meet and exceed market demands.

CompTIA Network+

CompTIA Network+ helps develop a career in IT infrastructure, covering troubleshooting, configuring, and managing networks.CompTIA Network+ validates the technical skills needed to securely establish, maintain and troubleshoot the critical networks that businesses rely on. Unlike other vendor-specific networking certifications, CompTIA Network+ prepares candidates to support networks on any platform. CompTIA Network+ is the only certification that covers the specific skills that network professionals need. Other certifications are so broad, they don't cover the hands-on skills and precise knowledge required in today's networking environments.CompTIA Network+ features flexible training options, including self-paced learning, live online training, custom training and labs to advance the career development of IT professionals in network administration

CompTIA Network+ is a vendor-neutral certification that validates the skills and knowledge of network technicians. It certifies that individuals have the skills to design, configure, manage, and troubleshoot network systems. The Network+ certification covers a wide range of topics related to networking, including network design, security, and troubleshooting. It also covers the basics of network infrastructure, including cabling, switches, routers, firewalls, and more advanced topics, such as virtualization and cloud computing.CompTIA Network+ is considered an entry-level certification for network technicians. However, it is also helpful for individuals who work in related fields, such as system administrators, security professionals, and IT managers.

To become CompTIA Network+ certified, individuals must pass a certification exam. The exam covers a wide range of topics related to network systems. It requires individuals to demonstrate their knowledge and skills in real-world scenarios. Having a CompTIA Network+ certification can be beneficial for individuals seeking to advance their careers in the field of networking. In addition, it demonstrates to employers that an individual has a solid foundation in networking and the skills necessary to support and manage network systems.

Certified Wireless Network Professional (CWNP)

CWNP, offer enterprise wireless certifications for entry-level professionals up to seasoned network experts. Each certification level is designed to benchmark your deepening understanding of RF technologies and applications of wireless networks.CWNP employs authorized training providers called CWNP Learning Centers to deliver instructor-led, video, and online LIVE training towards CWNP certifications. CWNP Learning Centers offer global training using the official CWNP curriculum taught by CWNT-certified instructors.CWNP publishes videos, white papers, blogs, and other materials that assist the networker in learning Wi-Fi technologies and preparing for CWNP exams.

Juniper Networks Certified Internet Associate (JNCIA)

The JNCIA -Junos certification is designed for networking professionals with beginner-intermediate networking knowledge. The written exam verifies your understanding of the core functionality of the Juniper Networks Junos OS. In addition, because JNCIA-Junos provides a core understanding of the Juniper Networks core operating system, it is the baseline certification for multiple certification tracks. These certifications test different networking aspects, such as network design, network security, wireless networking, cloud computing, and Linux networking, among others.

Areas where network experts are required

Network experts are in high demand in many industries and organizations, including Information technology (IT) departments. IT departments of large organizations require network experts to design, implement, and maintain their network infrastructure. Telecommunications companies also need network experts to design, build and maintain communication networks, including voice and data networks. Financial services companies need network experts to ensure the secure and efficient transfer of financial data. The healthcare industry involves network experts to manage the secure transfer of sensitive patient information between healthcare providers, insurance companies, and government agencies. Government agencies require network experts to design and maintain secure communication networks for critical operations. Educational institutions need network experts to design and maintain their networks to support e-learning and other technology-based initiatives. Retail and e-commerce companies require network experts to manage their networks for secure and efficient transactions. These are just a few examples of the many industries and organizations that require the services of network experts. The demand for network experts is expected to continue to grow as organizations increasingly rely on technology to support their operations

Expected salary for network experts.

The salary for computer network experts, also known as network engineers, can vary widely depending on several factors such as industry, location, experience, and education. According to data from the U.S. Bureau of Labor Statistics, the median annual salary for network and computer systems administrators was $84,810 as of May 2020. The salary range for network engineers can vary significantly based on factors such as industry and experience. For example, network engineers working in the telecommunications industry often earn higher salaries than those in other industries. Similarly, those with more experience or specialized certifications can command higher salaries than those just starting in the field.

In addition, location can play a big role in determining a network engineer's salary. Areas with a high cost of living or a large concentration of technology companies often offer higher salaries than other areas. For example, network engineers working in the San Francisco Bay Area or New York City generally earn higher salaries than those working in smaller cities or rural areas

Education can also impact a network engineer's salary. Those with advanced degrees such as a master's or doctorate in computer science or a related field may command higher salaries than those with just a bachelor's degree. While the median annual wage for network and computer systems administrators is around $84,000, the salary range for network engineers can vary widely based on industry, location, experience, and education.

Available free course online on computer networking,

There are several free online courses available for those interested in learning about computer networking

Table 3: Available free course online on computer networking

SN	INSTITUTION	COURSE NAME	LEVEL	LINK
1	University of Colorado System	Computer Communications Specialization	Intermediate Specialization 3-6 Months	https://www.coursera.org/specializations/computer-communications#about
2	Yonsei University	Introduction to TCP/IP	Beginner · Course · 1-3 Months	https://www.coursera.org/learn/tcpip
3	Google Career certificates	The Bits and Bytes of Computer Networking	Beginner · Course · 1-3 Months	https://www.coursera.org/learn/computer-networking
4	University of Colorado System	Fundamentals of Network Communication	Beginner · Course · 1-3 Months	https://www.coursera.org/learn/fundamentals-network-communications
5	IBM	Networking and Storage Essentials	Introductory :4 weeks:4–6 hours per week	https://www.edx.org/course/introduction-to-networking-and-storage?index=product&queryID=97b301c259019e0f55ba7df1539c740f&position=1

These free online courses can provide a good starting point for those interested in learning about computer networking and can help individuals determine if they would like to pursue further education in this field

Statistics on Computer Networks.

According to the U.S. Bureau of Labor Statistics, the demand for network and computer systems administrators is expected to grow 5% from 2019 to 2029, faster than the average for all occupations. As of 2021, the median salary for network and computer systems administrators in the United States is approximately $90,070 per year, according to the U.S. Bureau of Labor Statistics. A bachelor's degree in computer science, management information systems, or a related field is typically required for a network and computer systems administrator career. Some employers may also require a master's degree or certification. According to data from the National Center for Women & Information Technology, the network and computer systems administration field has a low representation of women, with women making up only 24% of the workforce in this field. The highest-paying industries for network and computer systems administrators are computer systems design and related services, finance and insurance, and health care. These statistics provide a general overview of network and computer systems administration, and the actual numbers may vary depending on factors such as location, experience, and company size.

The future of computer networking

The future of computer networking is expected to be shaped by several emerging technologies and trends, such as Software-defined networking (SDN), which aims to simplify network management and increase network flexibility by using software to control and configure network devices. This technology is expected to become more widespread in the future as organizations look for ways to improve their networks. Also, the growth of 5G networks is the next generation of wireless networks and is expected to offer faster speeds, lower latency, and improved network coverage. The widespread adoption of 5G networks is expected to have a significant impact on the future of computer networking. The Internet of Things (IoT) growth is expected to drive the demand for new networking technologies and solutions. Network experts will need to be able to design and manage networks that can handle the massive amounts of data generated by IoT devices.

Moreover, Cloud computing is expected to grow in popularity and will require network experts to design and maintain networks that can support cloud computing applications. In contrast, the growing threat of cyber attacks is expected to drive the demand for network experts with cybersecurity expertise. These are just a few of the many factors that will shape the future of computer networking. Network experts who stay up-to-date with the latest technologies and trends will be in high demand as organizations continue to rely on technology to support their operations.

04
SPECIALIST IN COMPUTER SECURITY

Computer security protects computer systems and networks from unauthorized access, theft, damage, and disruption. Computer security is essential because it protects sensitive information and systems from unauthorized access, theft, damage, or disruption. This includes personal and financial information, intellectual property, government and organizational secrets, and critical infrastructure. Without proper security measures, individuals and organizations are at risk of financial loss, reputational damage, and even national security threats. Additionally, as our reliance on technology continues to grow, the importance of computer security will only increase

Computer security aims to ensure confidentiality means keeping sensitive information secret from unauthorized parties. Integrity protects against unauthorized modification of data. Availability ensures that authorized users have access to the resources they need when they need them. Authentication is verifying the identity of a user before granting access to resources and authorization, which refers to controlling what actions a user can perform once they have been authenticated. To meet all the above standards, we must have someone responsible for security issues within organizations or companies

Specializations in Computer Security

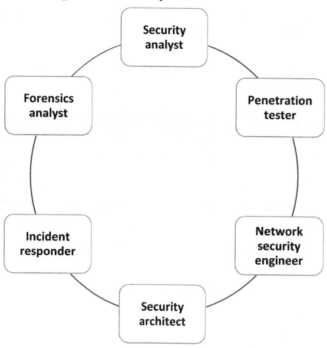

Figure 7 Specializations in Computer Security

- ◎ **Security analyst:** A security analyst is a professional who is responsible for evaluating and identifying potential threats to an organization's information systems, data, and assets. They perform security assessments, monitor security systems, analyze security data and events, and recommend solutions to improve security posture. Their goal is to prevent, detect and respond to cyber security incidents, protecting the organization from data breaches and unauthorized access.

- ◎ **Penetration tester:** A penetration tester is a security professional who performs simulated cyber attacks on computer systems, networks, or web applications to identify and exploit vulnerabilities. The goal of penetration testing is to simulate real-world attacks and assess an organization's defence mechanisms, allowing the identification and remediation of security weaknesses before they can be exploited by malicious actors. Penetration testers use a combination of manual and automated techniques to find, validate and report on security vulnerabilities, and work with organizations to develop remediation strategies to improve their overall security posture.

- ◎ **Network security engineer:** A network security engineer is a professional who is responsible for designing, implementing and maintaining the security of an organization's computer networks. They work to protect the network infrastructure from unauthorized access, data breaches, and other security threats by implementing security measures such as firewalls, intrusion detection systems, and encryption. Network security engineers also monitor security systems, perform security audits, and respond to security incidents. They stay up-to-date with the latest security technologies and threats and continuously assess and update the organization's security posture to ensure the protection of sensitive information and assets.

- ⊙ **Security Architect:** A security architect is a professional responsible for the overall design and planning of an organization's information security systems. They work to align the security strategy with the organization's goals and risk tolerance and ensure the security of information systems by integrating security measures into the overall technology architecture. Security architects identify potential security risks and design security solutions to mitigate those risks, such as firewalls, intrusion detection systems, and encryption. They also oversee the implementation of security measures, conduct security assessments, and evaluate the effectiveness of the organization's security posture. They play a key role in ensuring sensitive information and assets' confidentiality, integrity, and availability.

- ⊙ **Incident responder:** An incident responder is a professional responsible for quickly identifying, containing, and resolving security incidents within an organization. They are a critical component of an organization's security program, working to minimize the impact of security breaches and prevent the spread of damage. Incident responders use various tools and techniques to detect, analyze, and respond to security incidents, such as malware analysis, network forensics, and log analysis. They work closely with other security professionals, such as security analysts and network security engineers, to assess the impact of an incident, implement containment and remediation measures, and restore normal operations. Their goal is to return the organization to a secure state as quickly as possible while preserving evidence for further investigation.

- ⊙ **Forensics analyst**: A forensics analyst is a professional who specializes in analysing digital evidence in support of investigations and legal proceedings. They use specialized tools and techniques to acquire, preserve, and analyze digital data in a manner that is admissible in a court of law. Forensics analysts work in various settings, including law enforcement, corporate security, and legal organizations. They are critical in investigating cybercrime incidents such as data breaches, intellectual property theft, and cyberstalking. Their goal is to uncover and preserve digital evidence that can be used to support legal action and to aid in the understanding of the nature and extent of a security breach

Certification programs for Forensics Analysts may vary by vendor and technology, but some popular certifications include:

- Certified Computer Forensics Examiner (CCFE)
- Certified Computer Forensics Professional (CCFP)
- Certified Forensics Examiner (CFE)
- Certified Information Systems Security Professional (CISSP)

These certifications demonstrate a professional's expertise in digital forensics. They can be valuable for individuals seeking to advance their careers in this field. However, it is important to note that certifications are not the only indicator of a professional's knowledge and skills and that hands-on experience, continuous learning, and a strong portfolio of work are also important for success in this field.

Skills required by computer security experts

Computer security experts, also known as cybersecurity professionals, require various technical skills to protect computer systems and data from various threats effectively. One of the most fundamental skills is knowledge of programming languages such as Python, C, and C++. These languages are used to develop secure software and scripts for automating tasks such as vulnerability scanning and penetration testing. In addition to programming languages, knowledge of operating systems such as Windows, Linux, and macOS is crucial for security experts. This includes understanding how to configure and secure these systems and the ability to identify and remediate vulnerabilities. Networking skills are also critical, as security experts must be able to understand and analyze network traffic to identify and mitigate attacks. Another important technical skill for cybersecurity professionals is an understanding of cryptography. This includes knowledge of encryption algorithms, digital signatures, and key management. In addition, understanding how cryptography is used to secure data both in transit and at rest is essential for protecting sensitive information from unauthorized access.

Security experts must be familiar with various security tools and technologies, such as firewalls, intrusion detection/prevention systems, and security information and event management (SIEM) platforms. They must also be able to configure, maintain, and use these tools effectively to prevent, detect, and respond to security incidents.

A strong foundation in programming languages, operating systems, networking, cryptography, and security technologies is essential for computer security experts to be effective in their roles. The ability to continuously learn and adapt to new technologies and threats is also critical in this constantly evolving field.

Available Global Certification in Computer Security

Certified Information Systems Security Professional (CISSP)	**Certified Ethical Hacker (CEH)**
CompTIA Security+	**Certified Information Security Manager (CISM)**
Certified Cloud Security Professional (CCSP)	**Certified Expert Penetration Tester (CEPT)**
	Global Information Assurance Certification (GIAC)

Figure 8:Global Certifications in Computer Security.

⊙ Certified Information Systems Security Professional (CISSP)

The Certified Information Systems Security Professional (CISSP) [1]exam is a six-hour exam consisting of 250 questions that certify security professionals in ten different areas, access control systems and methodology, business continuity planning and disaster recovery planning, physical security, operations, security, management practices, telecommunications and networking security. Other areas important to the CISSP certification are cryptography, security architecture application and systems development, law, investigation, and ethics.

To become certified as a CISSP, you will need at least five years of full-time, paid work as a security analyst in two or more of the eight domains covered in the CISSP, such as cryptography and software development security. There are experience waivers available for those with college degrees and additional credentials if these are approved by the (ISC). You also can become an Associate of the (ISC) and earn the CISSP when you meet your experience requirement. The next step is to prepare for and pass the exam. You will need to have a score of a minimum of 700 out of 1000 points to pass the exam.

After passing the exam, you will need to have an endorsement in subscribing to the (ISC) Code of Ethics. You will have to have an endorsement from another (ISC) professional who can verify your professional experiences requirements such as length of employment, professional reputation,

---

[1] *https://www.isc2.org/Certifications/CISSP*

and continuing education as a security analyst. Obtaining a professional endorsement from a current member is the reason it is important to belong to professional organizations and to participate in professional seminars and events. These are useful career moves that are useful for networking with potential endorsers of your CISSP application.

◎ Certified Ethical Hacker (CEH)

The Certified Ethical Hacker (CEH) [2]provides an in-depth understanding of ethical hacking phases, various attack vectors, and preventative countermeasures. It will teach you how hackers think and act so you will be better positioned to set up your security infrastructure and defend against attacks. By providing an understanding of system weaknesses and vulnerabilities, the CEH course helps students learn to protect their organizations and strengthen their security controls to minimize the risk of a malicious attack.CEH was built to incorporate a hands-on environment and systematic process across each ethical hacking domain and methodology, allowing you to work toward proving the required knowledge and skills needed to achieve the CEH credential and perform the job of an ethical hacker. Now in its 12th version, CEH continues to evolve with the latest operating systems, tools, tactics, exploits, and technologies

Certified Ethical Hacker (CEH) is a certification that validates an individual's skills and knowledge in ethical hacking and security. It certifies that individuals have the necessary skills to identify and assess security threats to computer systems and networks and to implement measures to defend against those threats.CEH is a comprehensive certification that covers a wide range of topics related to ethical hacking, including network security, web application security, mobile security, and cloud security. It also covers the basics of hacking techniques, such as reconnaissance, scanning, and exploitation, as well as more advanced topics, such as reverse engineering and malware analysis.

CEH is designed for individuals who work in the field of information security, such as security analysts, penetration testers, security consultants, and network administrators. It is also valuable for individuals who work in related fields, such as software development and IT management, as it provides a deeper understanding of security risks and best practices. To become CEH certified, individuals must pass a certification exam. The exam covers a wide range of topics related to ethical hacking and security and requires individuals to demonstrate their knowledge and skills in real-world scenarios.

Having a CEH certification can be beneficial for individuals seeking to advance their careers in the field of information security. It demonstrates to employers that an individual has a strong understanding of security risks and the skills necessary to defend against them, and can help individuals stand out in a competitive job market.

◎ CompTIA Security+

CompTIA Security+ [3]is the first security certification a candidate should earn. It establishes

---

[2] *https://www.eccouncil.org/programs/certified-ethical-hacker-ceh/*
[3] *https://www.comptia.org/certifications/security*

the core knowledge required of any cybersecurity role and provides a springboard to intermediate-level cybersecurity jobs. Security+ incorporates best practices in hands-on troubleshooting, ensuring candidates have the practical security problem-solving skills required to assess the security posture of an enterprise environment and recommend and implement appropriate security solutions. To monitor and secure hybrid environments, including cloud, mobile, and IoT. To operate with an awareness of applicable laws and policies, including principles of governance, risk, and compliance and to identify, analyze, and respond to security events and incidents

Security+ is compliant with ISO 17024 standards and approved by the US DoD to meet directive 8140/8570.01-M requirements. Regulators and governments rely on ANSI accreditation because it provides confidence and trust in the outputs of an accredited program. Over 2.3 million CompTIA ISO/ANSI-accredited exams have been delivered since January 1, 2011.

⊙ Certified Information Security Manager (CISM)

ISACA's Certified Information Security Manager (CISM[4]) certification is for those with technical expertise and experience in IS/IT security and control who want to make a move from team player to manager. CISM can add credibility and confidence to your interactions with internal and external stakeholders, peers and regulators. ISACA's Certified Information Security Manager (CISM) certification brings credibility to your team and ensures alignment between the organization's information security program and its broader goals and objectives. CISM can validate your team's commitment to compliance, security and integrity and increase customer retention!

The Certified Information Security Manager (CISM) is a professional certification that validates an individual's expertise in information security management. It certifies that individuals have the necessary knowledge and experience to manage and oversee information security programs' development, implementation, and maintenance.CISM is designed for individuals who hold management positions in information security, such as information security officers, security directors, and risk management professionals. The certification covers a range of topics related to information security management, including risk management, information security governance, incident management, and security program development and management.

To become CISM certified, individuals must have at least five years of professional experience in information security management and pass a certification exam. The exam covers a wide range of topics related to information security management and requires individuals to demonstrate their knowledge and skills in real-world scenarios. Having a CISM certification can be beneficial for individuals seeking to advance their careers in the field of information security. It demonstrates to employers that an individual understands information security management practices and the skills necessary to lead and manage information security programs. Additionally, it can help individuals stand out in a competitive job market and may lead to higher salaries and career advancement opportunities.

⊙ Certified Cloud Security Professional (CCSP)

---

[4] *https://www.isaca.org/credentialing/cism*

Earning the globally recognized CCSP[5] cloud security certification is a proven way to build your career and better secure critical assets in the cloud. The CCSP shows you have the advanced technical skills and knowledge to design, manage and secure data, applications and infrastructure in the cloud using best practices, policies and procedures established by the cybersecurity experts at (ISC)². Prove your skills, advance your career, and gain support from a community of cybersecurity leaders here to help you throughout your professional journey.

The Certified Cloud Security Professional (CCSP) certification validates an individual's expertise in cloud security. It certifies that individuals have the necessary knowledge and experience to design, manage, and secure cloud computing environments.

CCSP is designed for individuals who work in cloud security, such as security architects, engineers, administrators, and consultants. The certification covers a range of topics related to cloud security, including cloud security architecture, cloud data security, cloud platform and infrastructure security, and cloud application security.

To become CCSP certified, individuals must have a minimum of five years of professional experience in information security, with at least three years of experience in cloud security, and must pass a certification exam. The exam covers a wide range of topics related to cloud security and requires individuals to demonstrate their knowledge and skills in real-world scenarios. Having a CCSP certification can be beneficial for individuals seeking to advance their careers in the field of cloud security. It demonstrates to employers that an individual has a strong understanding of cloud security practices and the skills necessary to secure cloud computing environments. Additionally, it can help individuals stand out in a competitive job market and may lead to higher salaries and career advancement opportunities.

◉ Certified Expert Penetration Tester (CEPT)

CEPT [6] The Certified Expert Penetration Tester (CEPT) is a professional certification that validates an individual's expertise in penetration testing. It certifies that individuals have the necessary knowledge and experience to identify and assess computer systems, networks, and applications vulnerabilities.CEPT is designed for individuals who work in the field of penetration testing, such as security consultants, security engineers, and security analysts. The certification covers a range of topics related to penetration testing, including network security, web application security, database security, and mobile application security.

To become CEPT certified, individuals must have a minimum of two years of professional experience in the field of information security and must pass a certification exam. The exam covers a wide range of topics related to penetration testing. It requires individuals to demonstrate their knowledge and skills in real-world scenarios. Having a CEPT certification can be beneficial for

---

[5] *https://www.isc2.org/Certifications/CCSP*
[6] *https://www.infosecinstitute.com/skills/learning-paths/certified-expert-penetration-tester-cept/*

individuals seeking to advance their careers in the field of information security. It demonstrates to employers that an individual understands penetration testing practices and the skills necessary to identify and assess vulnerabilities in computer systems, networks, and applications. Additionally, it can help individuals stand out in a competitive job market and may lead to higher salaries and career advancement opportunities.

⊙ **Global Information Assurance Certification (GIAC)**

GIAC[7] certifications span the breadth of infosec. Our certifications are concentrated in focus areas: offensive security, cyber defence, cloud security, DFIR, management, and ICS. Each focus area has multiple certifications testing various abilities and skill levels. Rather than skimming the surface of different skill sets, GIAC certifications are a mile deep for specialized job-focused tasks. This allows us to thoroughly validate a practitioner's abilities and likelihood of success in a real-world work environment. The Global Information Assurance Certification (GIAC) is a professional certification that validates an individual's expertise in information security. It certifies that individuals have the necessary knowledge and experience to implement, manage, and protect computer systems and networks.

GIAC offers various information security certifications covering various topics, including penetration testing, incident response, digital forensics, security management, and software security. Each certification requires individuals to pass a certification exam that tests their knowledge and skills in real-world scenarios. To become GIAC certified, individuals must have a minimum of two years of professional experience in the field of information security and must pass the relevant certification exam. The exams are designed to be practical and hands-on, and they test an individual's ability to apply their knowledge in real-world scenarios. Having a GIAC certification can be beneficial for individuals seeking to advance their careers in the field of information security. It demonstrates to employers that an individual understands information security practices and the skills necessary to protect computer systems and networks. Additionally, it can help individuals stand out in a competitive job market and may lead to higher salaries and career advancement opportunities.

Industries where computer security experts are highly required

In essence, all computer experts are responsible for computer security. However, those who are assigned Computer security duties are highly expected to make sure computer systems are free from all kinds of danger. These experts are needed in a variety of industries, including Financial services, where they must protect sensitive financial information and prevent financial fraud. In Healthcare where they protect patient information and comply with regulations such as HIPAA. In Government institutions to secure classified information and critical infrastructure. Also in Technology and software development, their duties are to secure software products and protect against cyber attacks. These experts are also needed in retail and e-commerce to protect customer information and prevent data breaches. In Telecommunications to secure network systems and protect against cyber attacks. In defence and military to secure classified information and protect against cyber warfare.In

---

[7] *https://www.giac.org/*

education to protect student information and secure educational systems and networks. These are just a few areas where security experts are highly needed, however, they are required in all sectors to use computerized systems so that we can have secured information assets.

Expected salary for computer security experts

The expected salary for a computer security expert can vary widely depending on location, industry, and experience level. According to Glassdoor, the average salary for a computer security expert in the United States is approximately $98,000 per year. However, some computer security experts, particularly those with specialized skills and significant experience, can earn much more. It's important to note that salaries can also vary based on the size and type of company and the level of responsibility and duties. For example, a senior security analyst in a large corporation may earn a higher salary than a junior security analyst in a smaller company.

Available free online courses on computer security

Table 4:Available free online courses on computer security

SN	Course Name	Level	Duration	Link	Organization
1	Introduction to Cybersecurity Tools & Cyber Attacks	Beginner	4 weeks	https://www.coursera.org/learn/introduction-cybersecurity-tools	Coursera
2	Cybersecurity Fundamentals	Beginner	8 weeks	https://www.coursera.org/learn/cybersecurity-fundamentals	Coursera
3	Cybersecurity and Its Ten Domains	Intermediate	14 weeks	https://www.coursera.org/learn/cyber-security-domains	Coursera
4	Usable Security	Advanced	8 weeks	https://www.coursera.org/learn/usable-security	Coursera
5	Cybersecurity Basics	Beginner	4 weeks	https://www.edx.org/course/cybersecurity-basics	edX
6	Cybersecurity Fundamentals	Beginner	6 weeks	https://www.edx.org/course/cybersecurity-fundamentals	edX
8	Computing: Information and Technology	Beginner	Self-paced	https://www.khanacademy.org/computing/computer-science	Khan Academy
9	Internet 101	Beginner	Self-paced	https://www.khanacademy.org/partner-content/internet-101	Khan Academy

It's important to note that while these courses can provide a solid introduction to computer security, they may not provide the level of hands-on experience needed for a career in the field. Some courses may also have a knowledge cutoff, so be sure to verify the course information and its relevance to the current state of the field.

Free resources on computer security technology

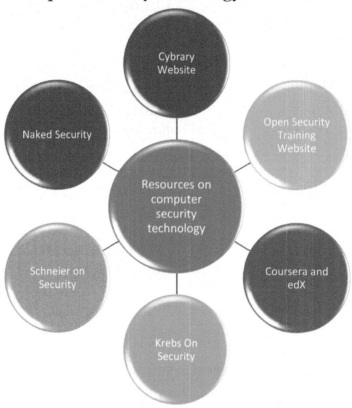

Figure 9:Free resources on computer security technology

There are several free resources available for learning about computer security technology. One of the most popular is the **website Cybrary**. It offers a range of free courses on topics like ethical hacking, network security, and incident response. Another option is the **Open Security Training** website, which provides a large selection of free online training courses and videos on topics such as exploit development and reverse engineering.

Websites like **Coursera and edX** offer free online courses on a range of computer security topics from top universities. These courses are often self-paced, allowing students to learn at their speed, and can be a great way to gain practical experience in the field.

For those who prefer to read, websites such as **KrebsOnSecurity**, **Schneier on Security**, and **Naked Security by Sophos** offer insightful articles on the latest security threats and best practices. These sites also often provide in-depth analysis of recent cyber attacks and breaches, as well as guidance on how to stay safe online. These resources provide a great starting point for anyone looking to learn more about computer security technology and are available to anyone with an internet connection.

Future of computer security

The future of computer security will be shaped by a range of trends and developments that are likely to impact the industry in various ways. One of the most important of these trends is the increasing use of artificial intelligence and machine learning. These technologies will enable real-time threat detection and response, providing critical insights into complex security data. This will allow organizations to quickly identify and respond to potential threats, reducing the risk of cyber-attacks and data breaches.

Another significant trend in computer security is the increasing focus on cloud security. With more and more organizations moving their systems and data to the cloud, securing these systems will become a top priority for the computer security industry. This will require the development of new security protocols and tools that are specifically designed for cloud environments. The Internet of Things (IoT) is another trend that is likely to impact the future of computer security. As the number of connected devices continues to grow, securing these devices will become increasingly important. This will require new approaches to security, including the use of encryption and other security measures to protect sensitive data.

Other trends in computer security include the development of new cybersecurity regulations and standards, the potential impact of quantum computing on cryptography and security, and the importance of human factors in protecting against cyber threats. In the years ahead, it will be critical for the computer security industry to remain vigilant and adaptable, as cyber threats continue to evolve and become more sophisticated

05
COMPUTER PROGRAMMERS

Computer programming is the process of designing, writing, testing, debugging, and maintaining the source code of computer programs. This code specifies the sequences of operations that a computer should perform to accomplish a specific task and is written in a high-level programming language, such as Python, C++, or Java. The goal of programming is to produce an executable program that solves a given problem and meets the desired requirements.

Computer programming is important because it is the primary method of creating software and applications that run on computers and other digital devices. It allows individuals and organizations to automate tasks, create new tools and technologies, and solve complex problems. It also plays a crucial role in many industries, such as finance, healthcare, and entertainment, and is essential for innovation in the digital age. Additionally, computer programming skills are highly sought after in the job market and can lead to a fulfilling and lucrative career. A computer programmer is a person who writes code in one or more programming languages to create software, applications, and systems that run on computers. They are responsible for designing, coding, testing, debugging, and maintaining the source code of computer programs

Different Roles in Computer Programming

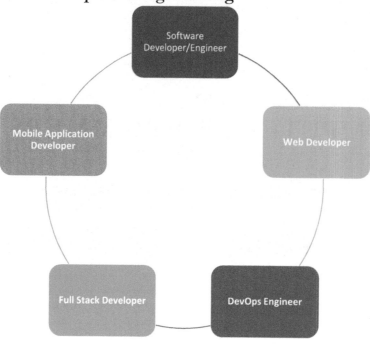

Figure 10:Different Roles in Computer Programming

Software Developer/Engineer: responsible for designing, coding, testing, and maintaining software applications. A software developer or software engineer is a professional who is responsible for designing, developing, testing, and maintaining software applications. They use programming languages and technologies to create software solutions that meet the needs of users. Software developers work on a variety of projects, ranging from web applications to mobile apps, desktop software, and more. They also play a key role in the software development lifecycle, including requirements gathering, design, coding, testing, and deployment. Software developers may work independently or as part of a team, and must stay up-to-date with the latest technologies and programming languages to continually improve their skills and knowledge.

Web Developer: focuses on building websites and web applications. A web developer is a professional who specializes in the development of web applications and websites. They use programming languages such as HTML, CSS, and JavaScript to create dynamic and interactive web pages, and may also use server-side scripting languages like PHP and Python to create more complex web applications. Web developers work on a variety of projects, from simple websites to complex e-commerce platforms, and may be involved in the entire web development lifecycle, from designing the user interface to coding, testing, and deploying the final product. They must have a strong understanding of web technologies, user experience design, and web accessibility, and must stay up-to-date with the latest tools and trends in web development to continuously improve their skills.

DevOps Engineer combines software development and IT operations to optimize the software delivery process. A DevOps Engineer is a professional who works at the intersection of software development and operations. They are responsible for automating the software development lifecycle and improving the collaboration between development and operations teams. DevOps Engineers use a combination of tools and practices to automate the process of software development, testing, deployment, and infrastructure management. They help to ensure the reliability, scalability, and security of software systems by implementing continuous integration and continuous delivery (CI/CD) pipelines, and by automating the provisioning and management of infrastructure. DevOps Engineers also work to identify and resolve technical issues and to continuously improve the software development process, ultimately enabling organizations to deliver high-quality software faster and more efficiently.

Full Stack Developer: familiar with all layers of software development, from front-end user interfaces to back-end systems and databases. A Full Stack Developer is a software developer who has a comprehensive understanding of both front-end and back-end development. They are capable of working on all aspects of a web application, from the user interface to the database, and can develop and maintain the entire application stack. Full Stack Developers are skilled in a variety of programming languages and web technologies, including HTML, CSS, JavaScript, and server-side scripting languages such as PHP, Ruby, or Python. They have a strong understanding of databases, server administration, and web security. Full Stack Developers are responsible for designing and implementing the complete web application, including the user interface, server-side logic, and data storage. They must have the ability to troubleshoot and debug complex issues and must have excellent problem-solving skills to find the best solutions for a given problem.

Mobile Application Developer: focuses on developing apps for mobile devices. A mobile application developer is a software developer who specializes in creating applications for mobile devices such as smartphones and tablets. They use programming languages and technologies specific to mobile platforms, such as Swift for iOS and Java for Android, to develop and maintain mobile applications. Mobile application developers must have a strong understanding of the unique design and user experience requirements of mobile devices, as well as the different capabilities and limitations of various mobile platforms. They are responsible for the entire mobile application development process, including design, coding, testing, and deployment, and must work closely with designers, product managers, and other stakeholders to ensure that the final product meets the needs of the users. Mobile application developers must stay up-to-date with the latest mobile technologies and trends and must continually improve their skills and knowledge to produce high-quality and innovative mobile applications

The skills required by computer programmer

A computer programmer must have different skills to allow him/her to perform his duties without problems. Some of the skills include being able to write and test code for software applications. Debugging and fixing errors in existing software and should be able to design, develop and maintain software systems. Collaborating with cross-functional teams to develop software solutions and Documenting code and technical specifications. Computer programmers must Stay up to date with emerging trends and technologies in software development. Furthermore, a programmer must have basic skills such as strong problem-solving skills. Proficiency in one or more programming languages.Good understanding of algorithms and data structures. Experience with software development methodologies. Ability to learn and adapt to new technologies quickly and good communication skills.Moreover. Must have attention to detail and the ability to produce high-quality, maintainable code.

Known programming languages and their use

A programmer doesn't need to know all programming languages. But knowing more than one language will be most advantageous for a programmer. Some of the most popular programming languages and their uses have been shown below.

- ❖ **Python**

Python is a high-level, interpreted programming language known for its simple and easy-to-read syntax. It was first released in 1991 and has since become one of the most popular programming languages in the world, used for a wide range of tasks from web development and scientific computing to data analysis and artificial intelligence.

One of the key features of Python is its support for multiple programming paradigms, including procedural, object-oriented, and functional programming. It also has a large standard library that includes modules for tasks such as connecting to web servers, reading and writing files, and working with data.

Python is open-source software, which means that anyone can use and modify the source code. This has led to the creation of a large and active community of users and developers who contribute to the language and its various libraries. Overall, Python is a versatile and powerful language that is well-suited for both beginners and experienced programmers.

- ❖ **Java**

Java is a high-level, object-oriented programming language that was first released in 1995. It is one of the most widely used programming languages in the world, particularly for building large-scale enterprise applications and developing mobile applications for Android. One of the key features of

46

Java is its "write once, run anywhere" (WORA) principle, which means that Java code can be run on any device or platform that has a Java Virtual Machine (JVM) installed, without having to recompile the code. This makes it an ideal choice for building cross-platform applications.Java is also known for its strong type checking, which helps to prevent many programming errors, and its garbage collection mechanism, which automatically frees up memory that is no longer being used by the program. In addition to its standard libraries, Java has a large and active community of developers who have created many third-party libraries and tools, making it easier for Java developers to accomplish complex tasks and integrate with other systems. Overall, Java is a robust and reliable language that is well-suited for building complex, scalable applications and for developing applications for the enterprise.

❖ C++

C++ is a high-level, general-purpose programming language that was first released in 1985 as an extension of the C programming language. It is widely used for developing operating systems, embedded systems, and high-performance applications such as games and simulations. One of the key features of C++ is its support for low-level programming, which makes it well-suited for tasks that require fine-grained control over system resources, such as memory and processor usage. C++ also supports object-oriented programming, which enables developers to encapsulate data and behaviour into objects, making it easier to write and maintain complex code. In addition to its built-in libraries, C++ has a large and active community of developers who have created many third-party libraries and tools, making it easier for C++ developers to accomplish complex tasks and integrate with other systems.

C++ is also known for its high performance and efficiency, as it can execute code faster than many other programming languages. However, this can also make C++ code more difficult to write and maintain, especially for beginners, as it requires a good understanding of system resources and memory management.C++ is a powerful and flexible language that is well-suited for developing high-performance applications and for low-level programming tasks.

❖ JavaScript

JavaScript is a high-level, interpreted programming language that was first released in 1995. It is primarily used for creating dynamic and interactive web pages, but it can also be used for server-side programming, desktop applications, and mobile applications. One of the key features of JavaScript is its ability to manipulate the Document Object Model (DOM), which is the web page's structure in real-time, allowing developers to create dynamic and interactive web pages. It is often used in conjunction with HTML and CSS to create the front end of web applications.JavaScript is an object-oriented language, and it supports functional programming, making it a versatile and flexible language for developing a wide range of applications. It has a large and active community of developers who have created many third-party libraries and tools, making it easier for JavaScript developers to accomplish complex tasks and integrate with other systems.JavaScript is a dynamic and popular language that is well-suited for creating interactive web pages and for developing web applications, as well as for other types of applications.

❖ C#

C# is a modern, object-oriented programming language that was first released in 2000. It is primarily used for developing Windows applications and games, but it can also be used for developing web, mobile, and desktop applications. One of the key features of C# is its strong type checking, which helps to prevent many programming errors. It also supports both object-oriented and component-based programming, making it a flexible and powerful language for developing a wide range of applications. C# is part of the .NET framework, which provides a large library of pre-built classes and tools that make it easier for C# developers to accomplish tasks such as reading and writing files, connecting to databases, and creating user interfaces. In addition to its standard libraries, C# has a large and active community of developers who have created many third-party libraries and tools, making it easier for C# developers to accomplish complex tasks and integrate with other systems. C# is a modern and versatile language that is well-suited for developing Windows applications and for building a wide range of other applications, including web, mobile, and desktop applications.

❖ Ruby

Ruby is a high-level, interpreted, dynamic programming language that was first released in 1995. It is known for its elegant syntax and its support for multiple programming paradigms, including procedural, object-oriented, and functional programming. One of the key features of Ruby is its support for metaprogramming, which allows developers to write code that generates or modifies other code at runtime. This makes it a powerful and flexible language for developing a wide range of applications. Ruby is also known for its focus on developer happiness, with a strong emphasis on readability and maintainability. It has a large and active community of developers who have created many third-party libraries and tools, making it easier for Ruby developers to accomplish complex tasks and integrate with other systems. Ruby is particularly well-suited for web development, and it is the language behind the Ruby on Rails framework, which is a popular choice for building dynamic, database-backed web applications. Ruby is a dynamic and elegant language that is well-suited for web development and a wide range of other applications, and it is known for its focus on developer happiness.

❖ Swift

Swift is a high-performance, general-purpose programming language developed by Apple Inc. and released in 2014. It is primarily used for developing iOS, iPadOS, macOS, watchOS, and tvOS applications. One of the key features of Swift is its focus on safety, with features such as type inference and automatic reference counting, which help prevent common programming errors. Swift is also fast, with performance comparable to low-level languages such as C++, and its syntax is concise and expressive, making it easier for developers to write and maintain code. Swift has a large and active community of developers who have created many third-party libraries and tools, making it easier for Swift developers to accomplish complex tasks and integrate with other systems. Swift is also designed to be easy to learn, especially for developers who are familiar with other modern programming languages. Its syntax is influenced by languages such as Python and Ruby, making it more accessible and intuitive for many developers.

Swift is a powerful and efficient language that is well-suited for developing iOS, macOS, watchOS, and tvOS applications, and its focus on safety and ease of use make it a great choice for many types of development projects.

❖ PHP

PHP is a server-side scripting language that was first released in 1995. It is primarily used for developing dynamic web applications, and it is estimated to be used by more than 80% of websites on the internet. One of the key features of PHP is its ease of use, with a syntax that is straightforward to learn, especially for developers who are familiar with other scripting languages. It also has a large and active community of developers who have created many third-party libraries and tools, making it easier for PHP developers to accomplish complex tasks and integrate with other systems.PHP is particularly well-suited for developing database-backed web applications, and it has a wide range of built-in functions for connecting to and manipulating databases. It can be used with a variety of databases, including MySQL, PostgreSQL, and Microsoft SQL Server. In addition to its ease of use and support for database-backed web applications, PHP is also known for its performance and scalability, making it a popular choice for large and complex web applications.PHP is a widely-used and versatile language that is well-suited for developing dynamic web applications, and its ease of use and support for database-backed applications make it a popular choice for many types of development projects.

❖ SQL

SQL (Structured Query Language) is a domain-specific language used to manage data held in a relational database management system (RDBMS) or for stream processing in a Relational Data Stream Management System (RDSMS). It is used to create, modify and extract data from databases.SQL is used to perform various operations on relational databases, including creating tables, inserting and updating data, retrieving data using queries, and deleting data. It provides a standard way of interacting with databases, and the syntax is consistent across different RDBMS, such as MySQL, Oracle, Microsoft SQL Server, and PostgreSQL.SQL is based on the relational model of data, which organizes data into tables with rows and columns. The relationships between the tables are defined using keys, and the data in the tables can be combined and retrieved using joins.SQL is widely used for managing data in a wide range of applications, including business intelligence, data warehousing, and e-commerce. With its ease of use and support for complex data manipulation and analysis, it is an essential tool for many data professionals and database administrators.SQL is a powerful and widely-used language for managing data in relational databases, and its consistent syntax and support for complex data manipulation make it a popular choice for many types of data-driven applications.

❖ R

R is a free, open-source programming language and software environment for statistical computing and graphics. It was developed by statisticians and data scientists, and it is widely used for data analysis, statistical modelling, and data visualization. R has a rich ecosystem of packages and libraries that extend its capabilities, making it a versatile and flexible tool for a wide range of data analysis tasks. It has built-in support for a variety of data types, including scalars, vectors, matrices, and data frames, and it also has a powerful set of functions for data manipulation, cleaning, and transformation. In addition to its capabilities for data analysis, R is also known for its strong support for data visualization, with a wide range of libraries for creating charts, plots, and graphs. These visualizations can be used to explore and understand data, and they can also be used to communicate results to others. R is widely used in many fields, including finance, healthcare, marketing, and academia, and it has a large and active community of users and developers who have created many packages and tools for solving a wide range of data analysis problems. R is a powerful and flexible language for data analysis and visualization, and its rich ecosystem of packages and libraries makes it a popular choice for many data-driven applications.

This is not an exhaustive list, but these are some of the most widely used programming languages today.

Global certifications for computer programmers

There are several certifications for computer programmers ,including

 Java SE 11 Developer

 Microsoft Certified: Azure Developer Associate

 Google Certified Professional Cloud Developer

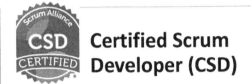 Certified Scrum Developer (CSD)

Figure 11:Available Certifications for Developers.

- **Java SE 11 Developer**[8]

Candidates who hold this certification have demonstrated proficiency in Java (Standard Edition) software development recognized by a wide range of worldwide industries. They have also exhibited thorough and broad knowledge of the Java programming language, coding practices and utilization of new features incorporated into Java SE 11. By passing the required exam, a certified individual proves tremendous fluency in Java SE and acquisition of the valuable professional skills required to be a Java software developer. This includes a deep understanding of object orientation, functional programming through lambda expressions and streams, and modularity.

Microsoft Certified: Azure Developer Associate

Candidates for the Azure Developer [9]Associate certification are cloud developers who participate in all phases of development ,from requirements definition and design to development, deployment, and maintenance. They partner with cloud DBAs, cloud administrators, and clients to implement solutions. Candidates should be proficient in Azure SDKs, data storage options, data connections, APIs, app authentication and authorization, compute and container deployment, debugging, performance tuning, and monitoring. Candidates should have 1-2 years of professional development experience and experience with Microsoft Azure. They should be able to program in an Azure-

---

[8] *https://education.oracle.com/java-se-11-developer/pexam_1Z0-819*
[9] *https://learn.microsoft.com/en-us/certifications/azure-developer/*

supported language and should be proficient using Azure CLI, Azure PowerShell, and other tools.

- **Google Certified Professional Cloud Developer**

The Google Certified Professional Cloud Developer certification is a professional certification that validates an individual's expertise in developing applications on the Google Cloud Platform. It certifies that individuals have the necessary knowledge and experience to design, develop, and manage applications using Google Cloud technologies.

The certification covers a range of topics related to cloud development, including Google Cloud architecture, application development, data storage and management, security, and deployment.

To become a Google Certified Professional Cloud Developer certified, individuals must have experience developing applications on the Google Cloud Platform and must pass a certification exam. The exam covers a wide range of topics related to cloud development and requires individuals to demonstrate their knowledge and skills in real-world scenarios.

Having a Google Certified Professional Cloud Developer certification can be beneficial for individuals seeking to advance their careers in cloud development. It demonstrates to employers that an individual has a strong understanding of Google Cloud technologies and the skills necessary to design, develop, and manage applications on the platform. Additionally, it can help individuals stand out in a competitive job market and may lead to higher salaries and career advancement opportunities.

- **Certified Scrum Developer (CSD)**

Strengthen your technical skills in agile product development. Certified Scrum Developers (CSD®) have demonstrated — through training that ensures they have a working understanding of Scrum and agile principles and have learned specialized agile engineering skills. The Certified Scrum Developer® course is designed for product developers who are working in a Scrum environment. The goal is to expose students to the most important tools and techniques needed to build good products iteratively and incrementally Scrum requires. These ideas are central to the entire field of agile product development.

In today's competitive job market, the Certified Scrum Developer training can set you apart from the pack. A successful Certified Scrum Developer® is committed to continuous improvement. The coursework and dedication needed to achieve a CSD sharpen your skills to help you become a better practitioner of Scrum and agile development. By earning a Certified Scrum Developer certification, you Learn the foundations of Scrum and the scope of the Certified Scrum Developer's role from the best minds in development agility. Demonstrate to employers and peers your understanding of core Scrum knowledge Expand your career opportunities by staying relevant and marketable across all industry sectors by adopting agile practices. Engage with a community of recognized Scrum experts who are committed to continuous improvement is important to note that while these certifications can demonstrate expertise and increase job prospects, practical experience and a strong portfolio of work are also highly valued in the industry.

❖ Industries where computer programmers are required most

Computer programmers are required in a variety of industries and fields, some of the most common areas are Software development they develop and maintain software applications for desktop, web, and mobile platforms. Also in Information Technology (IT) they are designing and implementing IT systems and infrastructure for organizations. Programmers are also required in Financial services where their duties include developing and maintaining software for banking and financial institutions. These experts also are important in the healthcare sector for developing and implementing healthcare IT systems, such as electronic health records (EHRs) and medical billing software. Developing and maintaining e-commerce platforms and payment systems in E-Commerce Sector. In Gaming, they are Developing video games for personal computers and gaming consoles. Similarly, in government, they are developing and maintaining software systems for government agencies and departments. And, in education, they develop educational software and systems for schools and universities. These are just a few examples, and there are many other areas where computer programmers are in demand.

❖ Expected salaries for computer programmers

The salary for a computer programmer can vary widely based on some factors, including the location where salaries can vary depending on the cost of living and local job market conditions. More experienced programmers typically earn higher salaries than those with less experience. Education with a higher degree in computer science or a related field may lead to a higher salary. Different industries may offer different salaries for computer programmers, with higher salaries often found in industries such as finance, healthcare, and technology. As of 2021, the average salary for computer programmers in the United States is around $80,000 per year. However, salaries can range from around $50,000 to over $120,000 depending on the factors listed above

Available free online courses on computer programming

There are many free online courses available for learning computer programming, some of the most popular platforms are listed in table 4 below.

Table 5:Available free online courses on computer programming

SN	Institution	Course Name	Level	Duration	Link
1	Coursera	Python for Everybody	Beginner	5 courses, 4-8 weeks each	https://www.coursera.org/specializations/python
2	Coursera	Programming for Everybody (Getting Started with Python)	Beginner	5 weeks	https://www.coursera.org/learn/python
3	Coursera	Java Programming and Software Engineering Fundamentals	Beginner	6 weeks	https://www.coursera.org/learn/java-programming
4	edX	Introduction to Computer Science and Programming Using Python	Beginner	9 weeks	https://www.edx.org/course/introduction-to-computer-science-and-programming-using-python-0
5	edX	Introduction to Programming in C	Beginner	5 weeks	https://www.edx.org/course/introduction-to-programming-in-c
8	Khan Academy	HTML/JS: Making webpages interactive with jQuery	Intermediate	Self-paced	https://www.khanacademy.org/computing/computer-programming

These are just a few examples, and there are many other resources available for learning computer programming online, both for free and for a fee.

Free resources and tools for computer programming

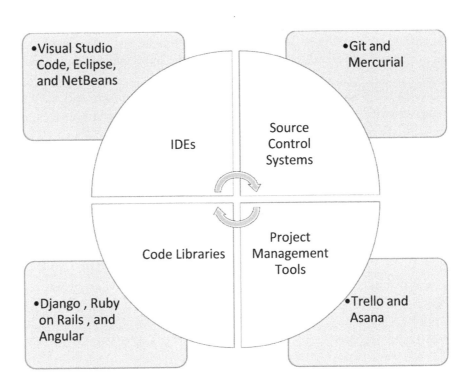

Figure 12:Free Resources for Developers.

Above are among many free resources and tools available for computer programming, including Integrated Development Environments (IDEs) such as Visual Studio Code, Eclipse, and NetBeans provide a comprehensive environment for writing, debugging, and testing code. Source control systems like Git and Mercurial. These tools allow programmers to manage and track changes to their code, collaborate with other developers, and maintain different versions of their code. Project management tools include Trello and Asana. These tools allow programmers to organize and track the progress of their projects and tasks. Online communities and forums: Sites like Stack Overflow, Reddit, and Quora provide a wealth of information and support for programmers, including answers to technical questions and advice on best practices.Code libraries and frameworks: Many programming languages have libraries and frameworks that provide pre-written code for common tasks and functions, such as Django for Python, Ruby on Rails for Ruby, and Angular for JavaScript

Learning Resources: Websites like Codecademy, Khan Academy, and W3Schools provide free tutorials and courses on various programming languages and software development concepts. These are just a few examples, and there are many other free resources and tools available for computer programming.

The future of computer programming

The field of software development is likely to undergo significant changes shortly due to advancements in artificial intelligence and machine learning, the increasing trend towards cloud computing, the growing popularity of mobile devices, the rising threat of cyber attacks, the adoption of blockchain technology, and the growth of the Internet of Things (IoT). These developments are expected to drive the development of new tools and services and to increase the demand for programmers with specific skill sets in these areas. As a result, software developers will need to stay informed and adapt to these trends to remain competitive in an ever-changing industry.

These trends are likely to shape the future of computer programming and have a significant impact on the skills and knowledge that programmers will need in the coming years.

06
COMPUTER ENGINEERS

Computer Engineering is a branch of electrical engineering that deals with the design and development of computer systems and networks. It combines the principles of electrical engineering with computer science to create integrated systems that can perform tasks such as data processing, communication, and storage. Computer engineers are involved in the design of computer hardware, software, and networks, as well as their integration and application in various systems

Roles of computer engineer

Computer engineers are responsible for designing, developing, and maintaining computer hardware, software, and systems. Their job duties can vary based on the industry they work in and the specific position they hold, but generally include:

- Design and development: Computer engineers are responsible for designing and developing computer systems, software, and hardware. This includes writing code, testing and debugging software, and developing algorithms and data structures.
- Maintenance and support: Once computer systems are designed and developed, computer engineers are responsible for maintaining and supporting them. They must troubleshoot any issues that arise and keep the systems up-to-date with the latest technology and software updates.
- Collaboration: Computer engineers often work in teams with other engineers, as well as other professionals such as project managers, clients, and stakeholders. They must collaborate with these individuals to ensure that computer systems are meeting the needs of the organization and to identify areas for improvement.

Other responsibilities of computer engineers may include researching new technologies and developing prototypes to test them, creating technical documentation, and providing training to end-users on how to use computer systems effectively. Overall, computer engineers play a critical role in developing and maintaining the technology that is essential to modern life.

Skills required by computer engineer

Computer engineers need to possess a mix of technical and soft skills to excel in their field. First and foremost, strong programming skills are essential, including knowledge of programming languages such as C, C++, Java, Python, and others. Additionally, they must have a good understanding of computer systems, including computer architecture, operating systems, networks, and databases.

Analytical thinking is another crucial skill for computer engineers, as they must be able to analyze and solve complex problems. Attention to detail is also critical, as even minor errors in code can cause significant problems. Computer engineers should also have project management skills, including the ability to manage multiple projects and meet deadlines. Effective communication skills are also essential for computer engineers, as they must interact with clients, colleagues, and other stakeholders. Creative thinking is another important skill for computer engineers, allowing them to come up with new solutions and innovations. Adaptability is also important, as new technologies and changing business requirements can require computer engineers to adapt quickly.

Computer engineers should possess critical thinking skills to evaluate and make decisions based on available data. They should also have good interpersonal skills and the ability to work well in a team environment. Overall, a combination of technical and soft skills is critical for computer engineers to succeed in their field and meet the demands of modern technology.

Certification in computer engineering.

A certification in computer engineering is a professional recognition that indicates a person has demonstrated a certain level of knowledge and skills in the field of computer engineering. There are several certifications offered by various organizations and industries, such as:

❖ **Certified Software Development Professional (CSDP)**

The Certified Software Development Professional (CSDP) is a certification program offered by the Institute of Electrical and Electronics Engineers (IEEE) Computer Society. The CSDP certification is aimed at software professionals who have several years of experience in software development and wish to demonstrate their expertise in software development methodologies, processes, and practices

To obtain the CSDP certification, candidates must have a minimum of five years of professional experience in software development, pass a written exam, and meet other eligibility requirements set by the IEEE Computer Society. The written exam covers a wide range of software development topics, including software development methodologies, software architecture, software testing, software maintenance, and project management.

The CSDP certification is recognized as a professional benchmark for software development professionals and is widely respected in the industry. It is designed to demonstrate a candidate's commitment to their profession and to provide evidence of their mastery of the software development process. Obtaining the CSDP certification can enhance an individual's career prospects, demonstrate their expertise to employers, and improve their professional standing.

❖ Certified Information Systems Security Professional (CISSP)

The Certified Information Systems Security Professional (CISSP) is a certification program offered by the International Information Systems Security Certification Consortium (ISC)^2. The CISSP certification is one of the most highly respected and widely recognized certifications in the information security industry.

The CISSP certification is designed for information security professionals who have extensive experience in the field and are responsible for designing, implementing, and managing an organization's information security program. To obtain the CISSP certification, candidates must have a minimum of five years of cumulative, paid work experience in two or more of the eight domains of the CISSP Common Body of Knowledge (CBK). The eight domains of the CBK include security and risk management, asset security, security engineering, communications and network security, identity and access management, security assessment and testing, security operations, and software development security. Candidates must also pass a comprehensive, six-hour written exam that tests their knowledge and understanding of the CISSP CBK. The CISSP certification is a rigorous and demanding program, and passing the exam is a significant accomplishment that demonstrates a candidate's expertise in information security.

Holding the CISSP certification is widely regarded as a sign of professional excellence and is recognized globally by employers, governments, and other organizations. The certification helps to establish credibility and trust with clients and stakeholders, and it provides a competitive advantage in the job market for information security professionals.

❖ Certified Information Systems Auditor (CISA) by ISACA

The Certified Information Systems Auditor (CISA) is a certification program offered by ISACA (formerly known as the Information Systems Audit and Control Association). The CISA certification is aimed at information technology (IT) auditors, control professionals, and security specialists who are responsible for auditing, controlling, monitoring, and assessing an organization's IT and business systems. To obtain the CISA certification, candidates must have at least five years of experience in IS audit, control, or security, and must pass a written exam that covers five domains of knowledge: the process of auditing information systems, governance and management of IT, information systems acquisition, development, and implementation, information systems operations, maintenance, and service management, and protection of information assets.

The CISA certification is widely recognized as the global standard for IS audit professionals. It demonstrates a candidate's expertise in information systems auditing, control, and security and provides evidence of their ability to assess an organization's information security and IT governance. The certification is highly valued by employers and can lead to career advancement and improved earning potential for information technology professionals. Holding the CISA certification also shows a commitment to continuing professional development and a dedication to the highest standards of professional conduct in the information technology industry.

❖ Oracle Certified Professional, Java SE 11 Developer by Oracle Corporation

The Oracle Certified Professional, Java SE 11 Developer certification is a professional-level certification program offered by Oracle Corporation. It is designed for software developers who have a strong understanding of the Java programming language and who wish to demonstrate their expertise in using the Java Standard Edition (SE) 11 platform.

To obtain the Oracle Certified Professional, Java SE 11 Developer certification, candidates must pass a written exam that tests their knowledge and understanding of the Java SE 11 platform and its features, including object-oriented programming, collections, generics, concurrency, and the Java Virtual Machine (JVM). The exam covers a wide range of topics, including Java syntax, data types, and control structures, as well as advanced topics such as Java collections, multithreaded programming, and JVM performance tuning. The Oracle Certified Professional, Java SE 11 Developer certification provides recognition of a candidate's expertise in using the Java SE 11 platform, and it is widely respected in the software development industry. It is a valuable asset for software developers who are looking to enhance their career prospects and demonstrate their knowledge and skills to employers.

Holding the Oracle Certified Professional, Java SE 11 Developer certification also shows a commitment to continuing professional development and a dedication to using industry-standard tools and technologies to develop high-quality software applications. It provides evidence of a candidate's ability to design, implement, and maintain applications that are reliable, efficient, and secure.

❖ **Microsoft Certified: Azure Developer Associate by Microsoft**

The Microsoft Certified: Azure Developer Associate certification is a professional-level certification program offered by Microsoft. It is designed for software developers who are looking to demonstrate their expertise in developing and deploying applications on the Microsoft Azure cloud platform.

To obtain the Azure Developer Associate certification, candidates must pass a written exam that tests their knowledge and understanding of key Azure services, including virtual machines, web apps, storage solutions, and networking. The exam also covers the use of Azure DevOps and other development tools to build, test, and deploy cloud-based applications. The Microsoft Certified: Azure Developer Associate certification is a valuable asset for software developers who are looking to specialize in cloud-based development and who want to demonstrate their expertise in using Azure services to build and deploy cloud-based applications. It is widely recognized in the software development industry and provides evidence of a candidate's ability to design, implement, and deploy scalable and secure cloud-based applications.

Holding the Azure Developer Associate certification also shows a commitment to continuing professional development and a dedication to using industry-standard tools and technologies to develop high-quality software applications. It provides a competitive advantage in the job market for software developers and can lead to career advancement and improved earning potential. The requirements for these certifications may include formal education, work experience, and passing a rigorous exam. Having a certification can help individuals advance their careers and increase their earning potential.

Areas where computer engineers are required

Computer engineers are highly sought after in various industries due to their skills and expertise in developing and maintaining computer systems, software, and hardware. One industry that highly demands computer engineers is the technology and software development, where they play a critical role in developing and improving systems and software for various applications. Another industry that requires computer engineers is telecommunications, where they develop and maintain communication networks, including telephone, cable, and satellite systems. In manufacturing, computer engineers are involved in the design, testing, and production of computer systems and components for various industries, from automotive to consumer electronics.

The healthcare industry also relies on computer engineers to design and develop medical devices and systems, including diagnostic equipment, patient monitoring systems, and electronic health records. Computer engineers are also in demand in finance, where they develop and maintain financial software and systems for banks and financial institutions.

In the gaming industry, computer engineers are involved in the design and development of video games and gaming systems. Lastly, in the aerospace and defence industry, computer engineers play a significant role in the design and development of advanced technology systems for aerospace and defence applications, including satellites, missiles, and aircraft systems. Computer engineers are in demand in various industries due to their skills and expertise in developing and maintaining computer systems and technology. The increasing reliance on technology in all aspects of modern life ensures that this trend is likely to continue in the future.

Expected salaries for computer engineers

The expected salary for a computer engineer can vary greatly depending on several factors such as location, experience, and industry. Salaries in cities such as San Francisco, New York, and Seattle tend to be higher due to the higher cost of living, while more experienced computer engineers typically earn higher salaries compared to entry-level engineers. Additionally, the technology and software development industry generally pays higher salaries compared to other industries. On average, computer engineers in the United States can expect to earn between $70,000 to $140,000 per year, with the exact salary depending on the specific job and location. It's worth noting that other factors such as education, skills, and demand for specific skills can also impact a computer engineer's salary. Ultimately, individuals interested in pursuing a career in computer engineering should research the industry and job market in their area to get a more accurate understanding of the potential salary range.

Available free online courses on computer engineering

There are several free online courses available for those interested in learning computer engineering. Some of the most popular platforms for free online courses

Table 6:Available free online courses on computer engineering

SN	Institution	Course Name	Level	Duration	Link
1	Coursera	Computer Architecture	Intermediate	4 weeks	https://www.coursera.org/learn/comparch
2	Coursera	Computer Networks	Intermediate	7 weeks	https://www.coursera.org/learn/computer-networks
3	Coursera	Computer Vision Basics	Intermediate	4 weeks	https://www.coursera.org/learn/computer-vision-basics
4	edX	Computer Science Essentials for Software Development	Beginner	10 weeks	https://www.edx.org/course/computer-science-essentials-for-software-development
5	edX	Introduction to Computer Engineering	Beginner	5 weeks	https://www.edx.org/course/introduction-to-computer-engineering
6	edX	Robotics	Intermediate	12 weeks	https://www.edx.org/course/robotics
7	Khan Academy	Algorithms	Intermediate	Self-paced	https://www.khanacademy.org/computing/computer-science
8	Khan Academy	The Internet	Intermediate	Self-paced	https://www.khanacademy.org/partner-content/code-org/internet-works

These courses provide an excellent opportunity to gain knowledge and skills in computer engineering without incurring any costs. However, they may not provide a comprehensive education or a formal certification, which is typically available through paid courses or degree programs.

Free resources and tools on computer engineering

❖ Compilers

GCC and Clang are popular open-source compilers for C and C++. GCC is a collection of compilers for multiple programming languages, including C, C++, Objective-C, Fortran, Ada, and others. It developed by the GNU Project and is considered one of the most widely used compilers in the open-source community. GCC is highly customizable and portable, making it a popular choice for a wide range of platforms and architectures. Clang is a compiler for the C, C++, and Objective-C programming languages developed by the LLVM Project. Clang is known for its fast compilation speeds and high-quality diagnostics, making it a popular choice for developers who want to improve their productivity. Clang is also used as the default compiler on macOS and is included with the Xcode development environment.

Both GCC and Clang are highly respected in the software development community and are used extensively in the development of both open-source and commercial software. They provide developers with powerful and flexible tools for compiling and optimizing their code, making them essential tools for software development in C and C++.

❖ Integrated Development Environments (IDEs)

Eclipse, Visual Studio Code, and NetBeans are popular open-source IDEs for software development. Integrated Development Environments (IDEs) are software applications that provide a comprehensive environment for software development. An IDE typically includes a source code editor, a compiler or interpreter, a debugger, and other tools and features that help streamline the software development process. Some of the most popular IDEs include:

- **Visual Studio Code (VSCode):** A free, open-source IDE developed by Microsoft that is widely used for web development, software development, and data science. It supports a wide range of programming languages, including Python, Java, C++, and more.
- **Eclipse**: A popular open-source IDE that is widely used for Java development. It also supports a range of other programming languages, including C++, Python, and more.
- **IntelliJ IDEA:** A commercial IDE developed by JetBrains that is widely used for Java development. It also supports a range of other programming languages, including Python, Kotlin, and more.
- **Xcode:** A commercial IDE developed by Apple that is used for iOS, iPadOS, macOS, watchOS, and tvOS development. It is widely used by developers who build software for Apple's platforms.
- **Android Studio:** A free, open-source IDE developed by Google that is used for Android app development.

IDEs provide developers with a comprehensive development environment that streamlines the software development process and helps improve productivity. They offer a wide range of features and tools, including source code editors, debuggers, compilers, and more, that help developers create high-quality software applications more efficiently.

❖ **Operating systems**

- **Linux:** One of the most widely used open-source operating systems, Linux is a Unix-like operating system that is highly customizable and flexible. It is used on a wide range of platforms, from servers and supercomputers to smartphones and embedded devices. Linux is well-known for its stability, security, and versatility, and it is widely used in the enterprise and scientific communities.
- **FreeBSD:** A free and open-source Unix-like operating system that is widely used as a server platform. FreeBSD is known for its stability and security, and it is widely used for web hosting, databases, and other server applications.
- **OpenBSD:** A free and open-source Unix-like operating system that is widely known for its security features. OpenBSD is often used as a firewall, VPN gateway, or secure web server.
- **NetBSD:** A free and open-source Unix-like operating system that is widely known for its portability and compatibility with a wide range of platforms and hardware architectures. NetBSD is often used in embedded systems and other resource-constrained environments.
- **Chrome OS:** A free and open-source operating system developed by Google that is based on the Linux kernel. Chrome OS is primarily used on Chromebooks, which are laptops designed for web-based applications and cloud computing.

Open-source operating systems provide users with the freedom to modify, distribute, and use the software as they see fit. They also provide a large community of developers who can contribute to the development and maintenance of the operating system, making them highly stable, secure, and reliable platforms for a wide range of applications.

❖ **Text editors**

Notepad++ and Sublime Text are popular text editors for coding. Notepad++ is a free and open-source text editor that is primarily used for coding in Windows. It supports a wide range of programming languages, including C, C++, Java, Python, and more. Notepad++ is known for its fast performance, powerful features, and customizable interface. Sublime Text is a proprietary, cross-platform text editor that is widely used for coding and web development. It supports a wide range of programming languages and provides a fast, intuitive interface and a wide range of features, including syntax highlighting, code completion, and a powerful built-in file explorer. Both Notepad++ and Sublime Text are highly respected in the software development community and are used extensively by developers to write, edit, and manage their code. They provide developers with fast and efficient text editing tools that help streamline the software development process and improve productivity.

❖ **Version control systems**

Version control systems are software tools that track changes made to a set of files over time. They allow developers to keep track of different versions of their code, collaborate with other developers, and revert to previous versions of the code if needed. Here are some of the most popular version control systems:

- **Git:** Git is a distributed version control system that is widely used for software development. It allows developers to keep track of changes made to their code, collaborate with other developers, and revert to previous versions of their code if needed. Git is fast, flexible, and secure, and it is used by a wide range of organizations and individuals for software development.
- **Subversion (SVN):** Subversion is a centralized version control system that is widely used for software development. It allows developers to keep track of changes made to their code, collaborate with other developers, and revert to previous versions of the code if needed. Subversion is known for its stability and reliability, and it is used by a wide range of organizations and individuals for software development.
- **Mercurial:** Mercurial is a distributed version control system that is similar to Git. It allows developers to keep track of changes made to their code, collaborate with other developers, and revert to previous versions of the code if needed. Mercurial is known for its simplicity, efficiency, and scalability, and it is used by a wide range of organizations and individuals for software development.
- **Apache Cassandra:** Apache Cassandra is a distributed NoSQL database management system that is designed to handle large amounts of data across many commodity servers. It provides a high level of scalability, reliability, and performance, and it is widely used for big data applications and real-time data streaming.

Version control systems are an essential tool for software development and are widely used by organizations and individuals to manage their code. They provide developers with a way to track changes made to their code over time, collaborate with other developers, and revert to previous versions of the code if needed, which helps to ensure that software projects are developed efficiently and effectively.

❖ **Online tutorials and forums**

Websites like Stack Overflow, GitHub, and Reddit offer a wealth of information and resources for computer engineers. Stack Overflow is a question-and-answer platform for software developers where users can ask and answer technical questions related to programming and software development. It has a large and active community of developers who are always ready to help answer questions and provide advice.GitHub is a web-based platform that allows users to store and manage their code, as well as collaborate with other developers. It also offers a vast library of open-source projects that developers can use and contribute to, as well as a large community of developers who can provide support and guidance.

Reddit is a social news and entertainment website that has many communities dedicated to specific topics, including software development. Reddit's software development community is a vibrant and active community of developers who share knowledge, ask questions, and provide support to one another.

These websites provide a wealth of information and resources for computer engineers and software developers, and they are essential tools for those looking to improve their skills and stay up-to-date with the latest developments in the field. They offer a platform for developers to collaborate, learn from each other, and find solutions to complex problems, which helps to advance the field of computer engineering and improve the quality of software development.

❖ **Project-based learning:**

Websites like Hackster and Instructables offer hands-on projects and tutorials for computer engineering and hardware development.

Hacksters is a community of engineers, makers, and hobbyists who share their knowledge and expertise through hands-on projects and tutorials. It offers a wide range of projects for users to build and experiment with, including projects related to computer engineering, hardware development, and the Internet of Things (IoT). Instructables is a similar website that provides a platform for users to share their projects and tutorials with the wider community. It offers a wealth of tutorials and projects for users to explore, ranging from simple hobby projects to complex engineering projects.

Project-based learning is a highly effective way for computer engineers and hardware developers to gain practical experience and deepen their knowledge of the field. By working on hands-on projects and experimenting with different technologies, engineers and developers can build their skills and expertise, and create real-world solutions to complex problems. These websites provide a valuable resource for computer engineers and hardware developers to access the latest knowledge, connect with other experts, and share their own experiences and projects.

These free resources and tools can provide an excellent foundation for learning computer engineering and developing practical skills. However, they may not provide the depth of knowledge and structure available through formal courses or degree programs.

The future of computer engineering

The field of computer engineering is constantly evolving and will be shaped by various trends shortly. One of the most significant trends in Artificial Intelligence and Machine Learning, which are expected to have a major impact on the field. AI and ML will enable advanced automation and decision-making, as well as improve data analysis and decision-making. Another key trend is the Internet of Things (IoT), which refers to the interconnected network of physical devices and objects embedded with electronics, software, sensors, and connectivity. As IoT continues to grow and evolve, it will lead to new applications and solutions that will change the way we live and work. Quantum Computing is also likely to play a major role in the future of computer engineering, particularly in fields such as cryptography, simulation, and optimization. As quantum computing technology becomes more advanced, it will revolutionize the way we approach complex problems and improve our ability to solve them. The widespread adoption of 5G networks and edge computing will also have a major impact on computer engineering, driving new applications and use cases such as real-time data processing, autonomous vehicles, and industrial IoT. Finally, cybersecurity will become increasingly important as the digital world continues to grow. Computer engineers will play a critical role in developing new solutions to protect against cyber threats and ensure the security of our digital infrastructure. With the rise of these trends, computer engineering will continue to be an exciting and dynamic field with many opportunities for growth and innovation.

In the future, computer engineers will need to be adaptable, knowledgeable about a wide range of technologies, and focused on delivering innovative solutions to meet the demands of a rapidly evolving digital landscape. Additionally, they will need to stay up-to-date with the latest developments in the field and be able to quickly learn new technologies as they emerge.

07
SPECIALIST IN USER SUPPORT

User support is important in the field of computers because it helps ensure that users can effectively and efficiently utilize technology to meet their needs. This can include assisting with technical issues, providing information and guidance on software and hardware usage, and offering training and education on how to use technology effectively.By providing user support, organizations can improve user satisfaction and productivity, reduce the number of technical issues, and minimize downtime and disruptions. Additionally, effective user support can help build trust and confidence in technology among users, promoting its widespread adoption and integration into daily operations.

Different roles in user support in computer

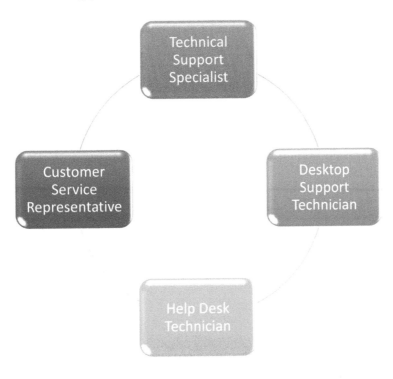

Figure 13Different roles in user support in computer

- **Technical Support Specialist**

A Technical Support Specialist is responsible for providing technical assistance to customers or clients regarding a particular product or service. They are typically the first point of contact for customers who are experiencing technical issues and need help resolving them. Technical Support Specialists are skilled problem solvers who possess a strong understanding of the technical aspects of the product or service they are supporting

Technical Support Specialists are required in a wide range of industries, including technology, software development, telecommunications, healthcare, finance, and manufacturing. Their role is to troubleshoot technical issues and provide solutions to customers in a timely and effective manner. They use their technical expertise to diagnose and resolve issues, as well as to provide advice and guidance to customers on how to best use the product or service they are supporting.

In addition to their technical expertise, Technical Support Specialists must possess strong communication and customer service skills. They must be able to communicate technical information clearly and concisely to non-technical customers, and they must be able to remain patient and professional while dealing with frustrated or upset customers. They must also be able to document customer interactions and technical issues in detail, as this information is often used to improve products or services and to provide feedback to development teams. Overall, Technical Support Specialists play a critical role in ensuring customer satisfaction and maintaining the reputation of the company they are working for.

- **Help Desk Technician**

A Help Desk Technician is responsible for providing technical support to end-users who are experiencing technical issues with hardware or software. They are the first point of contact for customers who need help with issues such as network connectivity, software installation, and printer problems. Help Desk Technicians use their technical expertise to troubleshoot issues and provide solutions to customers in a timely and effective manner.

Help Desk Technicians are required in a wide range of industries, including technology, software development, healthcare, finance, and government. Their role is to provide technical support to end-users and help them resolve issues quickly and efficiently. They use a variety of tools, including remote desktop software and knowledge base articles, to diagnose and resolve technical issues. They may also escalate more complex issues to higher-level technical support teams.

In addition to their technical expertise, Help Desk Technicians must possess strong communication and customer service skills. They must be able to communicate technical information clearly and concisely to non-technical customers, and they must be able to remain patient and professional while dealing with frustrated or upset customers. They must also be able to document customer interactions and technical issues in detail, as this information is often used to improve products or services and to provide feedback to development teams. Overall, Help Desk Technicians play a critical role in ensuring customer

- **Desktop Support Technician**

Information Security Analyst: An information security analyst is a professional who is responsible for maintaining the security and integrity of an organization's data and systems. They are tasked with identifying and addressing security threats and vulnerabilities and developing strategies to protect against cyber attacks, data breaches, and other forms of unauthorized access.

To become an information security analyst, you must possess a strong technical background in areas such as network security, cryptography, and computer programming. You must also have a deep understanding of industry best practices, standards, and regulations related to information security. Additionally, you should be able to assess risk, develop security policies and procedures, and communicate effectively with stakeholders to ensure that they are aware of potential security risks and how to mitigate them.

An information security analyst must be able to monitor network activity, analyze logs, and investigate incidents to determine the cause of security breaches or unauthorized access. They may also conduct vulnerability assessments, penetration testing, and security audits to identify weaknesses in the organization's security systems. Additionally, they may work with other teams to implement security measures such as firewalls, intrusion detection systems, and access control mechanisms to prevent unauthorized access to sensitive information. Overall, an information security analyst is a vital member of any organization's IT team, ensuring the confidentiality, integrity, and availability of critical data and systems.

- **Customer Service Representative**

A customer service representative (CSR) is a professional who provides assistance and support to customers with their inquiries, complaints, and concerns. CSRs are responsible for handling incoming calls, emails, chats, and other forms of communication from customers, ensuring that their issues are resolved efficiently and effectively.

To become a successful CSR, you must possess excellent communication and interpersonal skills, as well as a deep understanding of the products and services offered by the company. You must be able to listen carefully to customers' concerns, empathize with them, and offer appropriate solutions that meet their needs. You should also be able to handle difficult customers, diffuse tense situations, and maintain a positive attitude in all interactions.

A CSR must be knowledgeable about the company's policies, procedures, and products or services. They must be able to troubleshoot technical issues, provide basic product support, and provide accurate and helpful information to customers. Additionally, a CSR must be able to maintain accurate records of customer interactions, document any issues or concerns, and follow up with customers to ensure their satisfaction. CSR plays a crucial role in ensuring customer loyalty, retention, and satisfaction.

Skills required by user support expert

A user support expert is an individual who is responsible for providing technical support to users who are having difficulties with software, hardware, or systems. To be successful in this role, a user support expert must possess a combination of technical knowledge and soft skills.

Strong communication skills, both written and verbal, are essential for effective communication with users. The user support expert should be able to articulate technical information clearly and concisely to users who may have limited technical knowledge.

Technical knowledge of the specific software, hardware, or systems is also a key requirement for this role. The user support expert should have a deep understanding of the systems they are supporting and be able to diagnose and troubleshoot technical issues. Problem-solving skills are also essential for this role, as the user support expert must be able to find solutions to technical issues and resolve them promptly. This requires the ability to think critically and creatively, and to approach problems from different angles.

Empathy and patience are also critical for this role, as the user support expert must be able to handle difficult situations with understanding and compassion. The user support expert should be able to put themselves in the user's shoes and provide the support that is both effective and empathetic. Organizational and time management skills are also important, as the user support expert must be able to prioritize tasks, manage multiple support requests, and meet deadlines. This requires the ability to stay focused and organized, even in high-pressure situations. Adaptability is also essential for this role, as technology is constantly evolving and changing. The user support expert must be able to learn new technologies and tools quickly and adapt to changes in the work environment.

Attention to detail is also important, as the user support expert must be able to pay close attention to details, such as error messages and log files, to resolve technical issues.

Customer service orientation is critical for this role, as the user support expert must have a customer-focused mindset, with a desire to provide excellent service to users and resolve their issues as efficiently as possible. These skills, combined with technical knowledge, are what make a successful user support expert.

Available certifications in computer user support

There are several certifications in computer user support, some of the most popular ones are:

- **CompTIA A+**

CompTIA A+ [10]certified professionals are proven, problem solvers. They support today's core

---

[10] *https://www.comptia.org/certifications/a*

technologies from security to networking to virtualization and more. CompTIA A+ is the industry standard for launching IT careers into today's digital world. CompTIA A+ is the only industry-recognized credential with performance testing to prove pros can think on their feet to perform critical IT support tasks. It is trusted by employers around the world to identify the go-to person in end-point management & technical support roles. CompTIA A+ appears in more tech support job listings than any other IT credential. The CompTIA A+ Core Series requires candidates to pass two exams: Core 1 (220-1101) and Core 2 (220-1102) covering the following new content, emphasizing the technologies and skills IT pros need to support a hybrid workforce.

- **Microsoft Technology Associate (MTA)**

This is an entry-level certification for individuals interested in building a career in technology. MTA is a certification program from Microsoft designed to provide entry-level IT professionals with the fundamental technical skills needed to pursue a successful career in the field. The MTA program covers a range of basic IT concepts and skills, including operating systems, software development, database administration, and security. The certification is designed for individuals just starting in their IT careers, or for those looking to make a career change into the field of technology. Earning an MTA certification can demonstrate a basic level of competency in a specific technology area and provide a foundation for further study and career advancement. The certification is recognized globally and can be a valuable addition to a candidate's resume when seeking employment in the IT field.

- **Certified Computer User Support Technician (CCUST)**

The Certified Computer User Support Technician (CCUST) is a certification that validates the skills and knowledge of individuals who provide technical support to end-users in a professional setting. The CCUST certification program covers a range of topics, including computer hardware and software, operating systems, network systems, and troubleshooting techniques. The CCUST certification is designed for individuals who work in a technical support role and are responsible for assisting users with technical issues. The certification demonstrates a level of expertise in the field and shows that the individual has the skills and knowledge necessary to effectively support end-users.

Holding a CCUST certification can be beneficial for individuals looking to advance their careers in technical support or for those seeking employment in the field. It can demonstrate to potential employers that the individual has the necessary knowledge and skills to provide quality support to end-users and can help set them apart from other job candidates.

- **Certified Support Center Analyst (CSCA)**

The Certified Support Center Analyst (CSCA) is a certification that recognizes individuals who work in technical support and service centre environments. The CSCA certification program covers a range of topics, including customer service, communication skills, problem-solving, and technical knowledge. The certification is designed for individuals who work in technical support centres and are responsible for assisting customers with technical issues. The CSCA certification demonstrates a level of expertise in customer service and technical support and shows that the individual has the skills and knowledge necessary to effectively support customers.

Holding a CSCA certification can be beneficial for individuals looking to advance their careers in technical support or for those seeking employment in the field. It can demonstrate to potential employers that the individual has the necessary customer service and technical skills to provide quality support to customers and can help set them apart from other job candidates.

- **Apple Certified Support Professional (ACSP)**

A certification program for Apple support professionals. This certification gives you a competitive edge in today's evolving job market. It will enable you to benefit from the power of the Apple brand.

The Apple Certified Support Professional (ACSP) is a certification program offered by Apple Inc. to validate the technical knowledge and customer service skills of individuals who provide support for Apple products. The ACSP certification covers a range of topics, including the Mac operating system, Apple hardware, and applications. The certification is designed for individuals who work in technical support and are responsible for assisting customers with technical issues related to Apple products. The ACSP certification demonstrates a level of expertise in the field and shows that the individual has the skills and knowledge necessary to effectively support Apple customers.

Holding an ACSP certification can be beneficial for individuals looking to advance their careers in technical support for Apple products or for those seeking employment in the field. It can demonstrate to potential employers that the individual has the necessary knowledge and skills to provide quality support to Apple customers and can help set them apart from other job candidates.

- **HDI Customer Service Representative (HDI-CSR)**

HDI Customer Service Representative (HDI-CSR) training focuses on call handling best practices, communication [11]and listening techniques, documentation, problem-solving, and troubleshooting skills, conflict negotiation, and responses to difficult customer behaviours. This certification verifies that customer service professionals are knowledgeable in the skills and techniques required to provide exceptional customer service and support in both support centre and call centre environments. It ensures they understand how to assess customer needs while exceeding their expectations.

The HDI Customer Service Representative (HDI-CSR) is a certification offered by the Help Desk Institute (HDI), a leading organization in the technical support and service management industry. The HDI-CSR certification program is designed to validate the customer service and technical skills of

---

[11] *https://www.thinkhdi.com/education/courses/hdi-customer-service-representative.aspx#*

individuals who provide support to customers in a technical support centre environment. The HDI-CSR certification covers a range of topics, including customer service, communication skills, problem-solving, and technical knowledge. The certification is designed for individuals who work in technical support centres and are responsible for assisting customers with technical issues.

Holding an HDI-CSR certification can be beneficial for individuals looking to advance their careers in technical support or for those seeking employment in the field. It can demonstrate to potential employers that the individual has the necessary customer service and technical skills to provide quality support to customers and can help set them apart from other job candidates. The HDI-CSR certification is recognized as a standard of excellence in the technical support industry.

Industries where specialists in computer user support are required

Specialists in computer user support are required in a variety of settings, including in business organizations to provide technical support for employees and troubleshoot issues with computers, networks and other related systems. Government agencies provide technical support for employees and assist with the maintenance and repair of computer systems and networks.

Also, educational institutions provide support for students and faculty, troubleshoot computer-related issues and maintain educational technology systems. Similarly, Healthcare organizations support the use of electronic medical record systems and assist with the maintenance and repair of computer systems. Furthermore, call centres provide technical support to customers of technology companies via phone or chat. Moreover, Online businesses provide customer support through email or chat and troubleshoot technical issues with e-commerce websites and systems.

Expected salary for user support experts

The salary for a computer user support specialist can vary widely based on factors such as location, experience, industry, and specific job responsibilities. In general, the median salary in the United States for computer user support specialists is around $52,000 per year, with some earning as much as $80,000 or more with significant experience and advanced skills. It is also important to note that salaries for computer user support specialists can vary greatly by industry. For example, those working in the technology sector or for large corporations may earn higher salaries than those working in small businesses or non-profit organizations. Additionally, those working in cities with a high cost of living, such as San Francisco or New York, can expect to earn higher salaries than those working in smaller cities or rural areas.

Available free online courses on computer user support

There are many free online courses available for those interested in learning about computer user support. Here are a few popular options:

Table 7:Available free online courses on computer user support

SN	Institution	Course Name	Level	Duration	Link
1	Coursera	Technical Support Fundamentals	Beginner	5 weeks	https://www.coursera.org/learn/technical-support-fundamentals
2	Coursera	Google IT Support Professional Certificate	Beginner	5 courses, 8-14 weeks each	https://www.coursera.org/professional-certificates/google-it-support
3	edX	IT Support: Fundamentals	Beginner	16 weeks	https://www.edx.org/course/it-support-fundamentals
4	edX	IT Support: Networking Essentials	Intermediate	10 weeks	https://www.edx.org/course/it-support-networking-essentials
5	Khan Academy	Hour of Code	Beginner	Self-paced	https://www.khanacademy.org/hourofcode

These courses can be a great way to get started in computer user support or to expand your existing skills and knowledge.

Free resources and tools for user support experts

Below are free resources and tools available for computer user support specialists

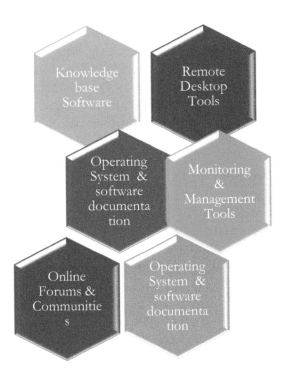

Figure 14:Resources for Support Experts

⊙ **Remote Desktop tools:**

Tools such as TeamViewer and AnyDesk allow for remote access to computers for troubleshooting and support.

Remote desktop tools like TeamViewer and AnyDesk are commonly used for remote access to computers for various purposes, including remote support, remote administration, remote collaboration, and more. These tools allow you to connect to a remote computer as if you were physically sitting in front of it, allowing you to control its mouse and keyboard, access its files and programs, and perform other tasks. This can be especially useful for resolving technical issues, providing remote training, or assisting remote workers with tasks on their work computers.

⊙ **Online forums and communities**

Sites like Reddit, Stack Overflow, and Spiceworks offer forums where computer support specialists can ask questions, find solutions to problems and connect with others in the field.

⊙ **Operating System and software documentation**

Official documentation and support resources provided by the operating system and software vendors, such as Microsoft, Apple, and Google, can be valuable resources for resolving issues. Operating systems and software documentation are important aspects of computer technology.

Documentation includes user manuals, reference guides, help files, and online resources that provide information on using, configuring, and troubleshooting an operating system or software application. It is intended to make the software more accessible and usable for users and to help them understand how the software works and how to get the most out of it. Documentation can also help troubleshoot and resolve technical issues and provide information on the latest features and upgrades. Good documentation is considered a key component of any software or operating system, as it helps users understand and effectively use the technology.

◉ Knowledge base software

Tools like Zendesk, Help Scout, and Freshdesk provide a centralized repository of information and support resources that can be used to assist users.

Knowledge base software, also known as help desk software or customer support software, is designed to help organizations manage customer inquiries and support requests. Tools like Zendesk, Help Scout, and Freshdesk are popular examples of knowledge-base software. These tools allow organizations to create a centralized repository of information that customers can access to find answers to common questions or issues. The knowledge base can include articles, FAQs, tutorials, and other types of content that can help customers resolve problems on their own without having to contact support.

In addition to the knowledge base, knowledge base software often includes features for managing support tickets, chat and email support, and customer service analytics. This makes it a comprehensive solution for organizations looking to improve their customer support processes and provide better service to their customers.

◉ Monitoring and management tools

Tools like Nagios and SolarWinds can be used to monitor computer systems and networks, helping support specialists to identify and resolve issues before they become major problems.

Monitoring and management tools like Nagios and SolarWinds are used to monitor and manage the performance and availability of various IT systems, including servers, network devices, applications, and services. These tools allow administrators to proactively identify and resolve problems before they impact users or cause downtime. They can monitor a variety of parameters, such as network traffic, CPU utilization, disk space, and more, and alert administrators when these parameters exceed specified thresholds. In addition to monitoring, these tools also provide management capabilities, such as remote administration, configuration management, and reporting. This allows administrators to quickly and efficiently resolve problems while also providing them with the information they need to optimize performance and ensure the availability and reliability of IT systems.

Monitoring and management tools play a crucial role in ensuring the health and reliability of IT systems and are essential tools for administrators in any organization that relies on technology.

These resources and tools can help computer user support specialists be more efficient, provide better support, and stay up-to-date with the latest developments in the field.

The future of computer user support

The future of computer user support is likely to be shaped by several trends, such as increased automation which is the use of artificial intelligence and machine learning to automate routine tasks, and support functions is likely to become more widespread, allowing support specialists to focus on more complex issues. With more people working remotely due to the COVID-19 pandemic, the demand for remote support tools and services is expected to grow. The shift to cloud-based solutions for storage, computing, and software delivery is likely to increase, leading to a growing need for support specialists who are knowledgeable about these technologies. As the threat of cyber attacks continues to grow, computer user support specialists will need to be increasingly focused on ensuring the security of computer systems and data. Companies are becoming increasingly focused on delivering a positive customer experience, and computer user support specialists will play a key role in achieving this goal by resolving issues quickly and effectively. In the future, computer user support specialists will need to be adaptable, knowledgeable about a wide range of technologies, and focused on delivering excellent customer service. Additionally, they will need to stay up-to-date with the latest developments in the field and be able to quickly learn new technologies as they emerge.

08
DATA ANALYSTS

Data analysis is the process of examining, cleaning, transforming, and modelling data to discover useful information, draw conclusions, and support decision-making. It involves using statistical, algorithmic, and visual methods to uncover patterns and insights in data and to identify relationships between variables. The end goal of data analysis is to improve understanding of a phenomenon or to support decision-making.

Data analysis is important because it helps to provide insights into data and identify patterns and relationships.to Support informed decision-making by turning data into actionable information.Not only that, but also to enhance understanding and uncover trends, opportunities, and areas for improvement. Data analysis helps to identify potential problems and risks and to evaluate the effectiveness of strategies and programs. Moreover, data analysis improves communication and collaboration by visualizing data in an accessible way and increases efficiency by automating repetitive tasks and identifying areas for optimization.

Different roles in data analysis

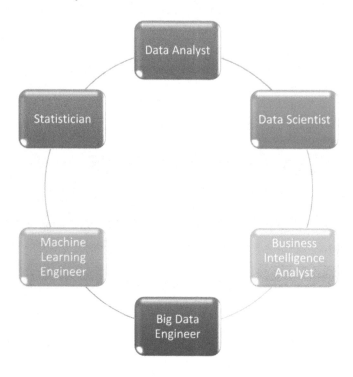

Figure 15:Different Roles in Data Analysis

◉ **Data Analyst**

A data analyst is a professional who is responsible for collecting, processing, and performing statistical analysis on data to uncover insights and inform business decisions.

Data analysts use various techniques, including data mining, data visualization, and machine learning, to extract insights from large and complex data sets. They then use these insights to inform business decisions, improve processes, and drive growth.

Data analysts work in a variety of industries, including finance, healthcare, retail, technology, and more. They may be employed by companies, consult for clients, or work for government agencies or non-profit organizations.

Some of the specific responsibilities of a data analyst can include the following:

- Collecting and importing data from various sources
- Cleaning and preprocessing data to ensure accuracy and consistency
- Performing exploratory data analysis to uncover patterns and trends
- Building predictive models and running simulations to support decision making
- Visualizing data and presenting insights to stakeholders
- Communicating complex findings in a clear and actionable manner

- Staying up-to-date with the latest data analysis tools and techniques.

Overall, data analysts play a critical role in today's data-driven world by providing valuable insights that help organizations make informed decisions and improve their performance

⊙ Data Scientist

A data scientist is a professional who uses statistical and machine-learning techniques to extract insights and knowledge from data. Data Scientists are focused on using advanced analytics techniques, such as machine learning, on making predictions or identify patterns in data. They use machine learning algorithms to build predictive models and make forecasts based on data. Data Scientists typically work with larger and more complex data sets, and they must have a deep understanding of data science and machine learning concepts. They must be able to understand business problems and identify opportunities for improvement, as well as communicate their findings to stakeholders. The role of a Data Scientist is more focused on the future, and they use data to make predictions and inform strategic decision-making.

⊙ Business Intelligence Analyst

A Business Intelligence (BI) Analyst is a professional who is responsible for using data and analytics to support decision-making and drive business growth.BI Analysts collect, process, and analyze data from various sources, such as sales, marketing, and financial data, to gain insights into business performance. They use BI tools, such as data visualization and dashboards, to present their findings in a clear and meaningful way. The role of a BI Analyst is to provide stakeholders with the information they need to make informed decisions. They must have a strong understanding of business processes and be able to communicate complex findings in a clear and actionable manner.BI Analysts can be found in a variety of industries, including finance, healthcare, retail, technology, and more. They may be employed by companies, consult for clients, or work for government agencies or non-profit organizations.

Some of the specific responsibilities of a BI Analyst can include the following:

- Collecting and importing data from various sources
- Cleaning and preprocessing data to ensure accuracy and consistency
- Building and maintaining dashboards and reports to visualize data
- Analyzing data to uncover patterns and trends
- Communicating complex findings in a clear and actionable manner
- Collaborating with stakeholders to identify business problems that can be solved with data
- Developing and testing new methods for data analysis
- Staying up-to-date with the latest BI tools and techniques.

Overall, BI Analysts play a critical role in today's data-driven world by providing valuable insights that help organizations make informed decisions and improve their performance.

◉ Big Data Engineer

A Big Data Engineer is a professional who is responsible for designing, building, and maintaining large-scale data processing systems. They work with big data technologies, such as Apache Hadoop, Apache Spark, and Apache Kafka, to process and analyze massive amounts of data from a variety of sources.

The role of a Big Data Engineer is to ensure that data is processed efficiently and accurately and that insights are extracted on time. They must have a deep understanding of big data technologies and be able to design and implement data processing pipelines that can handle large and complex data sets. Big Data Engineers can be found in a variety of industries, including finance, healthcare, retail, technology, and more. They may be employed by companies, consult for clients, or work for government agencies or non-profit organizations.

Some of the specific responsibilities of a Big Data Engineer can include the following:

- Designing and implementing data processing pipelines using big data technologies
- Ensuring data quality and accuracy
- Monitoring and maintaining data processing systems to ensure they are performing optimally
- Collaborating with data scientists and other stakeholders to identify business problems that can be solved with big data
- Building and maintaining data storage solutions, such as data lakes and data warehouses
- Developing and testing new methods for big data processing
- Staying up-to-date with the latest big data technologies and best practices.

Overall, Big Data Engineers play a critical role in today's data-driven world by enabling organizations to process and analyze large amounts of data in a timely and efficient manner. By doing so, they provide valuable insights that help organizations make informed decisions and improve their performance.

◉ Machine Learning Engineer

A Machine Learning (ML) Engineer is a professional who is responsible for developing and deploying ML models to solve real-world problems. They work with data scientists and other stakeholders to identify business problems that can be solved using ML and then build and deploy models to address those problems.ML Engineers must have a strong understanding of both ML algorithms and software engineering principles. They must be able to design and implement ML models that are accurate, scalable, and maintainable. They must also be familiar with big data technologies, such as Apache Hadoop and Apache Spark, to process and analyze large amounts of data.ML Engineers can be found in a variety of industries, including finance, healthcare, retail, technology, and more. They may be employed by companies, consult for clients, or work for government agencies or non-profit organizations.

Some of the specific responsibilities of an ML Engineer can include the following:

- Working with data scientists and other stakeholders to identify business problems that can be solved using ML
- Building and deploying ML models using tools such as TensorFlow, PyTorch, and scikit-learn
- Ensuring that ML models are accurate, scalable, and maintainable
- Monitoring and maintaining deployed ML models to ensure they are performing optimally
- Collaborating with data engineers to ensure that data is processed and stored efficiently
- Developing and testing new ML algorithms and models
- Staying up-to-date with the latest ML technologies and best practices.

Overall, ML Engineers play a critical role in today's data-driven world by providing organizations with the ability to leverage ML to solve real-world problems. By doing so, they provide valuable insights that help organizations make informed decisions and improve their performance.

◎ Statistician

A Statistician is a professional who is trained in the collection, analysis, interpretation, presentation, and dissemination of numerical data. Statisticians use mathematical and statistical methods to design experiments, analyze data, and draw conclusions about a population based on a sample. Statisticians work in a wide range of industries, including healthcare, finance, marketing, government, and more. They may be employed by companies, consult for clients, or work for government agencies or non-profit organizations.

Some of the specific responsibilities of a Statistician can include the following:

- Designing and conducting statistical studies to test hypotheses and draw inferences about a population
- Analyzing data using statistical software, such as R and SAS
- Interpreting results and communicating findings to stakeholders, including clients, colleagues, and management
- Developing statistical models and algorithms to solve real-world problems
- Collaborating with other researchers and professionals, such as data scientists and epidemiologists, to design and conduct studies
- Staying up-to-date with the latest statistical methods and best practices
- Providing expert advice and consultation on statistical matters.

Statisticians play a critical role in today's data-driven world by providing organizations with the ability to make informed decisions based on data and evidence. They use their expertise in mathematical and statistical methods to turn data into actionable insights that help organizations improve their performance.

Available certifications in data analysis

Some popular certifications in data analysis include:

- **Certified Analytics Professional (CAP)**

The Certified Analytics Professional (CAP) certification is a trusted, independent verification of the critical technical expertise and related soft skills possessed by accomplished analytics and data science professionals and valued by analytics-oriented organizations. As a vendor- and technology-neutral certification, CAP is a testament to an analytics professional's superior competency in the seven domains of analytics, providing a valuable platform for organizations to better identify, recruit, and retain top analytics talent, as well as for professionals to distinguish themselves in today's highly competitive analytics workforce.

- **Certified Business Intelligence Professional (CBIP)**

The CBIP is the industry's most in-demand credential for Data Professionals, along with the CDP-Certified Data Professional in Data Management. Significant promotions and salary increments have been granted to these credential holders. (BI) is an umbrella term that includes the applications, infrastructure and tools, and best practices that enable access to and analysis of information to improve and optimize decisions and performance.BI represents the tools and systems that play a key role in the strategic planning process within a corporation. These BI systems allow a company to gather, store, access and analyze corporate data to aid in decision-making.

- **Microsoft Certified: Azure Data Scientist Associate**

Candidates for the Azure Data Scientist Associate certification [12]should have subject matter expertise in applying data science and machine learning to implement and run machine learning workloads on Azure. Responsibilities for this role include designing and creating a suitable working environment for data science workloads; exploring data; training machine learning models; implementing pipelines; running jobs to prepare for production; and managing, deploying, and monitoring scalable machine learning solutions. A candidate for this certification should have knowledge and experience in data science by using Azure Machine Learning and MLflow.

- **Tableau Desktop Specialist**

This exam is for those who have foundational skills and understanding of Tableau Desktop and at least three months of applying this understanding in the product. Be sure to review the full Tableau Desktop Specialist Exam Prep Guide before registering. There are no required prerequisites for this exam.

- **Amazon Web Services Certified Big Data – Specialty**

The AWS Certified Big Data - Specialty (BDS-C00) examination is intended for individuals who perform complex big data analyses. This exam validates an examinee's technical skills and experience in designing and implementing AWS services to derive value from data. It validates an examinee's

---

[12] https://learn.microsoft.com/en-us/certifications/azure-data-scientist/

ability to: Implement core AWS big data services according to basic architectural best practices. Design and maintain big data.Leverage tools to automate data analysis.Recommended AWS Knowledge A minimum of 2 years of experience using AWS technology and AWS security best practices. Independently define AWS architecture and services and understand how they integrate. Define and architect AWS big data services and explain how they fit in the data lifecycle of collection, ingestion, storage, processing, and visualization.

- **Google Analytics Individual Qualification (IQ)**

The Google Analytics Individual Qualification (IQ) is a certification program offered by Google that validates the knowledge and expertise of individuals in the use of Google Analytics. The Google Analytics IQ certification covers a range of topics, including digital analytics principles, implementation, configuration, and management of Google Analytics. The certification is designed for individuals who work with Google Analytics, such as marketing professionals, web analysts, and digital marketers. The Google Analytics IQ certification demonstrates a level of expertise in using Google Analytics to gather and analyze data to make informed business decisions.

Holding a Google Analytics IQ certification can be beneficial for individuals looking to advance their careers in digital marketing or for those seeking employment in the field. It can demonstrate to potential employers that the individual has the necessary knowledge and skills to effectively use Google Analytics and can help set them apart from other job candidates. The Google Analytics IQ certification is recognized as a standard of excellence in the digital marketing industry.

- **IBM Certified Data Professional**

The badge earner is ready for a career in data science with demonstrated ability to solve real-world problems. They can apply Data Science methodology - work with Jupyter notebooks - create Python apps - access relational databases using SQL & Python - use Python libraries to generate data visualizations - perform data analysis using Pandas - construct & evaluate Machine Learning (ML) models using Scikit-learn & SciPy and apply data science & ML techniques to real location data sets.

Note that the specific certifications available may change over time, and new certifications may become available.

Skills required by data analyst

Data Analysts are required to have a strong set of technical skills to perform their job effectively. Some of these skills include proficiency in SQL for accessing and manipulating data in databases, knowledge of data visualization tools such as Tableau, PowerBI, or Matplotlib, experience in data wrangling and cleaning techniques, and familiarity with at least one programming language such as Python or R.

Additionally, data analysts should know statistical analysis and machine learning algorithms, an understanding of cloud computing platforms such as AWS, GCP, or Azure, and big data tools like Hadoop or Spark. They must also be able to work with various data storage systems and formats, including relational databases and NoSQL databases. Data Analysts need a strong set of skills beyond just technical abilities to excel in their role. Firstly, they should have strong analytical and problem-solving skills, which are crucial for discovering insights and finding solutions to complex problems. Additionally, familiarity with data warehousing concepts and databases is important.

Excellent communication skills are also critical for data analysts. They must be able to effectively present their insights and findings to stakeholders using clear and concise language. Knowledge of data mining and cleaning techniques is also necessary to ensure the accuracy of the data being analyzed. The ability to work with large datasets and knowledge of big data technologies are also key skills for data analysts. Understanding business operations and industry-specific terminology is important for context and to ensure that the insights and findings are relevant and valuable to the business. Attention to detail and the ability to perform quality assurance on data outputs are crucial for ensuring the reliability of the data and maintaining the credibility of the data analyst. Creativity and the ability to think outside the box are important for finding innovative solutions to complex problems.

It's important to note that the specific skills required for data analysts may vary depending on the specific role and industry. Therefore, data analysts should be adaptable and willing to continue learning and developing their technical skills to stay current in their field

Areas where data analysts are required

Data analysts are in high demand across many industries, including technology and software development, financial services and banking, healthcare, retail and e-commerce, government and public sector, telecommunications, transportation and logistics, energy and utilities, consulting and market research, and manufacturing and production. In these industries, data analysts play a critical role in analyzing large data sets to provide insights and recommendations that help organizations make informed decisions. They are responsible for gathering, cleaning, and analyzing data from a variety of sources, including customer and financial data, operational data, and market research data.

In the technology and software development industry, data analysts are needed to help companies make informed decisions about product development, pricing, and marketing strategies. In financial services and banking, data analysts help banks and other financial institutions manage risk, detect fraud, and identify growth opportunities. In healthcare, data analysts analyze patient data to identify patterns and trends that can inform treatment and research. In retail and e-commerce, data analysts help companies optimize their pricing and inventory strategies and improve customer experiences. In the government and public sector, data analysts help agencies improve services, reduce costs, and make more informed policy decisions.

Data analysts are in high demand because of the increasing amount of data that organizations are collecting and the need for insights and recommendations that can inform decision-making. To become a data analyst, a candidate typically needs a degree in a field such as mathematics, statistics, or computer science, as well as strong analytical and problem-solving skills, proficiency in programming and data analysis software, and the ability to communicate findings effectively to non-technical stakeholders.

Expected salaries for data analyst

The salary for a data analyst can vary widely depending on factors such as experience, industry, location, and education. On average, the median salary for a data analyst in the United States is around $68,000 per year, according to data from Glassdoor. However, salaries can range from $50,000 to $120,000 or more, depending on experience and other factors. For example, data analysts with experience in the technology industry or who hold advanced degrees may earn salaries at the higher end of this range, while those just starting in their careers may earn salaries on the lower end.

It's also important to keep in mind that salaries can vary widely based on the company and location. For example, data analysts in major cities such as San Francisco, New York, and Washington, D.C., may earn higher salaries than those working in smaller cities or rural areas.

Available free online course on data analysis

There are many free online courses available for individuals interested in learning about data analysis. Here are a few popular platforms that offer such courses:

Table 8:Available free online course on data analysis

SN	Institution	Course Name	Level	Duration	Link
1	Coursera	Data Analysis with Python	Intermediate	Four weeks	https://www.coursera.org/learn/data-analysis-with-python
2	Coursera	Applied Data Science with Python	Intermediate	Five courses, 4-6 weeks each	https://www.coursera.org/specializations/data-science-python
3	Coursera	Data Science Math Skills	Intermediate	Four weeks	https://www.coursera.org/learn/datascience mathskills
4	edX	Data Science Essentials	Beginner	Eight weeks	https://www.edx.org/course/data-science-essentials
5	edX	Data Analysis: Visualization and Dashboard Design	Intermediate	Six weeks	https://www.edx.org/course/data-analysis-visualization-and-dashboard-design
6	edX	Python Basics for Data Science	Beginner	Four weeks	https://www.edx.org/course/python-basics-for-data-science
7	Khan Academy	SQL	Intermediate	Self-paced	https://www.khanacademy.org/computing/computer-programming/sql

These courses can be a great way for individuals to learn about data analysis and develop the skills needed to succeed in the field. However, it's important to keep in mind that free courses may not have the same level of depth or rigour as paid courses.

Free resources and tools for data analysis

Below are various options available for free online for data analysis

R Programming: R is a popular open-source programming language for data analysis and statistical computing. It has a large community of users and developers and a vast library of packages for data analysis. R is a programming language and software environment for statistical computing and graphics. It is widely used for data analysis and has a large and active community of users, which contributes to its popularity and makes it a great choice for data analysis tasks. R has a variety of built-in functions and packages for data import, cleaning, manipulation, visualization, and analysis. It can handle large datasets and has advanced statistical modelling capabilities, making it a great choice for both simple and complex data analysis tasks. R has a user-friendly syntax and supports the creation of customized functions and packages, which makes it easy to automate tasks and streamline workflows. R also integrates well with other tools, such as databases, spreadsheets, and web technologies, making it a versatile and powerful tool for data analysis.

In addition, R has strong support for data visualization, with multiple libraries available for creating high-quality charts, graphs, and other types of visual representations of data. This can greatly enhance the interpretability and impact of your data analysis results. R is a valuable tool for anyone who works with data and is interested in data analysis. Whether you are a beginner or an experienced data analyst, R has something to offer and can help you tackle a wide range of data analysis tasks.

Python: Python is a widely-used programming language for data analysis, machine learning, and artificial intelligence. It has a large library of packages and tools for data analysis, including NumPy, Pandas, and Matplotlib. Python is a high-level programming language that is widely used for data analysis and has a large and active community of users. It is well-suited for data analysis tasks due to its simplicity, versatility, and abundance of libraries and tools available for data manipulation, analysis, and visualization.

Python has built-in support for reading and writing various data formats, including CSV, Excel, JSON, and SQL databases. Additionally, there are many libraries available for cleaning, transforming, and manipulating data, such as NumPy, Pandas, and sci-kit-learn. Python is also well-suited for data visualization, with libraries such as Matplotlib, Seaborn, and Plotly available for creating high-quality charts, graphs, and other types of visual representations of data. This makes it easier to understand and communicate your data analysis results. In addition, Python has a rich ecosystem of tools for machine learning, deep learning, and other forms of advanced data analysis. These tools, such as TensorFlow, Keras, and PyTorch, make it possible to build complex models and analyze large and complex datasets.

Python is a great choice for anyone interested in data analysis, whether you are a beginner or an experienced data analyst. It is easy to learn, versatile, and has a large and active community of users, making it a valuable tool for anyone working with data.

Excel: Excel is a widely-used spreadsheet software that has many built-in tools for data analysis, such as pivot tables, chart creation, and regression analysis. Excel is a widely used spreadsheet program that is well-suited for data analysis and visualization. It is a powerful tool that can be used for simple tasks, such as sorting and filtering data, as well as more complex tasks, such as creating pivot tables, charts, and graphs.

Excel provides a user-friendly interface for working with data, making it easy to import, clean, manipulate, and visualize data. It also supports a wide range of mathematical and statistical functions, making it possible to perform calculations and analyze data without having to write complex formulas or code. In addition, Excel provides a variety of tools for creating charts, graphs, and other visual representations of data. These tools allow you to quickly and easily summarize and visualize your data, making it easier to understand and communicate your results. One of the main advantages of Excel is that it is widely used and well-known, making it easy to share your data and results with others. Additionally, it integrates well with other Microsoft Office programs, such as Word and PowerPoint, making it easy to create professional-looking reports and presentations.

Excel is a valuable tool for data analysis, particularly for small to medium-sized datasets and simple to intermediate-level tasks. While it may not be as powerful as other data analysis tools, such as R or Python, it provides a user-friendly interface and is widely used, making it a great choice for many data analysis tasks.

Google Sheets: Google Sheets is a cloud-based spreadsheet software that has many of the same Google Sheets is cloud-based spreadsheet program that is parts of the Google Drive suite of productivity tools. It is a powerful tool for data analysis, particularly for small to medium-sized datasets, and is well-suited for simple to intermediate-level tasks. Google Sheets has a user-friendly interface and supports a wide range of functions and formulas, making it easy to import, clean, manipulate, and visualize data. It also provides a variety of tools for creating charts, graphs, and other visual representations of data, making it easier to understand and communicate your results.

One of the main advantages of Google Sheets is that it is cloud-based, meaning that you can access your data and analysis results from anywhere with an internet connection. This makes it easy to collaborate with others and share your data and results with others. Additionally, it integrates well with other Google Drive tools, such as Google Docs and Google Slides, making it easy to create professional-looking reports and presentations. Google Sheets also provides a variety of add-ons and extensions, which can be used to enhance the functionality of the program and add new features for data analysis. For example, you can use add-ons to import data from websites, perform advanced statistical analysis, and visualize data in new ways.

Google Sheets is a valuable tool for data analysis, particularly for small to medium-sized datasets and simple to intermediate-level tasks. Its user-friendly interface, cloud-based accessibility, and integration with other Google Drive tools make it a great choice for many data analysis tasks.

Tableau Public: Tableau Public is a free data visualization tool that allows users to connect to and analyze data from a wide range of sources. Tableau Public is a free data visualization tool that can be used to create interactive dashboards, charts, and graphs. It is designed to be easy to use and accessible to anyone, regardless of their technical expertise or experience with data analysis.

Tableau Public provides a drag-and-drop interface for working with data, making it easy to connect to a wide range of data sources, including spreadsheets, databases, and cloud-based data sources. It also provides a wide range of tools for cleaning and transforming data, making it possible to quickly and easily prepare your data for analysis. One of the key strengths of Tableau Public is its powerful visualization capabilities. It provides a variety of visualization types, including bar charts, line charts, scatter plots, and maps, making it possible to represent your data in a variety of ways. Additionally, Tableau Public provides a range of interactive features, such as the ability to filter, sort, and drill down into your data, making it easier to explore and understand your results.

Tableau Public is designed to be used for public data and is intended for non-commercial use. The data and visualizations created with Tableau Public are publicly accessible and can be easily shared with others. Tableau Public is a great choice for anyone looking for a powerful yet accessible data visualization tool. Its ease of use, powerful visualization capabilities, and ability to connect to a wide range of data sources make it a valuable tool for anyone working with data.

OpenRefine: OpenRefine is a free and open-source data cleaning tool that allows users to clean, transform, and normalize data.

OpenRefine is a free and open-source data cleaning and data wrangling tool. It is designed to help you clean and transform messy, complex data into a more organized and usable form. OpenRefine provides a user-friendly interface for working with data, making it easy to import, clean, manipulate, and export data. It supports a wide range of data formats, including spreadsheets, CSV files, and JSON files, making it possible to work with data from a variety of sources.

One of the key strengths of OpenRefine is its ability to handle messy and inconsistent data. It provides a variety of tools for cleaning and transforming data, such as the ability to remove duplicates, split and merge cells, and correct typos and inconsistencies in your data. It also provides a flexible scripting language, GREL (General Refine Expression Language), which allows you to write custom scripts to clean and manipulate your data in specific ways. OpenRefine is also designed to be flexible and extensible, making it possible to use a wide range of data types and use cases. It integrates with a variety of data storage and processing tools, including databases, spreadsheets, and cloud-based data platforms.

OpenRefine is a valuable tool for anyone working with messy, complex data. Its user-friendly interface, wide range of data cleaning and transformation tools, and flexible scripting language make it a great choice for data cleaning and data wrangling tasks.

Weka: Weka is a free and open-source machine learning software that allows users to perform data analysis and build predictive models.

Weka is a free and open-source software for machine learning and data mining. It is a suite of machine learning algorithms for solving a variety of data mining problems, including classification, regression, clustering, and association rule learning. Weka provides a graphical user interface for working with data, making it easy for users to interact with the software and apply machine learning algorithms to their data. It also provides a command-line interface for more advanced users who want to automate their data analysis tasks.

One of the key strengths of Weka is its wide range of machine-learning algorithms. It provides a variety of algorithms, including decision trees, neural networks, support vector machines, and many others, making it possible to tackle a wide range of data mining problems. It also provides tools for evaluating the performance of different algorithms, making it possible to compare the results of different models and choose the best one for your data.

Weka is designed to be flexible and extensible, making it possible to use a wide range of data types and use cases. It integrates with a variety of data storage and processing tools, including databases, spreadsheets, and cloud-based data platforms. Weka is a valuable tool for anyone working with machine learning and data mining. Its wide range of machine learning algorithms, user-friendly interface, and flexible integration options make it a great choice for solving a variety of data mining problems.

These resources and tools can be a great starting point for individuals who are interested in learning about data analysis or for those who are just starting in their careers. However, it's important to keep in mind that these free resources may not have the same level of functionality or support as paid tools.

The future of data analysis

The future of data analysis is expected to be shaped by several emerging trends, including:

The future of data analysis is likely to be characterized by the continued growth of big data, the increasing availability of cloud computing, the rise of artificial intelligence, and the increasing importance of data privacy and security. This will lead to more sophisticated data analysis tools, the development of new methods for processing and analyzing large and complex data sets, and the integration of data analysis into everyday business processes and decision-making. Additionally, there will be a growing emphasis on data literacy and the ability to interpret and communicate the insights obtained from data analysis.

09
DIGITAL MEDIA AND GRAPHICS EXPERTS

Digital media refers to media content that is created, stored, and distributed through digital technologies, including computers, the Internet, and mobile devices. Examples of digital media include images, videos, audio, text, and interactive content such as websites, apps, and online games. In contrast, graphics refers to a visual representation of information, data or ideas in the form of images, charts, illustrations, or animations. This includes both static and dynamic graphics, such as logos, illustrations, infographics, and video graphics. Digital graphics can be created using a variety of software tools, including raster graphics editors, vector graphics editors, 3D modelling software, and animation software. In digital media, graphics play a crucial role in creating visual interest and conveying information effectively.

A graphics professional is an individual who specializes in creating visual designs and illustrations using various tools and techniques, such as illustration software, image editing software, and computer-aided design (CAD) software. They use their skills to create designs for various purposes, such as advertising, branding, packaging, and web and mobile applications. A graphics professional may work as a freelancer, in-house for a company, or at an advertising or design agency. They may also be known as a graphic designer, visual designer, or digital artist.

Different roles in media and graphics

with a team of designers and developers to create visual representations of a brand or product, overseeing the overall look and feel of marketing and advertising campaigns.

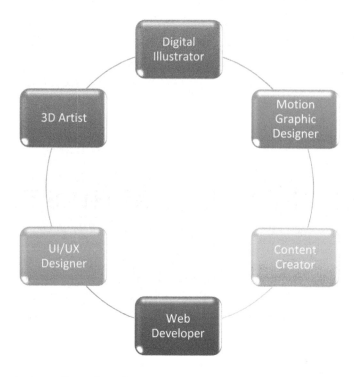

Figure 16Different roles in media and graphics

- **UI/UX Designer**

A UI/UX designer is a professional responsible for the design and development of the user interface (UI) and user experience (UX) of digital products such as websites, mobile applications, and software. They are responsible for creating and implementing designs that are both visually appealing and functional, ensuring that the product is easy to use and provides a positive user experience.

The role of a UI/UX designer involves a variety of tasks, including:

- Conducting user research to understand the target audience and their needs and behaviours

- Creating wireframes, prototypes, and high-fidelity mockups to visualize the product

- Designing the overall look and feel of the product, including the layout, colour scheme, and typography

- Creating and implementing design systems to ensure consistency across the product

- Working with developers to ensure that the design is properly implemented and functioning as intended

- Conducting user testing to gather feedback and iterate on the design

- Keeping up-to-date with the latest design trends and technologies.

A UI/UX designer should have a strong understanding of design principles, as well as the technical skills necessary to implement their designs, such as proficiency in design tools like Adobe Creative Suite or Sketch. They should also have excellent problem-solving skills and be able to think creatively and outside the box to find solutions to design challenges.

A UI/UX designer plays a critical role in ensuring that digital products are both visually appealing and functional, providing users with a positive experience and making it easier for them to achieve their goals.

- **Digital Illustrator**

A digital illustrator is an artist who creates illustrations using digital tools such as a computer, tablet, or graphics tablet. Digital illustration encompasses a wide range of styles and techniques, from hand-drawn illustrations that are scanned and coloured digitally to illustrations that are created entirely using digital tools. The role of a digital illustrator involves creating illustrations for a variety of media, including books, magazines, advertisements, and digital media such as websites and mobile applications. They work closely with clients and creative directors to understand their needs and create illustrations that meet the client's objectives

A digital illustrator should have a strong understanding of traditional illustration techniques, as well as the technical skills necessary to create digital illustrations, such as proficiency in illustration software such as Adobe Illustrator or Procreate. They should also have a strong sense of composition, colour, and form, as well as excellent drawing skills.

Steps for creating a digital illustration

1. Research and concept development to understand the project requirements and gather inspiration
2. Sketching and drawing to create the initial design
3. Refining the design and adding colour and details
4. Presenting the final illustration to the client for review and feedback
5. Making any necessary revisions to the illustration

Digital illustration is a rewarding and dynamic field that combines traditional illustration techniques with the latest digital tools and technology. Digital illustrators play a critical role in creating visually appealing and engaging illustrations that communicate ideas and tell stories in a variety of media.

- **Motion Graphic Designer**

A motion graphic designer is a professional who specializes in the design and animation of graphic elements for video and digital media. They use a combination of design, animation, and video production skills to create engaging and effective visual content that conveys information, tells stories and captures the attention of viewers.

The role of a motion graphic designer involves creating animations and visual effects for a variety of media, including television, film, advertisements, and digital media such as websites and social media platforms. They work closely with clients and creative directors to understand their needs and create motion graphics that meet the client's objectives.

A motion graphic designer should have a strong understanding of design principles, as well as the technical skills necessary to create motion graphics, such as proficiency in animation software such as Adobe After Effects or Cinema 4D. They should also have a strong sense of timing, spacing, and motion, as well as the ability to tell a story through animation.

The process of creating a motion graphic typically involves the following steps:

- Research and concept development to understand the project requirements and gather inspiration
- Sketching and storyboarding to create the initial design
- Creating and animating the graphic elements
- Adding sound, music, and special effects to enhance the animation
- Presenting the final motion graphic to the client for review and feedback
- Making any necessary revisions to the motion graphic.

Overall, motion graphic design is a dynamic and creative field that requires a combination of design and technical skills. Motion graphic designers play a critical role in creating engaging and effective visual content that captures the attention of viewers and communicates ideas in a variety of media.

- **Content Creator**

A content creator is a professional who creates and produces written, visual, or multimedia content for a variety of platforms, including websites, blogs, social media, and traditional media such as magazines and television. They are responsible for creating content that is engaging, informative, and relevant to the target audience, capturing the audience's attention and building brand awareness.

The role of a content creator involves a variety of tasks, including:

- Researching to understand the target audience and create content that meets their needs and interests
- Writing, editing, and producing articles, blog posts, videos, and other forms of content
- Creating visuals such as images, graphics, and videos to accompany the written content
- Optimizing content for search engines to improve visibility and drive traffic

- Promoting and sharing content through social media and other channels to reach a wider audience
- Collaborating with other team members, such as designers and marketers, to create integrated content campaigns
- Analyzing and tracking the performance of content to make informed decisions about future content creation.

A content creator should have excellent writing and communication skills, as well as the technical skills necessary to produce and publish content, such as proficiency in content management systems and multimedia editing software. They should also be knowledgeable about the latest trends and best practices in content creation and have a strong understanding of the target audience and their needs and interests.

Overall, a content creator plays a critical role in creating and producing high-quality content that captures the attention of the target audience and helps to build brand awareness and engagement.

- **Web Developer**

A web developer is a professional who creates and maintains websites and web applications. They are responsible for the technical aspects of a website, including its design, functionality, and security. Web developers work with a variety of technologies, including HTML, CSS, JavaScript, and back-end programming languages such as PHP, Ruby, and Python, to create and enhance websites and web applications.

The role of a web developer involves a variety of tasks, including:

- Working with clients and designers to understand the requirements for a website or web application
- Designing and building the structure and layout of a website or web application
- Writing code to implement features such as forms, dynamic content, and databases
- Ensuring that the website or web application is optimized for performance and security
- Testing the website or web application to ensure that it works as expected and fixing any bugs
- Maintaining and updating the website or web application to keep it up-to-date with the latest technologies and best practices
- Collaborating with other developers, designers, and stakeholders to ensure that the website or web application meets the needs of the client and the end-users.

A web developer should have strong technical skills, including a solid understanding of programming languages and web technologies, as well as the ability to write clean, efficient, and well-documented code. They should also be knowledgeable about the latest trends and best practices in web development and have strong attention to detail.

Overall, web development is a dynamic and fast-paced field that requires a combination of technical skills and creativity. Web developers play a critical role in creating and maintaining websites and web applications that are functional, user-friendly, and visually appealing and that meet the needs of the client and the end-users.

- **3D Artist**

A 3D artist is a professional who creates 3D models, animations, and visual effects for a variety of industries, including film, television, video games, architecture, product design, and virtual reality. They use computer software to design, model, texture, light, and render 3D objects and environments and to create animations and special effects.

The role of a 3D artist involves a variety of tasks, including:

- Working with a creative team to understand the project requirements and create concepts and storyboards
- Modelling 3D objects, characters, and environments, using techniques such as sculpting, rigging, and texturing
- Creating animations and special effects, including simulating physics, fire, water, and smoke
- Lighting and rendering 3D scenes to create photorealistic images and animations
- Collaborating with other artists, such as animators and compositors, to integrate 3D elements into live-action footage or 2D animations
- Ensuring that the 3D models and animations meet the project specifications and standards for quality and performance
- Staying up-to-date with the latest software and techniques in the 3D animation and visual effects industry.

A 3D artist should have strong technical skills, including a solid understanding of 3D modelling, animation, and rendering software, as well as a strong sense of design and composition. They should also be knowledgeable about the latest trends and best practices in 3D animation and visual effects and can work effectively in a fast-paced and deadline-driven environment.

3D artistry is a challenging and rewarding field that requires a combination of technical and creative skills. 3D artists play a critical role in creating stunning and immersive 3D visuals and animations that bring stories and ideas to life and captivate audiences. These are just a few of the many roles within the media and graphics industries, and the exact responsibilities and job titles can vary depending on the company or organization.

Skills required by media and graphics professionals

Media and graphics professionals are expected to have a blend of technical and creative skills. These skills include proficiency in graphic design software like Adobe Creative Suite, CorelDRAW, or GIMP. Additionally, a background in digital illustration and knowledge of tools such as vector graphics, raster graphics, and digital painting is crucial. Another important skill is UI design and an understanding of

UX design principles and wireframing tools such as Sketch or Figma. Web development is also crucial, with proficiency in HTML, CSS, and JavaScript and experience with CMSs such as WordPress or Shopify. In the realm of video and animation, knowledge of software such as Adobe After Effects, Autodesk Maya, or Blender is crucial. For 3D modelling and animation, proficiency in 3D software like Autodesk 3DS Max, Blender, or Cinema 4D is required.

Digital audio and video editing is also a critical skill, with knowledge of editing software like Adobe Premiere Pro, Final Cut Pro, or Avid Media Composer necessary. Finally, experience in printing and prepress technologies, including colour management, file preparation, and print production, is also important for these professionals.

It is also important for media and graphics professionals to stay up to date with the latest technologies and trends in their field and to continuously enhance their skills and knowledge

Available certifications in media and graphics

There are many certifications available for individuals interested in pursuing a career in the media and graphics industries. Here are some of the most popular certifications:

- **Adobe Certified Associate (ACA)**

ACA is a certification program offered by Adobe Systems that certifies individuals in various Adobe products, including Photoshop, Illustrator, and InDesign. The ACA certification is intended for individuals who are just starting their careers in digital media and graphic design or who are seeking to enhance their skills and knowledge of Adobe products. The ACA certification covers a range of Adobe software, including Adobe Photoshop, Illustrator, InDesign, and Dreamweaver. The certification program involves taking a certification exam that tests the individual's knowledge and ability to use Adobe software. Individuals who pass the exam receive an ACA certification, which is valid for two years.

The ACA certification is a recognized industry standard and can help individuals demonstrate their skills and knowledge to employers, clients, or customers. It can also help individuals stand out in a competitive job market and can lead to career advancement and higher earning potential.

- **Autodesk Certified User (ACU)**

Autodesk Certified User (ACU) is a certification program offered by Autodesk, Inc. for individuals who have demonstrated proficiency in using Autodesk software. The ACU certification is intended for individuals who are just starting their careers in design, engineering, and digital media or who are seeking to enhance their skills and knowledge in Autodesk products. The ACU certification covers a range of Autodesk software, including AutoCAD, Inventor, and Revit. The certification program involves taking a certification exam that tests the individual's knowledge and ability to use Autodesk software. Individuals who pass the exam receive an ACU certification, which is valid for two years.

The ACU certification is a recognized industry standard and can help individuals demonstrate their skills and knowledge to employers, clients, or customers. It can also help individuals stand out in a competitive job market and can lead to career advancement and higher earning potential.

- **Apple Certified Pro**

Apple Certified Pro is a certification program offered by Apple Inc. for individuals who have demonstrated proficiency in using Apple's professional software and hardware products. The Apple Certified Pro certification is intended for professionals who use Apple products in their work, such as audio and video professionals, graphic designers, and photographers. The Apple Certified Pro certification covers a range of Apple products, including Final Cut Pro X, Logic Pro X, and Motion. The certification program involves taking a certification exam that tests the individual's knowledge and ability to use the Apple software. Individuals who pass the exam receive an Apple Certified Pro certification, which is valid for three years.

The Apple Certified Pro certification is a recognized industry standard and can help individuals demonstrate their skills and knowledge to employers, clients, or customers. It can also help individuals stand out in a competitive job market and can lead to career advancement and higher earning potential.

- **Certified Internet Webmaster (CIW)**

Certified Internet Webmaster (CIW) is a certification program offered by the Certified Internet Web Professionals (CIW) organization for individuals who have demonstrated proficiency in web development and design, network technology, and security. The CIW certification is intended for individuals who work in web development, web design, and IT or who are seeking to enhance their skills and knowledge in these areas. The CIW certification covers a range of topics, including web design, web development, e-commerce, database design and management, security, and network technology. The certification program involves taking a certification exam that tests the individual's knowledge and ability to apply these concepts in a practical setting. Individuals who pass the exam receive a CIW certification, which is valid for two years.

The CIW certification is a recognized industry standard and can help individuals demonstrate their skills and knowledge to employers, clients, or customers. It can also help individuals stand out in a competitive job market and can lead to career advancement and higher earning potential. These are just a few of the many certifications available for media and graphics professionals, and the specific certifications will vary depending on the individual's area of focus and the industry they work in. It is important to research the specific certifications relevant to one's career goals, as well as the requirements and benefits of each certification.

Areas where digital media and graphics experts are required

Digital media and graphics experts are in high demand in a wide range of industries, from technology and entertainment to advertising and marketing. Some of the areas where digital media and graphics experts are required include web design and development, user experience (UX) design, motion graphics and animation, 3D modelling and visual effects (VFX), game design and development, graphic design, branding and marketing, virtual reality (VR) and augmented reality (AR), video production and post-production, interactive design and development, advertising and product design, user interface (UI) design, and data visualization and infographic design. Web design and development requires digital media and graphics experts to design and develop visually appealing and functional websites that are optimized for user experience and search engines. UX design focuses on creating intuitive and user-friendly interfaces and interactions for digital products, such as websites and mobile apps. Motion graphics and animation are used in a wide range of applications, from advertising and entertainment to education and training, to create engaging and interactive experiences.

In the entertainment industry, digital media and graphics experts are needed for 3D modelling and VFX to create realistic and visually stunning environments and characters for movies, TV shows, and video games. In the gaming industry, game design and development require digital media and graphics experts to create immersive and engaging gameplay experiences. In the marketing industry, digital media and graphics experts are needed for branding and marketing campaigns to create eye-catching graphics and visuals that help promote products and services. Overall, digital media and graphics experts play a critical role in creating effective and engaging digital experiences across a wide range of industries.

Expected salaries for digital media and graphics experts

The expected salary for digital media and graphics experts varies greatly depending on several factors, including location, years of experience, level of education, and specific areas of expertise. Some of the most popular roles in the field, such as web designer, UX designer, graphic designer, and video producer, typically have an average salary range of $40,000 to $85,000 per year.

However, for more specialized roles like motion graphics designer, 3D modeller, game developer, VR/AR developer, and UI designer, the salary can be significantly higher, with an average range of $60,000 to $130,000 per year. Similarly, branding and marketing specialists, as well as data visualization specialists, can earn an average salary of $50,000 to $100,000 per year. It's important to keep in mind that these are rough estimates, and actual salaries can vary greatly depending on the company and specific job offer.

Industries require digital media and graphics experts

Digital media and graphics experts are in high demand across a wide range of industries, reflecting the increasing importance of digital technologies and the growing need for effective communication and engagement with audiences through digital channels. This high demand can be seen in industries such as technology and software development, advertising and marketing, film and video production, gaming, and web and mobile development. The demand for digital media and graphics experts also extends to creative agencies, e-commerce, broadcasting and media, education and training, and healthcare and pharmaceuticals, among others. Additionally, industries such as retail and consumer products, automotive and transportation, and finance and banking also require the expertise of digital media and graphics professionals to help them effectively communicate and engage with their customers.

The increasing importance of digital technologies and the growing need for effective communication and engagement through digital channels have created high demand for digital media and graphics experts across a variety of industries. In these industries, digital media and graphics experts play a crucial role in creating and enhancing digital content, designing and developing user interfaces, and producing high-quality visual content.

Free online courses on digital media and graphics

There are several free online courses available for learning digital media and graphics, including:

Table 9:Free online courses on digital media and graphics

SN	Institution	Course Name	Level	Duration	Link
1	Coursera	3D Graphics for Web Developers	Intermediate	4 weeks	https://www.coursera.org/learn/3d-graphics-for-web-developers
2	Coursera	Computer Graphics	Intermediate	5 weeks	https://www.coursera.org/learn/computer-graphics
3	edX	Computer Graphics	Intermediate	10 weeks	https://www.edx.org/course/computer-graphics
4	Khan Academy	Computer Animation	Intermediate	Self-paced	https://www.khanacademy.org/partner-content/pixar/computer-animation
5	Coursera	Graphic Design	Beginner	4 weeks	https://www.coursera.org/learn/graphic-design
6	Coursera	Fundamentals of Graphic Design	Beginner	5 weeks	https://www.coursera.org/learn/fundamentals-of-graphic-design
7	Coursera	Introduction to Typography	Beginner	4 weeks	https://www.coursera.org/learn/typography
8	edX	Design Thinking Fundamentals	Beginner	4 weeks	https://www.edx.org/course/design-thinking-fundamentals

These courses offer a great opportunity to learn digital media and graphics skills at your own pace and can be a valuable resource for anyone looking to break into the field or improve their skills.

Free resources and tools for digital media and graphics

There are many free resources and tools available for digital media and graphics

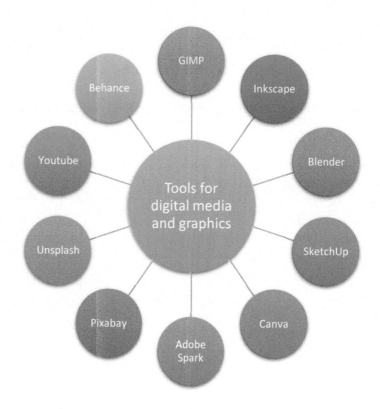

Figure 17:Free resources and tools for digital media and graphics

❖ **GIMP**

GIMP (GNU Image Manipulation Program) is a free, open-source image editing software program that is widely used for digital photo editing, graphic design, and digital painting. It is designed to be an alternative to commercial image editing software such as Adobe Photoshop and is available for various operating systems, including Windows, MacOS, and Linux.GIMP has a user-friendly interface and provides a wide range of features for image editings, such as colour correction, image composition, image retouching, and image manipulation. It also supports various image file formats and includes tools for working with layers, masks, and selections. Additionally, GIMP has a large community of users and developers who have contributed a wealth of plugins and tools to enhance the functionality of the software.

GIMP is a great option for individuals and organizations who want powerful and flexible image editing software that is also free to use. Whether you're a hobbyist, amateur photographer, graphic designer, or professional artist, GIMP provides a comprehensive suite of tools to help you create, edit, and manipulate digital images.

❖ **Inkscape**

Inkscape is a free, open-source vector graphics editor that is used for creating and editing scalable vector graphics (SVG) files. It is available for Windows, MacOS, and Linux operating systems.

Inkscape provides a user-friendly interface and a wide range of features for creating vector graphics, such as shape tools, text tools, and a powerful set of drawing tools. One of the strengths of Inkscape is its ability to create high-quality vector graphics that can be resized without losing quality, making it ideal for creating logos, icons, illustrations, and other graphics that need to be used in various sizes. Inkscape also supports a wide range of file formats, including SVG, PDF, EPS, and more, and can import and export files from other vector graphics software such as Adobe Illustrator.

Inkscape has a large and active user community, and there are many resources available, including tutorials, forums, and a repository of user-created extensions and add-ons. Whether you're a hobbyist, graphic designer, or professional artist, Inkscape provides a comprehensive suite of tools for creating, editing and manipulating vector graphics.

Blender

Blender is a free and open-source 3D creation software that is used for a wide range of tasks, including 3D modelling, animation, simulation, compositing, and motion graphics. It is available for Windows, MacOS, and Linux operating systems. Blender has a user-friendly interface and provides a wide range of features for creating and editing 3D graphics, including modelling tools, rigging tools, animation tools, and more. Blender is used by artists, animators, and visual effects professionals to create high-quality 3D content for film, television, video games, architecture, and product visualization. It supports a wide range of file formats, including its native format, the Blend file format, as well as other 3D file formats such as FBX, COLLADA, and STL.

Blender is highly customizable and has a large and active user community, with a wealth of resources available, including tutorials, forums, and a repository of user-created add-ons and plugins. Whether you're a beginner or an experienced 3D artist, Blender provides a powerful and flexible set of tools for creating and editing 3D graphics.

❖ **SketchUp**

SketchUp is a 3D modelling software for creating and visualizing 3D designs and models. It is used for a wide range of applications, including architecture, interior design, construction, engineering, and more. SketchUp is available in both free and paid versions, with the paid version offering additional features and capabilities.SketchUp has a user-friendly interface and provides a wide range of modelling tools, including the ability to create and manipulate 3D shapes, add text and annotations, and import and export a variety of file formats. It also has a large library of pre-built models and components that can be used in your designs, as well as a collection of plugins and extensions that can add additional functionality.

SketchUp is widely used in the architecture, engineering, and construction (AEC) industry, as well as by hobbyists, students, and educators. Whether you're a beginner or an experienced 3D modeller, SketchUp provides a flexible and intuitive set of tools for creating and visualizing 3D designs.

❖ Canva

Canva is a graphic design platform that provides an easy-to-use, drag-and-drop interface for creating a wide range of visual content, including graphics, presentations, posters, social media posts, and more. Canva is available in both free and paid versions, with the paid version offering additional features and capabilities. One of Canva's main strengths is its large library of templates, pre-made designs, and elements, including images, icons, shapes, and text styles, which can be easily customized to fit your needs. It also offers a variety of design tools and features, such as the ability to add and edit images, create charts and graphs, and add text and annotations to your designs.

Canva is widely used by individuals, businesses, and organizations for creating visually appealing and effective designs for various purposes, including marketing and advertising, social media, and branding. Whether you're a beginner or an experienced graphic designer, Canva provides a user-friendly and accessible platform for creating professional-looking designs.

❖ Adobe Spark

Adobe Spark is a suite of creative tools for creating and sharing visual content, including web pages, graphics, and videos. It is designed to be easy to use and accessible for people with little to no design experience and provides a range of templates, themes, and design elements to help users get started. Adobe Spark is part of the Adobe Creative Cloud suite of products and is available as a standalone product or as part of the Adobe Creative Cloud subscription. Adobe Spark allows users to create professional-looking designs and web pages quickly and easily without needing to know how to code. It offers a variety of design templates, pre-made graphics and icons, and the ability to add your images and text. It also provides tools for creating animations, adding video and audio to your designs, and incorporating interactive elements like buttons and forms.

Adobe Spark is widely used for a variety of purposes, including marketing and advertising, education, and personal projects. Whether you're creating graphics for social media, building a website, or putting together a visual presentation, Adobe Spark provides a powerful and accessible set of tools for creating visually engaging and impactful content.

❖ Pixabay

Pixabay is a website that provides a large collection of high-quality and royalty-free images, videos, and illustrations for personal and commercial use. It was created to provide an alternative to stock photo agencies and make high-quality images and videos available to anyone, anywhere.

One of the main advantages of Pixabay is that all of the content on the site is free to use, even for commercial purposes, without the need to pay royalties or licensing fees. This makes it an attractive option for businesses, bloggers, and others who need high-quality images and videos but don't want to pay the high costs associated with stock photo agencies. In addition to offering free images and videos, Pixabay also provides a user-friendly search interface and a range of tools for finding the right content for your needs. You can search for images and videos based on keywords, colour, category, and other criteria and then preview and download the content directly from the site.

Whether you're a professional graphic designer, marketer, or just someone looking for high-quality images and videos for personal use, Pixabay provides a vast and growing collection of content that is available to use at no cost.

❖ Unsplash

Unsplash is a website that offers a large collection of high-quality and royalty-free images that can be used for personal or commercial purposes. The site was created to provide a platform for photographers to share their work and make it accessible to a wider audience, and today it is one of the largest sources of free stock photos on the internet.

One of the main benefits of Unsplash is that all of the images on the site are available to use for free, without the need to pay royalties or licensing fees. This makes it an attractive option for businesses, bloggers, and others who need high-quality images but don't want to pay the high costs associated with stock photo agencies. In addition to offering free images, Unsplash also provides a user-friendly search interface and a range of tools for finding the right content for your needs. You can search for images based on keywords, colour, category, and other criteria and then preview and download the content directly from the site.

Whether you're a professional graphic designer, marketer, or just someone looking for high-quality images for personal use, Unsplash provides a vast and growing collection of content that is available to use for free. The site is updated regularly with new photos from a community of talented photographers, making it an essential resource for anyone in need of beautiful and inspiring images.

❖ YouTube

YouTube is indeed a great resource for learning digital media and graphics. With its vast collection of tutorials, how-to videos, and other educational content, it's easy to find the information you need to learn new skills and improve your existing ones. In addition to tutorials and other instructional videos, you can also find a wealth of resources on YouTube, including live streams and webinars, product demos, and case studies. Many content creators and experts in the field also use YouTube to share their work and offer insights and tips to others in the community. Furthermore, YouTube is also a platform for sharing your content. Whether you're a professional or just starting, you can use YouTube to showcase your work and build a following. With its large and diverse audience, it's an excellent way to reach potential customers, collaborators, and fans and to gain exposure for your digital media and graphics skills.

YouTube is a powerful tool that offers a wealth of resources and opportunities for anyone interested in learning and growing their skills in digital media and graphics. Whether you're just getting started or looking to take your skills to the next level, it's worth exploring.

❖ Behance

Behance is an online platform and social network that is focused on showcasing creative work and connecting artists and designers with potential clients, collaborators, and fans. It is a popular destination for professionals and enthusiasts in the fields of graphic design, web design, photography, illustration, and other creative arts. On Behance, users can create portfolios to showcase their work, connect with others in their community, and share their projects with a wider audience. Behance is also a great resource for discovering new talent and staying up-to-date on the latest trends in the digital media and graphics fields. In addition to being a platform for showcasing work and connecting with others, Behance also offers some tools and resources for creative professionals, including job listings, creative challenges, and educational content. This makes it an excellent resource for anyone looking to build their skills, make new connections, or find new opportunities in the digital media and graphics fields. Behance is a valuable resource for anyone interested in digital media and graphics. Whether you're just starting, looking to showcase your work, or seeking new opportunities, it's worth exploring.

These tools and resources can be a great starting point for anyone looking to learn digital media and graphics skills or to complete projects on a budget.

The future of digital media and graphics

As technology continues to evolve and advance, the future of digital media and graphics is poised for significant growth and transformation. The increasing demand for digital content and advancements in technology are driving this change and shaping the future of this field. Virtual and Augmented Reality (VR and AR) technologies are expected to become increasingly widespread, providing consumers and businesses with new and immersive experiences. With VR and AR, users will be able to interact with digital content more tangibly and realistically, creating a more engaging and memorable experience. Artificial Intelligence (AI) and Machine Learning (ML) are being integrated into digital media and graphics tools, making it easier for creators to create and manipulate content, automate tasks, and create more personalized experiences for users. This integration of AI and ML technologies will allow for a more efficient and personalized experience for users, as well as greater access to high-quality content.

The growth of 5G networks and edge computing is also expected to drive innovation in digital media and graphics. This growth will enable faster and more immersive experiences for users and greater access to high-quality content. With the increased speed and capabilities of 5G networks and edge computing, digital media and graphics will become even more dynamic and interactive. Interactive and dynamic content is also likely to continue to grow in popularity, providing users and customers with a more engaging and personalized experience. The use of big data and machine learning algorithms will also continue to advance, providing users with more personalized and contextual experiences based on their interests and behaviours. The future of digital media and graphics is poised for significant growth and transformation, driven by advancements in technology and a focus on creating more engaging and personalized experiences for users. Whether it be through VR and AR, AI and ML, 5G and edge computing, or interactive and dynamic content, the future of digital media and graphics promises to be an exciting and dynamic one.

10
AI AND ROBOTICS EXPERTS

Artificial Intelligence (AI) refers to the simulation of human intelligence in machines that are designed to think and act like humans. The field of AI research was founded on the belief that a machine can be made to think like a human if it is provided with sufficient information and processing power. Robotics is the branch of technology that deals with the design, construction, operation, and use of robots, as well as computer systems for their control, sensory feedback, and information processing. Robots can be used to perform tasks that are too dangerous, difficult, or tedious for humans, such as exploring hazardous environments, performing surgeries, or assembling products. Together, AI and Robotics form a powerful combination that has the potential to revolutionize the way we live and work. AI can be used to make robots more intelligent and capable, while robots can be used to perform tasks that would be impossible for AI systems alone.

Why AI?

Artificial Intelligence (AI) is important because it has the potential to greatly improve many aspects of our lives, including healthcare, education, transportation, and communication, to name a few. In healthcare, AI can be used to analyze large amounts of medical data to help doctors make more accurate diagnoses and to develop personalized treatment plans. In education, AI can be used to personalize learning experiences for students, provide real-time feedback to teachers, and help educators make data-driven decisions.

In transportation, AI can be used to optimize traffic flow, reduce accidents, and improve the efficiency of transportation systems. In communication, AI can be used to enhance natural language processing, improve the accuracy of machine translation, and develop more sophisticated virtual assistants. Additionally, AI has the potential to help solve some of the world's most pressing problems, such as climate change, poverty, and inequality, by providing new tools and insights to tackle these complex issues.

AI has the potential to bring about significant benefits and improvements across a wide range of industries and domains and to have a profound impact on society as a whole

Different roles in AI and robotics

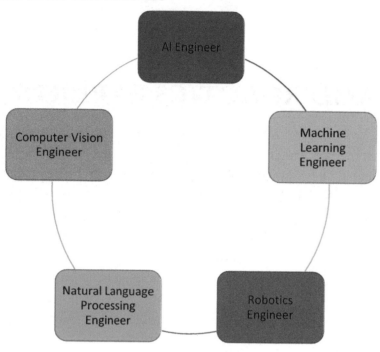

Figure 18:Different roles in LA and robotics

There are many roles in Artificial Intelligence (AI) and Robotics, including

AI Engineer: An AI engineer is a professional who is responsible for developing, designing, and implementing various artificial intelligence (AI) solutions. They typically work in software engineering, data science, or machine learning fields and have a strong background in computer science, mathematics, and statistics. The primary goal of an AI engineer is to create intelligent systems that can perform tasks and make decisions with little to no human intervention. AI engineers are also responsible for integrating these systems with other technologies and ensuring they meet the needs of users.

To become an AI engineer, a candidate typically needs a solid foundation in computer science, including knowledge of programming languages, data structures, and algorithms. A strong understanding of math and statistics is also important, as AI models rely heavily on mathematical concepts like linear algebra and calculus. In addition, AI engineers must be familiar with machine learning techniques and deep learning frameworks like TensorFlow or PyTorch.

In addition to technical skills, an AI engineer must also possess strong problem-solving and critical-thinking skills. AI engineers must be able to identify the root cause of problems and develop solutions that address those issues. They must also be able to work collaboratively with other professionals, including data scientists, software developers, and business analysts, to develop comprehensive AI systems that meet the needs of users. Overall, AI engineers are critical in developing intelligent systems that can make businesses and organizations more efficient and effective.

Machine Learning Engineer: A machine learning engineer is a professional who is responsible for designing, developing, and implementing machine learning systems. These systems use artificial intelligence (AI) algorithms to learn from data, identify patterns, and make predictions or decisions without being explicitly programmed. Machine learning engineers typically have a strong background in computer science, mathematics, and statistics, and they work with data scientists and other professionals to develop effective machine learning models and systems. The responsibilities of a machine learning engineer can vary depending on the organization and the specific project they are working on. However, some of their primary responsibilities may include data collection and preprocessing, model selection and training, hyperparameter tuning, model deployment, and ongoing performance monitoring and maintenance. They may work on a range of projects, from natural language processing and computer vision to recommendation systems and predictive modelling.

To become a machine learning engineer, a candidate typically needs a bachelor's or master's degree in computer science, mathematics, or a related field. They must have a strong foundation in programming, particularly in languages such as Python, Java, or C++. They must also be familiar with machine learning algorithms and frameworks, such as scikit-learn, TensorFlow, or PyTorch. Additionally, machine learning engineers must possess strong problem-solving and critical thinking skills, as well as excellent communication and collaboration skills, to work effectively with other professionals. Overall, machine learning engineers play a critical role in developing intelligent systems that can improve the efficiency and effectiveness of businesses and organizations.

Robotics Engineer: A robotics engineer is a professional who is responsible for designing, building, and testing robots and robotic systems. They work in a variety of industries, including manufacturing, healthcare, and defence, to develop robots that can perform tasks such as assembly, packaging, surgery, and exploration. Robotics engineers typically have a strong background in mechanical engineering, electrical engineering, and computer science, and they work with other professionals, such as software developers and data scientists, to develop effective robotic systems. The responsibilities of a robotics engineer can vary depending on the organization and the specific project they are working on. However, some of their primary responsibilities may include designing and testing mechanical components and systems, programming robots and their control systems, integrating hardware and software, and testing and troubleshooting robots to ensure they function properly. Robotics engineers may also be involved in the design of artificial intelligence algorithms that enable robots to learn and make decisions.

To become a robotics engineer, a candidate typically needs a bachelor's or master's degree in mechanical engineering, electrical engineering, or a related field. They must have a strong foundation in programming, particularly in languages such as C++ or Python, and be familiar with robotics platforms such as ROS (Robot Operating System). Additionally, robotics engineers must possess strong problem-solving and critical thinking skills, as well as excellent communication and collaboration skills, to work effectively with other professionals. Overall, robotics engineers play a critical role in developing robotic systems that can improve the efficiency and effectiveness of businesses and organizations in a wide range of industries.

Natural Language Processing Engineer: A natural language processing (NLP) engineer is a professional who specializes in developing systems that can interpret and analyze human language. These systems use artificial intelligence (AI) algorithms to understand and process text and speech data, allowing for a range of applications, such as language translation, sentiment analysis, and chatbots. NLP engineers typically have a strong background in computer science, linguistics, and statistics, and they work with other professionals, such as data scientists and software developers, to develop effective NLP systems. The responsibilities of an NLP engineer can vary depending on the organization and the specific project they are working on. However, some of their primary responsibilities may include data collection and preprocessing, developing machine learning models, building natural language generation systems, and testing and deploying NLP systems. They may work on a range of projects, from analyzing social media data to building conversational interfaces for customer service.

To become an NLP engineer, a candidate typically needs a bachelor's or master's degree in computer science, linguistics, or a related field. They must have a strong foundation in programming, particularly in languages such as Python or Java, and be familiar with machine learning and deep learning algorithms and frameworks, such as scikit-learn, TensorFlow, or PyTorch. Additionally, NLP engineers must possess strong problem-solving and critical thinking skills, as well as excellent communication and collaboration skills, to work effectively with other professionals. Overall, NLP engineers play a critical role in developing intelligent systems that can improve the efficiency and effectiveness of businesses and organizations that work with natural language data.

Computer Vision Engineer: A computer vision engineer is a professional who is responsible for designing and developing computer vision systems that can analyze and interpret images and videos. These systems use artificial intelligence (AI) algorithms to learn from visual data, identify patterns, and make predictions or decisions without being explicitly programmed. Computer vision engineers typically have a strong background in computer science, mathematics, and statistics, and they work with other professionals, such as data scientists and software developers, to develop effective computer vision models and systems. The responsibilities of a computer vision engineer can vary depending on the organization and the specific project they are working on. However, some of their primary responsibilities may include designing and testing image and video processing algorithms, developing machine learning models for image and video analysis, integrating hardware and software, and testing and troubleshooting computer vision systems to ensure they function properly. They may work on a range of projects, from object recognition and tracking to facial recognition and augmented reality.

To become a computer vision engineer, a candidate typically needs a bachelor's or master's degree in computer science, electrical engineering, or a related field. They must have a strong foundation in programming, particularly in languages such as Python, Java, or C++, and be familiar with computer vision algorithms and frameworks such as OpenCV, TensorFlow, or PyTorch. Additionally, computer vision engineers must possess strong problem-solving and critical thinking skills, as well as excellent communication and collaboration skills, to work effectively with other professionals. Overall, computer vision engineers play a critical role in developing intelligent systems that can improve the efficiency and effectiveness of businesses and organizations that work with visual data.

These are just a few of the many roles in AI and Robotics. The field is rapidly evolving, and new roles and specialities are emerging all the time

Global Certifications in AI and Robotics

There are several certifications available in Artificial Intelligence (AI) and Robotics, including:

❖ **Certified Artificial Intelligence Professional (CAIP)**

The Certified Artificial Intelligence Professional (CAIP) is a certification program that recognizes individuals who have demonstrated a high level of expertise in the field of artificial intelligence (AI). The certification program is designed to validate the skills and knowledge of AI professionals, helping organizations to identify and hire individuals who have the necessary skills and experience to work with AI technologies and implement AI solutions. The CAIP certification is awarded by the Institute of Electrical and Electronics Engineers (IEEE), a professional organization that is dedicated to advancing technology for the benefit of humanity. The certification covers a wide range of topics related to AI, including machine learning, deep learning, computer vision, natural language processing, and AI ethics.

To become a CAIP, individuals must pass a comprehensive examination that tests their knowledge and understanding of AI technologies and their applications. The certification is valid for three years, after which individuals must renew their certification by demonstrating ongoing professional development and continuing education. The CAIP certification is recognized globally and can be a valuable asset for individuals working in the field of AI, as well as organizations looking to hire AI professionals. The certification provides individuals with the opportunity to showcase their expertise and skills and can help to advance their careers in the rapidly growing field of AI.

❖ **Certified Machine Learning Professional (CMLP)**

The Certified Machine Learning Professional (CMLP) is a certification program that recognizes individuals who have demonstrated a high level of expertise in the field of machine learning. The certification program is designed to validate the skills and knowledge of machine learning professionals, helping organizations to identify and hire individuals who have the necessary skills and experience to work with machine learning technologies and implement machine learning solutions. The CMLP certification is awarded by professional organizations or educational institutions that specialize in machine learning and artificial intelligence. The certification covers a wide range of topics related to machine learning, including supervised and unsupervised learning, deep learning, data visualization, and model evaluation. To become a CMLP, individuals must pass a comprehensive examination that tests their knowledge and understanding of machine learning technologies and their applications. The certification is valid for a specified period, after which individuals must renew their certification by demonstrating ongoing professional development and continuing education.

The CMLP certification is recognized globally and can be a valuable asset for individuals working in the field of machine learning, as well as organizations looking to hire machine learning professionals. The certification provides individuals with the opportunity to showcase their expertise and skills and can help to advance their careers in the rapidly growing field of machine learning. Additionally, organizations that employ certified machine learning professionals can benefit from their expertise and knowledge, helping to ensure the success of their machine learning initiatives.

❖ **AWS Certified Machine Learning - Specialty**

The AWS Certified Machine Learning - Specialty certification is a certification program offered by Amazon Web Services (AWS) that recognizes individuals who have demonstrated a high level of expertise in designing, deploying and operating machine learning (ML) solutions on the AWS platform. The certification program is designed for individuals who have experience working with ML and big data technologies and who are interested in demonstrating their skills and knowledge in the field. To become AWS Certified in Machine Learning, individuals must pass a comprehensive examination that tests their knowledge and understanding of AWS services and tools related to ML, such as Amazon SageMaker, AWS Glue, and Amazon Kinesis. The certification covers a wide range of topics, including ML concepts, data preparation and processing, model training and deployment, and monitoring and optimization.

The AWS Certified Machine Learning - Specialty certification is a valuable asset for individuals working in the field of ML, as well as organizations looking to hire ML professionals who have expertise in the AWS platform. The certification provides individuals with the opportunity to showcase their skills and knowledge and can help to advance their careers in the rapidly growing field of ML and cloud computing. Additionally, organizations that employ certified machine learning professionals can benefit from their expertise and knowledge, helping to ensure the success of their ML initiatives on the AWS platform.

❖ **IBM Watson AI Engineer**

The IBM Watson AI Engineer certification is a program offered by IBM that recognizes individuals who have demonstrated a high level of expertise in designing, building, and deploying AI solutions using IBM Watson technologies. The certification program is designed for individuals who have experience working with AI and machine learning technologies and who are interested in demonstrating their skills and knowledge in the field. To become an IBM Watson AI Engineer, individuals must pass a comprehensive examination that tests their knowledge and understanding of

IBM Watson services and tools, such as Watson Studio, Watson Natural Language Processing, and Watson Knowledge Studio. The certification covers a wide range of topics, including AI concepts, data preparation and processing, model training and deployment, and monitoring and optimization.

The IBM Watson AI Engineer certification is a valuable asset for individuals working in the field of AI, as well as organizations looking to hire AI professionals who have expertise in IBM Watson technologies. The certification provides individuals with the opportunity to showcase their skills and knowledge and can help to advance their careers in the rapidly growing field of AI and machine learning. Additionally, organizations that employ certified Watson AI Engineers can benefit from their expertise and knowledge, helping to ensure the success of their AI initiatives using IBM Watson technologies.

❖ Microsoft Certified: Azure AI Engineer Associate

The Microsoft Certified: Azure AI Engineer Associate certification is a program offered by Microsoft that recognizes individuals who have demonstrated a high level of expertise in designing and implementing AI solutions on the Microsoft Azure platform. The certification program is designed for individuals who have experience working with AI and machine learning technologies and who are interested in demonstrating their skills and knowledge in the field. To become a Microsoft Certified: Azure AI Engineer Associate, individuals must pass a comprehensive examination that tests their knowledge and understanding of Microsoft Azure services and tools related to AI, such as Azure Cognitive Services, Azure Machine Learning, and Azure Databricks. The certification covers a wide range of topics, including AI concepts, data preparation and processing, model training and deployment, and monitoring and optimization.

The Microsoft Certified: Azure AI Engineer Associate certification is a valuable asset for individuals working in the field of AI, as well as organizations looking to hire AI professionals who have expertise in the Microsoft Azure platform. The certification provides individuals with the opportunity to showcase their skills and knowledge and can help to advance their careers in the rapidly growing field of AI and cloud computing. Additionally, organizations that employ certified Azure AI Engineers can benefit from their expertise and knowledge, helping to ensure the success of their AI initiatives on the Microsoft Azure platform.

❖ Robotics Engineer Professional Certificate Program

The Robotics Engineer, Professional Certificate Program, is a comprehensive training and certification program designed for individuals who are interested in pursuing a career in robotics engineering. The program typically covers a wide range of topics, including robotics fundamentals, control systems, robotics programming, and advanced robotics technologies such as artificial intelligence and machine learning.

The program is designed for individuals with a background in engineering, computer science, or a related field. Participants typically have some prior experience in programming and electronics and are expected to have a solid understanding of basic math and physics concepts. Upon completion of the program, participants may be eligible to take a certification exam, which will test their knowledge and understanding of the key concepts covered in the program. Upon passing the exam, participants will be awarded a professional certificate in Robotics Engineering, which can be used to demonstrate their skills and expertise in the field.

The Robotics Engineer, Professional Certificate Program, can be an excellent opportunity for individuals looking to gain expertise in robotics engineering and advance their careers in the field. The program provides hands-on experience with a wide range of robotics technologies and can help individuals develop the skills and knowledge needed to succeed as robotics engineers.

❖ **ROBO Global Robotics and Automation Index ETF**

The ROBO Global Robotics and Automation Index ETF is a type of exchange-traded fund (ETF) that invests in companies involved in the robotics and automation industry. The fund is designed to provide investors with exposure to the growth and innovation in the global robotics and automation market.

The ROBO Global Robotics and Automation Index ETF tracks the performance of the ROBO Global Robotics and Automation Index, which is a proprietary index comprised of companies involved in various aspects of the robotics and automation industry, such as industrial robotics, medical robotics, and unmanned aerial vehicles. Investing in the ROBO Global Robotics and Automation Index ETF can provide investors with diversified exposure to the robotics and automation industry, as the fund invests in a broad range of companies involved in the sector. The ETF offers a convenient way for investors to gain exposure to the industry without having to purchase individual stocks. Like other ETFs, the ROBO Global Robotics and Automation Index ETF is bought and sold on stock exchanges and can be purchased through a broker or a brokerage platform. The fund is designed for long-term investment and may be a suitable option for investors who are looking for exposure to growth and innovation in the robotics and automation industry. However, as with any investment, it is important to carefully consider the risks and potential rewards before making a decision.

These are just a few of the many certifications available in AI and Robotics. It is important to consider your career goals and the specific skills and knowledge you need to achieve them when choosing a certification program

Skills required by AI and Robotics expert

Artificial Intelligence (AI) and Robotics are highly technical fields that require a range of technical skills. Firstly, experts in these fields need to be proficient in programming languages such as Python, R, C++, and Java, which are commonly used in the field. They also need to have a deep understanding of machine learning algorithms, including decision trees, random forests, neural networks, and support vector machines. These experts must be able to apply these algorithms to solve real-world problems. Secondly, AI and Robotics experts need to be able to collect, clean and analyze large amounts of data. They also need to use data visualization techniques to uncover insights and make data-driven decisions. This requires expertise in data analysis and visualization, which is an essential skill for AI and Robotics experts.

Thirdly, Robotics experts need to have a deep understanding of robotics concepts, including kinematics, dynamics, and control. They should be able to design, build, and program robots to perform a variety of tasks. They also need to be skilled in Natural Language Processing (NLP) and Computer Vision. NLP experts must have a deep understanding of NLP concepts, including syntax, semantics, and pragmatics. Computer Vision experts, on the other hand, need to have a deep understanding of computer vision concepts, including image processing, pattern recognition, and object recognition. Fourthly, AI experts need to have a deep understanding of deep learning concepts, including Convolutional Neural Networks (CNNs), Recurrent Neural Networks (RNNs), and Generative Adversarial Networks (GANs). They should also be able to develop and implement deep learning models.

AI and Robotics experts need to be skilled software developers with experience using software development methodologies, version control systems, and software testing tools. Besides technical skills, AI and Robotics experts must have strong problem-solving skills, the ability to work well in a team, and strong communication and presentation skills. This combination of skills is essential for success in the fields of AI and Robotics.

Industries areas where IA and robotics experts are required

The demand for expertise in Artificial Intelligence (AI) and robotics is increasing across several industries. In the manufacturing and logistics sector, for example, robotics and AI are being used to automate tasks such as material handling and assembly line operations. This allows companies to increase efficiency, reduce costs, and improve product quality. In the healthcare industry, AI and robotics are being leveraged to develop new medical technologies, such as telemedicine systems and robotics-assisted surgery. This has the potential to greatly improve patient outcomes and reduce healthcare costs.

The finance industry is also utilizing AI, using it to automate tasks such as fraud detection, risk management, and portfolio optimization. This helps financial institutions to make more informed decisions, manage risks, and improve customer experiences. In the retail industry, AI and robotics are being used to enhance the shopping experience, for example, through personalization, recommendation systems, and autonomous checkout systems. This helps retailers to better understand their customers and offer them more personalized and convenient experiences.AI robotics are also having a major impact in the transportation sector, where they are being used in the development of autonomous vehicles and intelligent traffic management systems. This has the potential to greatly improve safety and reduce traffic congestion. The security industry is also utilizing

AI and robotics, for example, through the use of advanced surveillance systems, biometric identification, and threat detection. This helps to improve security and reduce the risk of crime and terrorism. In the energy and environment sector, AI and robotics are being used to improve energy efficiency and reduce environmental impact, for example, through the development of smart grid systems. This helps to promote sustainability and reduce the negative impact of human activities on the environment.

These are just a few examples of how AI and robotics are being applied to various industries, but it is clear that they are having a profound impact on the global economy and society.

Expected salaries for AI and robotics experts

The salaries of AI and robotics experts can also be influenced by the demand for specific skills and certifications. As the field continues to evolve, having expertise in areas such as machine learning, deep learning, computer vision, and robotics can increase an individual's earning potential. It is also worth mentioning that the salaries for AI and robotics experts can also depend on the type of organization they work for, with those working for large technology companies, consultancies, or government agencies often earning higher salaries than those working in smaller startups or non-profit organizations.

AI and robotics are rapidly growing field that offers a wide range of career opportunities and high earning potential. The exact salary that an AI and robotics expert can expect to earn will depend on some factors, including their education, experience, industry, location, and specific skills and certifications. Despite the variability in salaries, the demand for AI and robotics experts is expected to remain high, making it an attractive career option for those with interest in technology and innovation.

With these factors in mind, AI and robotics experts can typically expect to earn salaries in the range of $80,000 to $200,000 or more, with top earners in some industries earning significantly more. It is important to note that the demand for AI and robotics experts is high and expected to continue to grow in the coming years, making it a lucrative and rapidly growing field.

Available free online courses on AI and robotics

There are several free online courses available for those interested in learning about Artificial Intelligence (AI) and Robotics. Some popular platforms offering such courses include:

Table 10:Available free online courses on IA and robotics

SN	Institution	Course Name	Level	Duration	Link
1	Coursera	Introduction to Robotics	Intermediate	4 weeks	https://www.coursera.org/learn/introduction-to-robotics
2	Coursera	Robotics Specialization	Intermediate	4 courses, 4-6 weeks each	https://www.coursera.org/specializations/robotics
3	Coursera	Fundamentals of Robot Mechanics	Intermediate	4 weeks	https://www.coursera.org/learn/robot-mechanics
4	edX	Robotics	Intermediate	12 weeks	https://www.edx.org/course/robotics
5	edX	Autonomous Navigation for Flying Robots	Intermediate	6 weeks	https://www.edx.org/course/autonomous-navigation-for-flying-robots
6	Khan Academy	Intro to JS: Drawing & Animation	Beginner	Self-paced	https://www.khanacademy.org/computing/computer-programming/programming
7	Coursera	Machine Learning	Intermediate	11 weeks	https://www.coursera.org/learn/machine-learning
8	Coursera	Deep Learning Specialization	Intermediate	5 courses, 4-12 weeks each	https://www.coursera.org/specializations/deep-learning
9	Coursera	Neural Networks and Deep Learning	Intermediate	4 weeks	https://www.coursera.org/learn/neural-networks-deep-learning
10	edX	Artificial Intelligence	Intermediate	12 weeks	https://www.edx.org/course/artificial-intelligence-ai

These are just a few examples, but there are many other free online courses available for those interested in learning about AI and robotics. It is important to do some research and carefully evaluate the quality of the course and the instructor before enrolling in a free online course.

Free resources and tools for AI and robotics knowledge

There are several free resources and tools available for those interested in learning about Artificial Intelligence (AI) and Robotics. Some popular resources include:

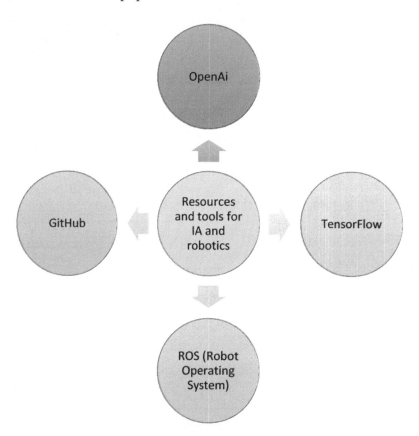

Figure 19:Free resources and tools for IA and robotics knowledge

OpenAI is a non-profit artificial intelligence research organization founded in 2015 to promote and develop friendly AI responsibly. The organization is based in San Francisco and is focused on advancing the field of AI through cutting-edge research and development while also working to ensure that AI technologies are developed and used in ways that are safe and beneficial for humanity.OpenAI was founded by a group of high-profile entrepreneurs and researchers, including Elon Musk, Sam Altman, Greg Brockman, Ilya Sutskever, and Wojciech Zaremba, among others. The organization is focused on developing and promoting AI technologies that can be used for a wide range of applications, including natural language processing, computer vision, robotics, and autonomous systems, among others.

124

OpenAI is widely recognized as a leader in the field of AI, and its research and development efforts have been widely covered in the media. The organization has made numerous breakthroughs in the field of AI, including the development of GPT-3, one of the largest and most advanced language models to date. OpenAI's work in AI has the potential to greatly benefit humanity, and the organization is widely regarded as one of the most influential players in the field of AI research and development.

TensorFlow is an open-source software library for machine learning and artificial intelligence developed by Google Brain Team. It is used for a variety of tasks, such as image classification, language translation, and sentiment analysis. TensorFlow has a comprehensive, flexible ecosystem of tools, libraries, and community resources that makes it one of the most popular deep learning platforms in use today. It is designed to be used on a wide range of devices, including desktop computers, mobile devices, and large-scale cloud-based systems. TensorFlow has a strong community of developers, researchers, and practitioners who contribute to its development, making it a well-supported platform for building and deploying machine learning models.

ROS (Robot Operating System) is an open-source framework for developing robotic systems. It provides a standardized way to write software for robots, making it easier to build, reuse, and share code across different robotics projects. ROS is designed to support a wide range of robotic platforms, including ground robots, aerial drones, and humanoid robots, among others.

ROS provides a collection of tools, libraries, and services that make it easier to build, test, and deploy robotic systems. For example, ROS provides standard message-passing libraries that allow robots to communicate with each other and with the outside world. It also provides a visual debugger and a simulator, which makes it easier to test and debug robotic systems.ROS is designed to be highly modular, allowing developers to build complex systems by composing smaller, reusable components. This helps to promote collaboration and reuse of code, making it easier for developers to build more advanced systems and bring new robotic technologies to market.

ROS has a large, active community of developers and users who contribute to its development and provide support for one another. This makes it a well-supported platform for developing robotic systems and provides a rich ecosystem of software and hardware components that can be leveraged to build advanced systems.

GitHub is a web-based platform for version control and collaboration that makes it easier for individuals and teams to work together on software projects. It was founded in 2008 and was acquired by Microsoft in 2018. GitHub provides a platform for developers to store and manage their code, track changes, and collaborate with others on projects. The platform also offers features such as bug tracking, project management, and team communication tools. Additionally, GitHub has become a hub for open-source software development, with millions of users sharing and contributing to projects. The platform has become an essential tool for developers around the world, and its popularity continues to grow as more people embrace the open-source model of software development. AI Stack Exchange: AI Stack Exchange is a question-and-answer platform for AI and machine learning professionals. It is a great resource for finding answers to specific questions and connecting with other experts in the field.

These are just a few examples, but there are many other free resources and tools available for those interested in learning about AI and robotics. It is important to carefully evaluate the quality and reliability of the resource or tool before using it to ensure it will meet your needs.

The Future of AI and Robotics

The future of Artificial Intelligence (AI) and Robotics is expected to be greatly impactful and transformative, with many experts predicting that these technologies will play a significant role in shaping the future of society, the economy, and many other aspects of our lives. Some of the key areas where AI and Robotics are expected to have a major impact in the future include:

- ✓ Automation: AI and robotics are expected to automate many tasks and processes across a wide range of industries, including manufacturing, transportation, healthcare, and many others. This is likely to lead to increased productivity and efficiency, as well as the elimination of many manual and repetitive tasks.
- ✓ Healthcare: AI and robotics are expected to play a major role in revolutionizing healthcare, including the development of new treatments, diagnostics, and medical devices, as well as improving the delivery of care and making healthcare more accessible and affordable.
- ✓ Transportation: AI and robotics are expected to play a significant role in the future of transportation, including the development of autonomous vehicles, drones, and other forms of smart transportation systems. This is likely to lead to increased safety, efficiency, and convenience in the transportation sector.
- ✓ Manufacturing: AI and robotics are expected to revolutionize manufacturing, including the development of smart factories that are highly automated and able to adapt to changing market demands and conditions. This is likely to lead to increased competitiveness and innovation in the manufacturing sector.
- ✓ Security: AI and robotics are expected to play a major role in enhancing security, including the development of smart surveillance systems, autonomous security robots, and advanced biometric systems for identification and authentication.

The future of AI and Robotics is expected to be exciting and dynamic, with many opportunities for innovation, growth, and impact. However, it is also important to consider the potential challenges and ethical implications of these technologies and to ensure that they are developed and used responsibly and sustainably

11

SYSTEM ANALYSTS

System Analysis and Design is the process of defining, developing and implementing an information system that meets the requirements of a specific organization. The main goal of this process is to create a solution that meets the business needs of the organization and to improve its efficiency, effectiveness, and profitability.

The steps involved in the System Analysis and Design process include the following:

- Requirements Gathering and Analysis: This is the first step in the process, where the system requirements are collected from stakeholders, analyzed and documented.
- Feasibility Study: This step assesses the feasibility of the proposed system based on factors such as technical, economic, and operational feasibility.
- System Design: This step involves creating a detailed design of the system, including its architecture, user interface, database design, and data flow diagrams.
- Implementation: This step involves the actual development of the system and testing it to ensure it meets the requirements.
- Maintenance: This step involves ongoing support and maintenance of the system to ensure it continues to meet the organization's changing needs.

The System Analysis and Design process is an iterative process and may involve multiple iterations and refinements before the final solution is deployed. The process requires close collaboration between the business stakeholders, developers, and the IT team to ensure a successful outcome.

Who is the system analyst

A System Analyst is a professional responsible for analyzing, designing, and implementing information systems for organizations. They play a critical role in bridging the gap between the business and technical aspects of an organization. The main duties of a System Analyst include the following:

- Gathering and analyzing the requirements of the business stakeholders to determine the best solution for their needs.

- Designing and developing the system architecture, data flow diagrams, and user interfaces.

- Coordinating with the IT team and developers to ensure the solution is implemented correctly.

- Conducting feasibility studies and risk assessments to determine the viability of proposed systems.

- Providing ongoing support and maintenance to ensure the system continues to meet the organization's evolving needs.

The System Analyst must possess a strong understanding of both business processes and technical systems and should have excellent analytical, communication, and problem-solving skills. They are often involved in projects from start to finish, working closely with stakeholders to ensure the solution meets their needs and is delivered on time and within budget.

Different roles in system analysis and design

The System Analysis and Design process typically involves multiple roles, each with its specific responsibilities. Some of the key roles involved in the process include

Business Stakeholders: Business stakeholders in system development are individuals or groups within an organization who have a vested interest in the successful development and implementation of technology systems. They may include executives, managers, employees, and customers.

The role of business stakeholders in system development is to provide input and guidance on the development of technology systems and to ensure that these systems align with the overall goals and objectives of the organization. They work closely with development teams and project managers to identify and prioritize business requirements and to ensure that technology solutions are tailored to meet the specific needs of the organization.

A typical day for a business stakeholder in system development might involve attending meetings with development teams and project managers, reviewing project plans and progress reports, and providing feedback on the development of technology systems. They may also be involved in testing and evaluating the systems to ensure that they meet the needs of the business and in making decisions about the allocation of resources and the direction of the project.

Business stakeholders play a critical role in ensuring the success of technology projects, as they provide a broader perspective on the needs and goals of the organization. To be effective, business stakeholders must have a good understanding of the organization's goals and objectives, as well as an understanding of the technology systems being developed. They must also be able to communicate effectively with technical and non-technical stakeholders and be able to make decisions that balance the needs of the business with the capabilities of the technology.

System Analysts: Systems analysts are professionals who study a company or organization's current computer systems and procedures and then design solutions to help the organization work more efficiently and effectively. They are often involved in the development, deployment, and maintenance of a variety of information systems, such as enterprise resource planning (ERP) systems, customer relationship management (CRM) systems, and business intelligence systems

The role of a systems analyst typically involves working closely with stakeholders in an organization, including management, employees, and end-users, to understand their needs and requirements. Based on this understanding, the systems analyst will then design and implement new systems or modify existing systems to meet these needs. In addition to technical skills, systems analysts must have strong communication and problem-solving abilities, as they are often required to translate technical concepts into language that non-technical stakeholders can understand.

In today's rapidly evolving technology landscape, the role of a systems analyst is becoming increasingly important as organizations look to improve their operations and stay competitive. Systems analysts must stay up-to-date with the latest technology trends and developments to provide the best solutions for their clients.

Project Managers: Project managers in system development are responsible for leading and managing technology projects from start to finish. They play a critical role in ensuring that projects are completed on time, within budget, and to the satisfaction of stakeholders.

The role of a project manager in system development requires a unique combination of technical and leadership skills. On the technical side, project managers should have a solid understanding of the systems and technologies involved in the project, as well as the development process. On the leadership side, project managers must be able to effectively communicate with team members, stakeholders, and clients and must be able to make decisions and manage risks that arise during the project.

A typical day for a project manager in system development might involve overseeing the work of development teams, tracking project progress and budget, communicating with stakeholders, and making decisions related to project scope, schedule, and resources. They must also be able to identify and manage potential risks and be prepared to take corrective action if necessary.

Project managers in system development play a key role in ensuring the success of technology projects, and their contributions can have a significant impact on an organization's bottom line. They must be able to lead cross-functional teams and must have excellent communication and leadership skills to be successful in this role.

Quality Assurance (QA) Testers: Quality assurance (QA) testers play a critical role in ensuring that software and other technology products meet high standards of quality and performance. They are responsible for evaluating the functionality, reliability, and overall quality of these products before they are released to the market.

The role of a QA tester involves designing, executing, and automating test cases to identify and document defects or bugs in the software. They work closely with development teams to ensure that software meets the requirements specified by the client or end-user. QA testers also develop test plans and test cases, as well as test metrics and reports, to evaluate the quality of the software and to communicate the results to the development team and other stakeholders.

To be successful as a QA tester, one must have strong attention to detail and be able to think critically about how software behaves in different scenarios. They should have a solid understanding of software development methodologies and be able to work well in a team environment. In addition, they must be able to effectively communicate their findings and recommendations to development teams and other stakeholders.

Quality assurance testing is an important step in the software development process, and QA testers play a vital role in ensuring that software is delivered to customers with high levels of quality and performance. By identifying and documenting defects early in the development process, QA testers can help reduce the cost and time associated with fixing problems down the road.

Technical Writers: Technical writers in system development play a crucial role in communicating complex technical information to a wide range of stakeholders, including end-users, developers, and other technical personnel. They are responsible for creating documentation, such as user manuals, installation guides, and online help systems, that explain how to use and maintain software and other technology products.

The role of a technical writer in system development requires a unique combination of technical and writing skills. Technical writers must have a deep understanding of the systems and technologies they are documenting, as well as the ability to communicate this information in a clear, concise, and accessible manner. They work closely with development teams, subject matter experts, and end-users to gather information and ensure that the documentation accurately reflects the product and its intended use.

A typical day for a technical writer in system development might involve researching and writing technical documentation, editing and revising existing documents, collaborating with development teams and other stakeholders, and testing the software to ensure that the documentation accurately reflects its functionality. They must also be able to create and maintain documentation standards and use tools such as screen capture software and HTML editors to create visually appealing and interactive documents.

Technical writers play an important role in ensuring that technology products are used effectively and efficiently. By creating clear and comprehensive documentation, they can help users get the most out of these products and can support the development teams in their efforts to deliver high-quality products. To be successful as a technical writer in system development, one must have strong technical and writing skills, as well as the ability to work well in a team environment and to effectively communicate complex information to a wide range of audiences.

All these roles work together to ensure the success of the System Analysis and Design process, and effective communication and collaboration among the team members are crucial for a successful outcome.

Technical skills required by system analysts

System Analysts are required to possess a range of technical skills to be effective in their role. Firstly, they must be proficient in requirements gathering and analysis, which involves collecting and analyzing requirements from stakeholders and then translating them into a detailed design that meets the business needs. They should also know software architecture, system design, and data flow diagrams, as well as experience in designing and developing user interfaces. In addition to this, System Analysts must have knowledge of databases and be familiar with database design and administration, as well as working with SQL and other database management systems. They must also possess knowledge of at least one programming language, such as Java, Python, or C++, and be able to write code to implement the system.

System Analysts must also know software development methodologies, such as Agile or Waterfall, and be experienced in following a structured development process. They should also know software testing methodologies, tools, and techniques, as well as experience in creating and executing test cases. Moreover, System Analysts need to know project management methodologies, tools, and techniques and the ability to manage projects and ensure they are delivered on time and within budget. They should also have strong communication, collaboration, and interpersonal skills, as well as the ability to communicate effectively with stakeholders and team members.

Having a mix of both technical and business skills is critical for System Analysts to be successful in their role. Additionally, they should be able to continuously upgrade their technical skills as technology evolves to keep up with industry trends and developments.

Available certifications in system analysis and design

There are several certifications available for System Analysts, which can demonstrate their knowledge and skills in the field. Some of the most popular certifications include:

◉ Certified Systems Analysis Professional (CSAP)

The Certified Systems Analysis Professional (CSAP) is a professional certification that recognizes individuals who have demonstrated mastery in the field of systems analysis. This certification is offered by the International Institute of Business Analysis (IIBA), a professional association that supports the development and recognition of business analysis professionals worldwide.

To become a Certified Systems Analysis Professional (CSAP), individuals must meet the eligibility requirements set by the IIBA, which typically include several years of experience in business analysis and a certain level of education. They must also pass an examination that assesses their knowledge and skills in the areas of business analysis planning and monitoring, elicitation and collaboration, requirements life cycle management, strategy analysis, and requirements analysis and design definition. The CSAP certification is designed for professionals who are involved in the development and implementation of technology systems and who work with stakeholders to identify and prioritize business requirements. This certification is considered a valuable credential for systems analysts, project managers, business analysts, and other professionals involved in the development of technology systems.

By obtaining the CSAP certification, individuals demonstrate their commitment to excellence in the field of systems analysis and their ability to deliver value to their organizations and stakeholders. The CSAP certification provides recognition for their skills and expertise and can help them advance their careers and increase their earning potential.

◉ Certified Business Analysis Professional (CBAP)

The Certified Business Analysis Professional (CBAP) is a professional certification offered by the International Institute of Business Analysis (IIBA), a professional association that supports the development and recognition of business analysis professionals worldwide. The CBAP certification is designed to recognize individuals who have demonstrated mastery in the field of business analysis.

To become a Certified Business Analysis Professional (CBAP), individuals must meet the eligibility requirements set by the IIBA, which typically include several years of experience in business analysis and a certain level of education. They must also pass an examination that assesses their knowledge and skills in the areas of business analysis planning and monitoring, elicitation and collaboration, requirements life cycle management, strategy analysis, and requirements analysis and design definition. The CBAP certification is designed for professionals who work with stakeholders to identify and prioritize business requirements and who are involved in the development and implementation of technology systems. This certification is considered a valuable credential for business analysts, project managers, systems analysts, and other professionals involved in the development of technology systems.

By obtaining the CBAP certification, individuals demonstrate their commitment to excellence in the field of business analysis and their ability to deliver value to their organizations and stakeholders. The CBAP certification provides recognition for their skills and expertise and can help them advance their careers and increase their earning potential. The CBAP certification is widely recognized in the industry and can help individuals stand out in a competitive job market.

⊙ Certified Software Development Professional (CSDP)

The Certified Software Development Professional (CSDP) is a professional certification that recognizes individuals who have demonstrated mastery in the field of software development. This certification is offered by the Institute of Electrical and Electronics Engineers (IEEE) Computer Society, a professional organization that supports the development and recognition of computer professionals worldwide.

To become a Certified Software Development Professional (CSDP), individuals must meet the eligibility requirements set by the IEEE Computer Society, which typically include several years of experience in software development and a certain level of education. They must also pass an examination that assesses their knowledge and skills in the areas of software development life cycle, software design, software construction, software testing, and software maintenance and evolution. The CSDP certification is designed for software development professionals who are involved in the design, development, and maintenance of software systems. This certification is considered a valuable credential for software developers, software engineers, software architects, and other professionals involved in the software development process.

By obtaining the CSDP certification, individuals demonstrate their commitment to excellence in the field of software development and their ability to deliver high-quality software systems. The CSDP certification provides recognition for their skills and expertise and can help them advance their careers and increase their earning potential. The CSDP certification is widely recognized in the industry and can help individuals stand out in a competitive job market.

⊙ **Project Management Professional (PMP):**

The Project Management Professional (PMP) is a professional certification that recognizes individuals who have demonstrated mastery in the field of project management. This certification is offered by the Project Management Institute (PMI), a professional association that supports the development and recognition of project management professionals worldwide.

To become a Project Management Professional (PMP), individuals must meet the eligibility requirements set by the PMI, which typically include several years of project management experience and a certain level of education. They must also pass an examination that assesses their knowledge and skills in the areas of initiation, planning, executing, monitoring and controlling, and closing of projects, as well as their understanding of the project management framework, processes, and best practices.

The PMP certification is designed for project management professionals who lead and direct projects across a variety of industries and sectors. This certification is considered a valuable credential for project managers, project coordinators, program managers, and other professionals involved in the planning, execution, and delivery of projects. By obtaining the PMP certification, individuals demonstrate their commitment to excellence in the field of project management and their ability to deliver projects successfully. The PMP certification provides recognition for their skills and expertise and can help them advance their careers and increase their earning potential. The PMP certification is widely recognized in the industry and is considered a standard for project management professionals.

⊙ **Certified Information Systems Security Professional (CISSP)**

The Certified Information Systems Security Professional (CISSP) is a professional certification that recognizes individuals who have demonstrated mastery in the field of information security. This certification is offered by the International Information System Security Certification Consortium (ISC)², a non-profit organization that supports the development and recognition of information security professionals worldwide. To become a Certified Information Systems Security Professional (CISSP), individuals must meet the eligibility requirements set by (ISC)², which typically include several years of experience in information security and a certain level of education. They must also pass an examination that assesses their knowledge and skills in the areas of security and risk management, asset security, security engineering, communications and network security, identity and access management, security assessment and testing, security operations, and software development security.

The CISSP certification is designed for information security professionals who are involved in the design, development, and implementation of information security systems and processes. This certification is considered a valuable credential for information security officers, security consultants, security architects, and other professionals involved in the protection of information systems and data. By obtaining the CISSP certification, individuals demonstrate their commitment to excellence in the field of information security and their ability to implement and manage security systems. The CISSP certification provides recognition for their skills and expertise and can help them advance their careers and increase their earning potential. The CISSP certification is widely recognized in the industry and is considered a standard for information security professionals.

These certifications can be a valuable addition to a System Analyst's resume, demonstrating their expertise and commitment to the field. The certifications are recognized globally and can help professionals advance their careers and increase their earning potential

Areas where system analysts are required

System analysts play a critical role in a variety of industries and fields, as they are responsible for analyzing complex systems and processes to identify areas for improvement and develop solutions to improve efficiency, performance, and functionality. They work closely with stakeholders to understand their needs and requirements and use their expertise to design and develop systems that meet those needs.

In the Information Technology (IT) industry, system analysts play a vital role in the development and maintenance of software and hardware systems. They work closely with software developers, hardware engineers, and other IT professionals to design and implement systems that meet the needs of organizations. They also analyze existing systems to identify areas for improvement and recommend and implement solutions to resolve any issues.

In the healthcare industry, system analysts work to design and develop healthcare information systems that support patient care, clinical decision-making, and the administration of healthcare organizations. They also play a key role in ensuring the security and privacy of patient information and ensuring that healthcare systems comply with relevant regulations and standards. System analysts in the healthcare industry are critical to improving patient outcomes and the overall efficiency and effectiveness of healthcare delivery. In government, education, manufacturing, telecommunications, retail and e-commerce, transportation and logistics, energy and utilities, and other industries, system analysts work to support and improve the operations of organizations and support the needs of stakeholders.

Expected salaries for system analyst

The salary for a system analyst can vary widely based on factors such as location, experience, and specific industry. In the United States, the average salary for a system analyst is around $87,000 per year, according to Glassdoor. However, the salary can range from $60,000 to $120,000 or more, depending on the individual's experience and qualifications.

In other countries, the salary can be different based on the local economy and the cost of living. For example, a system analyst in Canada may earn an average salary of around CAD 70,000, while in the

UK, the average salary is around £45,000. It's worth noting that salaries for system analysts can vary significantly depending on the size and type of the organization, as well as the specific responsibilities and level of experience of the individual.

Available free online courses for system analysts

There are many free online courses available for system analysts; here are some popular platforms to explore

Table 11:Free online courses for system analysts

SN	Institution	Course Name	Level	Duration	Link
1	Coursera	Systems Analysis and Design	Intermediate	6 weeks	https://www.coursera.org/learn/systems-analysis-design
2	Coursera	Object Oriented Design	Intermediate	4 weeks	https://www.coursera.org/learn/object-oriented-design
3	edX	Software Construction: Object-Oriented Design	Intermediate	5 weeks	https://www.edx.org/course/software-construction-object-oriented-design
4	edX	System Design for Supply Chain Management	Intermediate	6 weeks	https://www.edx.org/course/system-design-for-supply-chain-management
5	Khan Academy	Computer Science Principles: Digital Information	Beginner	Self-paced	https://www.khanacademy.org/computing/computer-science

It is recommended to thoroughly review the course content, instructor qualifications, and student feedback before enrolling in any free online course.

Free resources and tools for system analysis and design

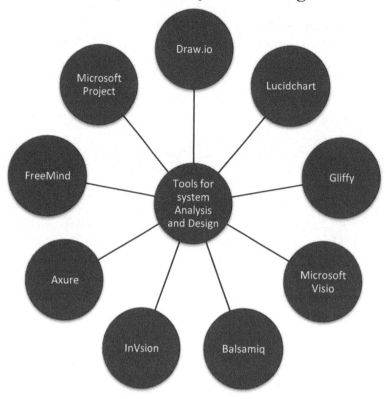

Figure 21:Free resources and tools for system analysis and design

There are many free resources and tools available for system analysis and design, including:

- **Draw.io**

Draw.io is a free online diagramming and flowchart tool that allows users to create a variety of diagrams and flowcharts, including flowcharts, network diagrams, UML diagrams, and mind maps. Draw.io is an easy-to-use tool that provides a simple, intuitive interface for creating diagrams and flowcharts. With Draw.io, users can easily drag and drop shapes, add text and images, and customize the appearance of their diagrams and flowcharts.

One of the key features of Draw.io is its ability to integrate with various cloud-based platforms, including Google Drive, Dropbox, and OneDrive. This allows users to save their diagrams and flowcharts to the cloud and access them from anywhere with an internet connection. Draw.io also supports real-time collaboration, which makes it ideal for team projects and group work. In addition to its ease of use and cloud integration, Draw.io offers a wide range of shapes, templates, and other resources to help users create professional-looking diagrams and flowcharts. It also provides various customization options, including colour schemes, line styles, and shape styles, which allow users to tailor their diagrams and flowcharts to their specific needs.

Draw.io is a versatile and user-friendly tool that offers a convenient and affordable way to create and share diagrams and flowcharts. It is well-suited for a variety of uses, from simple brainstorming and problem-solving sessions to complex project planning and management.

- **Lucidchart**

Lucidchart is a cloud-based diagramming and flowchart tool that provides users with an intuitive and powerful platform for creating a variety of diagrams and flowcharts, including flowcharts, wireframes, mind maps, and organizational charts. With its drag-and-drop interface and extensive library of shapes and templates, Lucidchart makes it easy for users to create professional-looking diagrams and flowcharts. One of the key benefits of Lucidchart is its integration with a variety of popular tools, including Google Drive, Microsoft Office, and Atlassian Confluence. This allows users to easily import and export diagrams and flowcharts and collaborate with others in real-time. Additionally, Lucidchart provides robust collaboration and commenting features, making it ideal for team projects and group work. Lucidchart also offers a wide range of customization options, including colour schemes, line styles, and shape styles. Users can also import custom images and logos and add text and annotations to their diagrams and flowcharts. Additionally, Lucidchart provides a powerful and flexible shape library, which includes shapes for a variety of domains, including technology, business, and healthcare.

Lucidchart is a comprehensive and user-friendly diagramming and flowchart tool that provides users with the tools they need to create professional-looking diagrams and flowcharts. Whether you're working on a simple brainstorming session, a complex project plan, or anything in between, Lucidchart makes it easy to create diagrams and flowcharts that are both visually appealing and effective in communicating your ideas.

- **Gliffy**

Gliffy is a cloud-based diagramming and flowchart tool that provides a simple and intuitive platform for creating a variety of diagrams and flowcharts, including flowcharts, network diagrams, wireframes, and mind maps. With its drag-and-drop interface and extensive library of shapes and templates, Gliffy makes it easy for users to create professional-looking diagrams and flowcharts, even if they have limited experience with design or graphic tools.

One of the key benefits of Gliffy is its integration with popular tools, such as Confluence, Jira, and Google Drive. This allows users to easily import and export diagrams and flowcharts and collaborate with others in real-time. Additionally, Gliffy provides robust collaboration and commenting features, making it ideal for team projects and group work. Gliffy also offers a wide range of customization options, including colour schemes, line styles, and shape styles. Users can also import custom images and logos and add text and annotations to their diagrams and flowcharts. Additionally, Gliffy provides a powerful and flexible shape library, which includes shapes for a variety of domains, including technology, business, and healthcare.

Gliffy is a comprehensive and user-friendly diagramming and flowchart tool that provides users with the tools they need to create professional-looking diagrams and flowcharts. Whether you're working on a simple brainstorming session, a complex project plan, or anything in between, Gliffy makes it easy to create diagrams and flowcharts that are both visually appealing and effective in communicating your ideas.

- **Microsoft Visio**

Microsoft Visio is a powerful and comprehensive diagramming and flowchart tool that provides users with the tools they need to create professional-looking diagrams, flowcharts, and technical illustrations. Visio is designed to be both easy to use and feature-rich, making it ideal for a wide range of users, including business professionals, technical specialists, and IT departments. One of the key benefits of Visio is its integration with other Microsoft Office applications, such as Word, Excel, and PowerPoint. This allows users to easily include Visio diagrams in their other Microsoft Office documents and to take advantage of the collaboration and sharing features provided by Microsoft Office. Additionally, Visio provides a wide range of templates, including flowcharts, network diagrams, and organizational charts, which make it easy for users to create professional-looking diagrams with minimal effort. Visio also provides a powerful and flexible set of tools for customizing and modifying diagrams. Users can easily add and modify shapes, text, and other elements and can also import custom images and logos. Additionally, Visio provides robust sharing and collaboration features, making it ideal for team projects and group work.

Microsoft Visio is a comprehensive and user-friendly diagramming and flowchart tool that provides users with the tools they need to create professional-looking diagrams and flowcharts. Whether you're working on a simple brainstorming session, a complex project plan, or anything in between, Visio makes it easy to create diagrams and flowcharts that are both visually appealing and effective in communicating your ideas.

- **Balsamiq**

Balsamiq is a rapid wireframing tool that provides a simple and intuitive platform for creating low-fidelity wireframes and prototypes. With its drag-and-drop interface and extensive library of pre-built UI elements and templates, Balsamiq makes it easy for users to create wireframes for websites, mobile apps, and software applications.

One of the key benefits of Balsamiq is its focus on rapid prototyping. Balsamiq is designed to be fast and easy to use, so users can quickly iterate on their wireframes and prototypes and get feedback from stakeholders and team members. Additionally, Balsamiq provides robust collaboration and sharing features, making it ideal for team projects and group work. Balsamiq also provides a wide range of customization options, including the ability to add custom UI elements, text, and annotations. Users can also import custom images and logos and can choose from a range of pre-built templates and UI elements to help speed up the wireframing process.

Balsamiq is a fast and intuitive rapid wireframing tool that provides users with the tools they need to create low-fidelity wireframes and prototypes. Whether you're working on a new website, a mobile app, or any other type of software application, Balsamiq makes it easy to create wireframes and prototypes that are both fast and effective in communicating your ideas.

- **InVision**

InVision is a digital product design platform that provides a comprehensive suite of tools for creating interactive prototypes, animations, and design systems. With its intuitive drag-and-drop interface and extensive library of pre-built UI elements, InVision makes it easy for designers to bring their ideas to life and create immersive user experiences.

One of the key benefits of InVision is its focus on collaboration. InVision provides a range of tools and features that make it easy for designers, developers, and stakeholders to work together and share feedback on designs in real-time. Whether you're working in a team or with stakeholders remotely, InVision makes it easy to collaborate on designs and get the feedback you need to improve and refine your designs.InVision also provides a wide range of advanced design and animation tools, including the ability to add animations, micro-interactions, and transitions to your prototypes. Additionally, InVision provides robust asset management and design system tools, making it ideal for large-scale projects and design systems that need to be consistent and scalable.

InVision is a comprehensive digital product design platform that provides users with the tools they need to create interactive prototypes, animations, and design systems. Whether you're working on a new website, a mobile app, or any other type of digital product, InVision makes it easy to bring your ideas to life and create immersive user experiences.

- **Axure**

Axure is a wireframing, prototyping, and documentation tool that provides a comprehensive suite of tools for creating interactive wireframes, prototypes, and documentation for websites, mobile apps, and software applications. With its drag-and-drop interface and extensive library of pre-built UI elements, Axure makes it easy for users to create high-fidelity wireframes and prototypes that accurately reflect their design ideas.

One of the key benefits of Axure is its versatility. Axure provides a range of tools and features that make it ideal for a wide range of design and development projects, from basic wireframes to complex prototypes and documentation. Additionally, Axure provides robust collaboration and sharing features, making it ideal for team projects and group work. Axure also provides a wide range of advanced design and interaction tools, including the ability to add interactions, animations, and dynamic content to your prototypes. Additionally, Axure provides a robust documentation and design system tool, making it ideal for creating detailed specifications and design systems that need to be consistent and scalable.

Axure is a versatile wireframing, prototyping, and documentation tool that provides users with the tools they need to create high-fidelity wireframes, prototypes, and documentation. Whether you're working on a new website, a mobile app, or any other type of software application, Axure makes it easy to create accurate and detailed designs that accurately reflect your ideas.

- **FreeMind**

FreeMind is a free and open-source mind-mapping tool that allows users to create visual diagrams and hierarchically organize information. With FreeMind, users can create maps that show the relationships between ideas, concepts, and information clearly and intuitively. This makes it ideal for organizing and visualizing complex information, such as project plans, research notes, and brainstorming sessions. One of the key benefits of FreeMind is its flexibility. FreeMind provides a range of tools and features that make it easy to create and customize maps to fit your specific needs. For example, users can add images, links, and notes to their maps and change the appearance and layout of their maps to suit their style and preferences.FreeMind also provides a range of collaboration and sharing features, making it ideal for group projects and team brainstorming sessions. For example, users can share their maps with others and collaborate on them in real-time, making it easy to work together and exchange ideas.

FreeMind is a powerful and flexible mind-mapping tool that provides users with the tools they need to create and organize information visually and intuitively. Whether you're working on a project plan, conducting research, or brainstorming ideas, FreeMind makes it easy to visualize and organize complex information.

- **Microsoft Project**

Microsoft Project is a project management software tool that provides a comprehensive suite of tools for planning, tracking, and reporting on projects. With Microsoft Project, project managers can create detailed project plans, set schedules and deadlines, and track progress to ensure that projects are completed on time and within budget. One of the key benefits of Microsoft Project is its versatility. Microsoft Project provides a range of tools and features that make it ideal for a wide range of project management needs, from the basic task and resource management to complex project portfolio management. Additionally, Microsoft Project integrates with other Microsoft products, such as Microsoft Teams and SharePoint, making it easy to collaborate with team members and share project information.

Microsoft Project also provides a range of advanced project management tools, including the ability to perform what-if analysis, create resource utilization reports, and generate custom reports based on specific project data. This makes it ideal for organizations that need to make informed decisions about their projects and resources. Microsoft Project is a comprehensive project management software tool that provides project managers with the tools they need to plan, track, and report on projects. Whether you're managing a small project or a large project portfolio, Microsoft Project makes it easy to stay organized, stay on top of deadlines, and make informed decisions about your projects.

These tools and resources can be useful for system analysts in designing, documenting, and communicating the specifications and requirements for a system.

The Future of system analysis and Design

The future of system analysis and design is expected to be impacted by some factors, including advancements in technology, changes in business practices, and increasing demand for innovative and efficient systems. The field of system analysis and design is constantly evolving, and several key trends and developments are shaping the direction of the industry. One such trend is the increasing use of Artificial Intelligence and Machine Learning, which is expected to transform the way systems are analyzed and designed. AI and machine learning can enable more sophisticated and automated analysis of complex systems and data, making it easier for organizations to develop and deploy new systems and applications. Another important trend is the growing adoption of cloud computing, which enables organizations to access and analyze large amounts of data in real-time and to rapidly deploy new systems and applications. This trend is driving the need for systems that can integrate and automate business processes across a variety of functions and departments.

DevOps is also becoming increasingly important in the field of system analysis and design. DevOps practices allow organizations to develop, test, and deploy systems more quickly and efficiently, helping to speed up the development and deployment process and reduce the risk of errors or bugs. The growing trend of digital transformation is also driving the need for systems that can integrate and automate business processes across a variety of functions and departments. Digital transformation is a process by which organizations use digital technologies to create new business models, products, and services and to enhance the overall customer experience.

The focus on user experience (UX) design is becoming increasingly important in system analysis and design as organizations seek to create systems that are easy to use, intuitive, and engaging for end users. This trend is driven by the growing importance of user-centred design, which emphasizes the importance of designing systems with the end user in mind.

12
DIGITAL MARKETING AND SOCIAL NETWORKS EXPERTS

Digital Marketing is the process of promoting a product, service, or brand through digital channels such as search engines, websites, social media, email, and mobile apps. The goal of digital marketing is to reach and engage customers through the use of digital technologies. Social Network Advertising refers to the use of social media platforms such as Facebook, Instagram, Twitter, and LinkedIn to promote products, services, or brands. Social media advertising allows companies to target specific audiences based on their demographic, geographic, and behavioural characteristics

Digital marketing and social network advertising encompass a variety of strategies and techniques that companies can use to connect with potential customers online. One of the most important components is search engine optimization (SEO), which involves optimizing a website to rank higher in search engine results pages (SERPs). This can include keyword research, on-page optimization, and link building to improve website visibility and drive more traffic. Content marketing is another key component of digital marketing, involving the creation and distribution of high-quality content that is relevant and valuable to a specific audience. By providing informative and engaging content, companies can attract and retain customers and build trust and loyalty over time.

Pay-per-click (PPC) advertising is another popular strategy, allowing companies to bid on keywords related to their products or services and pay only when users click on their ads. This can be an effective way to drive targeted traffic to a website and generate leads or sales. Email marketing remains a powerful tool for reaching and engaging with customers, allowing companies to promote their products or services through targeted, personalized emails. By segmenting email lists and tailoring messages to specific groups, companies can improve the effectiveness of their campaigns and build stronger relationships with their customers. Influencer marketing has become increasingly popular in recent years as companies leverage the power of social media influencers to promote their products or services to large and engaged audiences. Social media advertising, meanwhile, involves using platforms like Facebook, Instagram, and Twitter to promote products or services and reach and engage with target audiences.

Digital marketing and social network advertising provide a range of tools and strategies that companies can use to reach new customers and grow their businesses online. By combining multiple tactics and measuring results over time, companies can create effective campaigns that drive leads, sales, and brand awareness.

Importance of digital marketing and social media

Digital marketing and social media have revolutionized the way businesses approach marketing. With the increased reach offered by these channels, companies can target larger and more diverse audiences than ever before. This has led to a shift towards more targeted advertising, with companies using demographic, interest, and behaviour data to improve the effectiveness of their marketing efforts. In addition, the cost-effectiveness of digital marketing and social media has made it possible for businesses to reach a global audience while minimizing their marketing spend.

Customer engagement has also improved through the use of digital marketing and social media. Companies can now engage with customers in real-time, building relationships and creating a sense of community around their brand. This has been made possible by the rich data-driven insights that these channels offer. Through the analysis of customer behaviour and preferences, businesses can make data-driven decisions to improve their marketing strategies.

Moreover, digital marketing and social media have been shown to have a positive impact on sales and brand awareness. By reaching a large, targeted audience and engaging with customers in new and innovative ways, businesses can increase sales and grow their brands. With these benefits, digital marketing and social media have become essential components of a successful marketing strategy. Companies that ignore these channels risk falling behind in an increasingly digital world.

Different roles in digital marketing and social media field

There are many different roles within the field of digital marketing and social media, each with its unique responsibilities and skillset

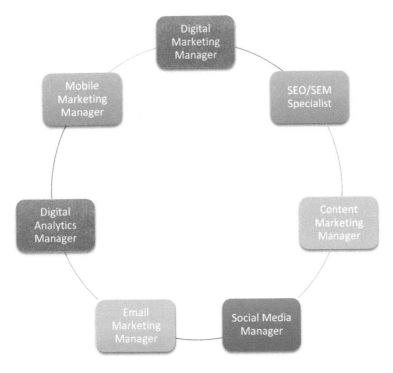

Figure 22:Different roles in digital marketing and social media field.

❖ **Digital Marketing Manager**

A Digital Marketing Manager is a professional responsible for overseeing the digital marketing efforts of a company. The role typically involves creating and implementing digital marketing strategies, managing digital marketing campaigns, analyzing data and metrics, and staying up-to-date with the latest digital marketing trends and technologies. The specific responsibilities of a Digital Marketing Manager can vary depending on the size and type of organization, but some common tasks include the following:

- Developing and executing comprehensive digital marketing plans and campaigns

- Managing the company's social media presence and online reputation

- Implementing and analyzing search engine optimization (SEO) and pay-per-click (PPC) advertising campaigns

- Conducting market research to stay informed about industry trends and competitor activity

- Developing and managing email marketing campaigns

- Collaborating with other teams, such as product development, sales, and customer service, to ensure a seamless customer experience

- Monitoring and reporting on the effectiveness of digital marketing efforts and making data-driven decisions to improve performance.

To be a successful Digital Marketing Manager, one typically needs a combination of marketing and technical skills, including experience with digital marketing tactics, strong analytical and project management abilities, excellent communication and leadership skills, and a deep understanding of the latest digital marketing technologies and trends.

❖ SEO/SEM Specialist

An SEO/SEM Specialist is a professional who focuses on optimizing websites for search engines and managing paid search advertising campaigns. This role is critical for improving a company's visibility in search engine results pages (SERPs) and driving traffic to its website.

Some of the main responsibilities of an SEO/SEM Specialist include the following:

- Conducting keyword research to determine the most effective target keywords for search engine optimization (SEO) and pay-per-click (PPC) advertising campaigns

- Optimizing websites for search engines by implementing best practices for on-page and off-page SEO, such as meta tags, header tags, and backlinking strategies

- Managing PPC advertising campaigns, including setting up and optimizing ad campaigns on platforms such as Google Ads and Bing Ads

- Analyzing data and metrics to continually improve the performance of SEO and PPC campaigns

- Staying up-to-date with the latest changes in search engine algorithms and best practices for SEO and PPC advertising

- Collaborating with other teams, such as content creation and website development, to ensure that the company's digital presence is optimized for search engines

- Communicating with clients or stakeholders to provide reports on the performance of SEO and PPC campaigns and to make recommendations for future optimization efforts.

To be successful as an SEO/SEM Specialist, one typically needs a strong understanding of search engine optimization and pay-per-click advertising, as well as experience with data analysis and project management. Additionally, an understanding of HTML, CSS, and JavaScript is often helpful, as well as experience with web analytics tools such as Google Analytics.

❖ Content Marketing Manager

A Content Marketing Manager is a professional who is responsible for developing and executing a content marketing strategy to support a company's overall marketing goals. The role involves creating and managing content that educates, informs, and engages target audiences, with the ultimate goal of driving customer engagement, lead generation, and sales.

Some of the main responsibilities of a Content Marketing Manager include the following:

- Developing and executing a content marketing strategy that aligns with the company's overall marketing goals

- Creating and managing a content calendar to ensure a steady flow of high-quality, relevant content

- Developing various types of content, including blog posts, whitepapers, ebooks, infographics, videos, and social media posts

- Managing a team of writers, designers, and other content creators to produce high-quality content

- Conducting market research to stay informed about industry trends and competitor activity

- Collaborating with other teams, such as product development, sales, and customer service, to ensure that content accurately reflects the company's offerings and customer needs

- Measuring and reporting on the performance of content marketing efforts, using analytics to make data-driven decisions to improve performance

- Staying up-to-date with the latest content marketing trends and technologies to ensure that the company's content marketing efforts are cutting-edge and effective.

To be successful as a Content Marketing Manager, one typically needs strong writing and editing skills, as well as experience with content creation and management. Excellent project management and leadership skills are also critical, as well as a deep understanding of the target audience and the ability to create content that resonates with them. Additionally, experience with analytics and data-driven decision-making is often helpful.

❖ Social Media Manager

A Social Media Manager is a professional who is responsible for overseeing an organization's social media presence and strategy. The role involves creating and executing social media campaigns, engaging with followers, and measuring the impact of social media efforts on the organization's overall marketing and business goals.

Some of the main responsibilities of a Social Media Manager include the following:

- Developing and executing a social media strategy that aligns with the organization's overall marketing goals

- Creating and publishing engaging and relevant content on social media platforms, such as Facebook, Instagram, Twitter, and LinkedIn

- Engaging with followers by responding to comments and messages and proactively seeking out opportunities to connect with potential customers and partners

- Monitoring and reporting on the performance of social media efforts, using analytics to make data-driven decisions to improve performance

- Staying up-to-date with the latest social media trends and best practices to ensure that the organization's social media efforts are cutting-edge and effective

- Collaborating with other teams, such as product development, sales, and customer service, to ensure that the organization's social media presence accurately reflects its offerings and customer needs

- Conducting market research to stay informed about industry trends and competitor activity.

To be successful as a Social Media Manager, one typically needs strong written and verbal communication skills, as well as experience with social media platforms and tools. Excellent project management and organizational skills are also critical, as well as the ability to create and publish engaging content that resonates with the target audience. Additionally, experience with analytics and data-driven decision-making is often helpful.

❖ **Email Marketing Manager**

An Email Marketing Manager is a professional who is responsible for creating and executing email marketing campaigns to support an organization's overall marketing goals. The role involves managing email lists, creating email content, and analyzing the performance of email campaigns to drive customer engagement and sales.

Some of the main responsibilities of an Email Marketing Manager include the following:

- Developing and executing an email marketing strategy that aligns with the organization's overall marketing goals

- Creating and managing email lists, including segmenting lists based on customer behaviour and demographics

- Developing and designing email content, including newsletters, promotional emails, transactional emails, and automated email campaigns

- Managing the deployment of email campaigns, including testing and optimizing for deliverability and engagement

- Analyzing the performance of email campaigns, using analytics to make data-driven decisions to improve performance

- Staying up-to-date with the latest email marketing trends and best practices to ensure that the organization's email marketing efforts are cutting-edge and effective

- Collaborating with other teams, such as product development, sales, and customer service, to ensure that email content accurately reflects the organization's offerings and customer needs.

To be successful as an Email Marketing Manager, one typically needs experience with email marketing platforms and tools, as well as strong writing and design skills. Excellent project management and organizational skills are also critical, as well as the ability to analyze data and make data-driven decisions. Additionally, experience with HTML, CSS and responsive design is often helpful.

❖ **Digital Analytics Manager**

A Digital Analytics Manager is a professional who is responsible for collecting, analyzing, and reporting on data from a company's digital marketing efforts. The role involves using analytics tools to track key metrics, such as website traffic, conversion rates, and customer engagement, and using this data to inform decisions about future marketing activities.

Some of the main responsibilities of a Digital Analytics Manager include the following:

- Developing and executing a digital analytics strategy that aligns with the company's overall marketing goals

- Implementing and maintaining analytics tools, such as Google Analytics, to track key metrics

- Collecting and analyzing data from various sources, including website traffic, social media, email marketing, and advertising campaigns

- Creating reports and dashboards to communicate the results of digital analytics efforts to key stakeholders, including senior leaders and other teams within the company

- Using data to inform decisions about future marketing activities, such as adjusting the mix of channels and tactics and optimizing campaigns for better performance

- Collaborating with other teams, such as product development and customer service, to ensure that data is being used to drive business decisions across the organization

- Staying up-to-date with the latest digital analytics trends and best practices to ensure that the company's digital analytics efforts are cutting-edge and effective.

To be successful as a Digital Analytics Manager, one typically needs a strong understanding of data analysis and experience with analytics tools and platforms. Excellent communication and presentation skills are also critical, as the role often involves communicating complex data insights to non-technical stakeholders. Additionally, experience with data visualization, SQL, and programming languages such as Python or R is often helpful.

❖ Mobile Marketing Manager

A Mobile Marketing Manager is a professional who is responsible for developing and executing mobile marketing strategies to reach and engage customers on mobile devices. The role involves creating and managing mobile campaigns, tracking and analyzing performance, and optimizing strategies to meet business goals.

Some of the main responsibilities of a Mobile Marketing Manager include the following:

- Developing and executing a mobile marketing strategy that aligns with the organization's overall marketing goals

- Creating and managing mobile advertising campaigns, such as in-app advertisements, mobile search ads, and push notifications

- Developing and optimizing mobile-friendly email campaigns and websites

- Tracking and analyzing the performance of mobile campaigns, using data to make data-driven decisions and continually optimising strategies for better results

- Staying up-to-date with the latest mobile marketing trends and best practices to ensure that the organization's mobile marketing efforts are cutting-edge and effective

- Collaborating with other teams, such as product development and customer service, to ensure that mobile campaigns accurately reflect the organization's offerings and customer needs

- Conducting market research to understand customer behaviour on mobile devices and stay informed about industry trends and competitor activity.

To be successful as a Mobile Marketing Manager, one typically needs experience with mobile marketing platforms and tools, as well as a strong understanding of mobile consumer behaviour. Excellent project management and organizational skills are also critical, as well as the ability to analyze data and make data-driven decisions. Additionally, experience with mobile design and user experience (UX) is often helpful.

Technical skills required by digital marketing and social media expert

Digital marketing and social media experts should have a strong understanding of marketing and communication principles. They should be able to develop and execute effective marketing campaigns, create engaging content, and analyze and interpret data to inform decision-making.

Another important skill for digital marketing and social media experts is project management. They should be able to manage multiple projects and deadlines simultaneously and work collaboratively with team members and clients to ensure the successful execution of digital marketing strategies.

In addition to technical and project management skills, digital marketing and social media experts should also have strong communication and interpersonal skills. They must be able to work effectively with team members, clients, and stakeholders and have the ability to clearly and effectively communicate complex ideas and data.

Lastly, digital marketing and social media experts should be adaptable and able to keep up with the latest trends and changes in the digital marketing landscape. This requires a commitment to ongoing learning and professional development, as well as a willingness to experiment with new technologies and strategies.

Available certification in digital media and social network marketing

There are several certifications available in digital media and social network marketing:

◉ Hootsuite Social Media Marketing Certification

Hootsuite Social Media Marketing Certification is a certification program offered by Hootsuite, a leading social media management platform. The certification is designed to validate an individual's knowledge and skills in using social media to achieve business goals, such as increasing brand awareness, generating leads, and boosting engagement.

The Hootsuite Social Media Marketing Certification program covers a range of topics, including social media strategy, content creation and management, advertising, and measurement and analysis. To earn the certification, individuals must complete a series of online courses and pass a final exam.

Holding the Hootsuite Social Media Marketing Certification can demonstrate to employers and clients that an individual has a strong understanding of social media marketing and the ability to use Hootsuite and other tools to drive business results. It can also help individuals stand out in a competitive job market and showcase their commitment to professional development.

It is worth noting that the Hootsuite Social Media Marketing Certification is not an industry-wide recognized certification, but it is highly regarded within the Hootsuite community and is a useful credential for those who are looking to specialize in using Hootsuite for social media marketing purposes.

◉ Hubspot Inbound Marketing Certification

The HubSpot Inbound Marketing Certification is a certification program offered by HubSpot, a leading provider of inbound marketing software. The certification is designed to validate an individual's knowledge and skills in using inbound marketing techniques to attract, engage, and delight customers.

The HubSpot Inbound Marketing Certification program covers a range of topics, including inbound marketing strategy, content creation and optimization, lead generation, and measurement and analysis. To earn the certification, individuals must complete a series of online courses and pass a final exam.

Holding the HubSpot Inbound Marketing Certification can demonstrate to employers and clients that an individual has a strong understanding of inbound marketing best practices and the ability to use HubSpot and other tools to drive business results. It can also help individuals stand out in a competitive job market and showcase their commitment to professional development.

It is worth noting that the HubSpot Inbound Marketing Certification is not an industry-wide recognized certification, but it is highly regarded within the HubSpot community and is a useful credential for those who specialize in using the HubSpot platform for inbound marketing purposes.

◉ Facebook Blueprint

Facebook Blueprint is a digital marketing certification program offered by Facebook. The program provides individuals and businesses with the skills and knowledge they need to effectively advertise and market on the Facebook platform.

Facebook Blueprint covers a wide range of topics, including creating and managing Facebook ads, using Facebook's targeting and optimization tools, and measuring the results of Facebook campaigns. The program consists of online courses and exams, and individuals can earn certifications in areas such as Facebook Certified Planning Professional and Facebook Certified Buying Professional.

Holding a Facebook Blueprint certification demonstrates a deep understanding of Facebook advertising and marketing and can help individuals stand out in a competitive job market. It can also be a valuable asset for businesses looking to advertise on Facebook, as it assures that their marketing partner has the skills and knowledge needed to create effective campaigns.

Facebook Blueprint is widely recognized as a valuable certification for digital marketers, and it is recognized as an industry-leading certification by Facebook. It is a useful credential for those who specialize in advertising on the Facebook platform, and it can help individuals and businesses stay up-to-date with the latest best practices and trends in Facebook marketing.

⊙ Google Ads Certification

The Google Ads Certification is a certification program offered by Google for individuals who want to demonstrate their knowledge and proficiency in using Google Ads, Google's advertising platform. The program is designed to validate an individual's skills in creating, managing, and optimizing Google Ads campaigns.

The Google Ads Certification covers a range of topics, including setting up and managing search and display campaigns, targeting and bidding strategies, and performance analysis and optimization. To earn the certification, individuals must pass two exams: the Google Ads Fundamentals exam and one of the advanced exams in either search, display, video, shopping, or mobile advertising.

Holding a Google Ads Certification demonstrates a deep understanding of Google Ads and the ability to effectively use the platform to drive business results. It can also help individuals stand out in a competitive job market and showcase their commitment to professional development.

The Google Ads Certification is widely recognized as a valuable certification for digital marketers, and it is recognized as an industry-leading certification by Google. It is a useful credential for those who specialize in advertising on Google's advertising platform, and it can help individuals and businesses stay up-to-date with the latest best practices and trends in Google Ads.

⊙ Twitter Flight School Certification

Twitter Flight School is a certification program offered by Twitter for individuals who want to demonstrate their knowledge and proficiency in using Twitter for advertising and marketing. The program provides individuals and businesses with the skills and knowledge they need to effectively use Twitter to reach their target audience and achieve their marketing goals.

Twitter Flight School covers a wide range of topics, including creating and managing Twitter Ads campaigns, targeting and optimization, and performance analysis and measurement. The program consists of online courses and exams, and individuals can earn certifications in areas such as Twitter Ads Manager and Twitter Analytics.

Holding a Twitter Flight School certification demonstrates a deep understanding of Twitter advertising and marketing and can help individuals stand out in a competitive job market. It can also be a valuable asset for businesses looking to advertise on Twitter, as it assures that their marketing partner has the skills and knowledge needed to create effective campaigns.

Twitter Flight School is widely recognized as a valuable certification for digital marketers, and it is recognized as an industry-leading certification by Twitter. It is a useful credential for those who specialize in advertising on the Twitter platform, and it can help individuals and businesses stay up-to-date with the latest best practices and trends in Twitter marketing.

◉ Instagram Partner Program Certification

The Instagram Partner Program is a certification program offered by Instagram for individuals who want to demonstrate their knowledge and proficiency in using Instagram for advertising and marketing. The program provides individuals and businesses with the skills and knowledge they need to effectively use Instagram to reach their target audience and achieve their marketing goals.

The Instagram Partner Program covers a wide range of topics, including creating and managing Instagram Ads campaigns, targeting and optimization, and performance analysis and measurement. The program consists of online courses and exams, and individuals can earn certifications in areas such as Instagram Ads Manager and Instagram Analytics.

Holding an Instagram Partner Program certification demonstrates a deep understanding of Instagram advertising and marketing and can help individuals stand out in a competitive job market. It can also be a valuable asset for businesses looking to advertise on Instagram, as it assures that their marketing partner has the skills and knowledge needed to create effective campaigns.

The Instagram Partner Program is widely recognized as a valuable certification for digital marketers, and it is recognized as an industry-leading certification by Instagram. It is a useful credential for those who specialize in advertising on the Instagram platform, and it can help individuals and businesses stay up-to-date with the latest best practices and trends in Instagram marketing.

◉ Digital Marketing Institute (DMI) Professional Diploma in Digital Marketing

The Digital Marketing Institute (DMI) Professional Diploma in Digital Marketing is a comprehensive training and certification program for individuals who want to build their skills and knowledge in digital marketing. The program covers a range of digital marketing topics, including search engine optimization (SEO), search engine marketing (SEM), social media marketing, email marketing, content marketing, mobile marketing, and digital analytics.

The DMI Professional Diploma in Digital Marketing is designed to provide individuals with a broad understanding of digital marketing, as well as the skills and knowledge needed to effectively implement digital marketing strategies and tactics. The program consists of online courses, live webinars, and hands-on projects, and it is taught by industry experts.

Holding a DMI Professional Diploma in Digital Marketing demonstrates a deep understanding of digital marketing, and can help individuals stand out in a competitive job market. It can also be a valuable asset for businesses looking to build their digital marketing capabilities, as it assures that their marketing team has the skills and knowledge needed to implement effective digital marketing strategies.

The DMI Professional Diploma in Digital Marketing is widely recognized as a valuable certification for digital marketers, and it is recognized as an industry-leading certification by the Digital Marketing Institute. It is a useful credential for those who want to specialize in digital marketing, and it can help individuals and businesses stay up-to-date with the latest best practices and trends in digital marketing.

These certifications provide recognition for individuals who have demonstrated proficiency in the respective platforms and digital marketing strategies

Industry areas where digital marketing and social media experts are required

Digital marketing and social media experts are in high demand across a wide range of industries. One area where their expertise is particularly valuable is e-commerce. With more and more consumers turning to online shopping, businesses in this industry need skilled professionals to help them navigate the complexities of online marketing and social media. Healthcare is another industry where digital marketing and social media experts are needed, as healthcare providers look to reach patients and build their brand through online channels.

In addition to e-commerce and healthcare, digital marketing and social media experts are also in demand in finance and banking, retail, tourism and hospitality, food and beverage, fashion and beauty, technology and telecommunications, automotive, education and training, and non-profit and social causes. In these industries, digital marketing and social media experts can help businesses increase their online visibility, build brand awareness, and engage with customers in meaningful ways. As the importance of digital channels continues to grow, the need for skilled professionals in this field is only set to increase, making it an exciting and rewarding career path for those with a passion for marketing and technology.

Expected salaries for digital marketing and social media experts

The salary for digital marketing and social media experts varies widely based on some factors. These factors include the individual's level of experience, the specific job role they hold, the size of the company they work for, and the location of the company. As a rough estimate, an entry-level digital marketing specialist can expect to earn between $40,000 and $60,000 per year. A mid-level digital marketing manager can expect to earn between $70,000 and $100,000 per year, while a senior digital marketing strategist can expect to earn between $100,000 and $150,000 per year.

For social media roles, a social media manager can expect to earn between $50,000 and $80,000 per year, while a social media strategist can expect to earn between $70,000 and $120,000 per year. It's important to note that these figures are rough estimates and can vary based on some additional factors, including an individual's educational background, certifications, and industry specialization.

Overall, salaries in the digital marketing and social media field are generally competitive and continue to grow as demand for these skills increases. As businesses increasingly turn to digital channels to reach their target audiences, the need for skilled digital marketing and social media professionals is only set to increase, making it an exciting and rewarding field to pursue.

Available free online courses on digital marketing and social media

Here are some free online courses on digital marketing and social media:

Table 12:Free online Courses on digital marketing and social media

S N	Institution	Course Name	Level	Duration	Link
1	Coursera	Digital Marketing	Beginner	4 weeks	https://www.coursera.org/learn/digital-marketing
2	Coursera	Social Media Marketing	Beginner	4 weeks	https://www.coursera.org/learn/social-media-marketing
3	edX	Marketing Analytics: Marketing Measurement Strategy	Intermediate	6 weeks	https://www.edx.org/course/marketing-analytics-marketing-measurement-strategy
4	edX	Social Media Data Analytics	Intermediate	4 weeks	https://www.edx.org/course/social-media-data-analytics
5	Khan Academy	Entrepreneurship	Beginner	Self-paced	https://www.khanacademy.org/partner-content/pixar/entrepreneurship

While these courses are free, some of them may require a fee for certifications or additional materials.

Free resources and tools for digital marketing and social media

Figure 23:Free resources and tools for digital marketing and social media

Here are some free resources and tools for digital marketing and social media:

❖ **Google Analytics**

Google Analytics is a web analytics service offered by Google that helps individuals and businesses track and analyze their website traffic. With Google Analytics, users can track key metrics such as the number of visitors to their website, the source of the traffic, and the most popular pages.

Google Analytics also provides detailed information about the behaviour of website visitors, including how long they stay on the site, what pages they visit, and what actions they take. This information can be used to improve the user experience and optimize website content for better engagement and conversion rates.

Google Analytics is widely used by digital marketers, webmasters, and businesses of all sizes to understand the performance of their websites and to make data-driven decisions. The platform provides a range of features, including custom reports, real-time analytics, and integration with other Google tools, such as Google AdWords.

Getting certified in Google Analytics demonstrates a deep understanding of the platform and its features, and it can help individuals stand out in a competitive job market. The certification covers a range of topics, including how to set up and configure Google Analytics, how to use analytics to measure website performance, and how to use analytics data to inform and improve digital marketing strategies.

❖ Google My Business

Google My Business is a free tool offered by Google that helps businesses manage their online presence across Google, including Google Search and Google Maps. With Google My Business, businesses can create a listing that includes information such as their address, phone number, hours of operation, and photos of their products or services. Google My Business is designed to help businesses connect with potential customers and make it easier for people to find them online. When someone searches for a business on Google, the Google My Business listing will appear in the search results, providing potential customers with key information about the business.

The Google My Business listing also allows businesses to respond to reviews, post updates, and connect with their audience through Google Posts. This helps businesses build a strong online presence, engage with their customers, and drive more traffic to their websites. Getting certified in Google My Business demonstrates a deep understanding of the platform and its features, and it can help individuals stand out in a competitive job market. The certification covers a range of topics, including how to set up and manage a Google My Business listing, how to optimize the listing for search engines, and how to use Google My Business to engage with customers and build a strong online presence.

❖ Hootsuite

Hootsuite is a social media management platform that helps individuals and businesses manage their social media presence across multiple networks, including Facebook, Twitter, Instagram, LinkedIn, and more. With Hootsuite, users can schedule and publish posts, monitor their social media accounts for engagement, and analyze their social media performance.

Hootsuite provides a range of features that make it easier for businesses and individuals to manage their social media presence, including the ability to manage multiple profiles from a single dashboard, a content library for storing and organizing assets, and a range of analytics and reporting tools. Hootsuite is widely used by digital marketers, social media managers, and businesses of all sizes to improve their social media performance and build stronger relationships with their customers and followers. The platform is easy to use, and it offers a range of integrations with other tools and platforms, making it a popular choice for those looking to streamline their social media management.

Getting certified in Hootsuite demonstrates a deep understanding of the platform and its features, and it can help individuals stand out in a competitive job market. The certification covers a range of topics, including how to use Hootsuite to manage and schedule social media posts, how to use the platform to monitor and engage with followers, and how to use Hootsuite's analytics and reporting tools to measure and improve social media performance.

❖ Mailchimp

Mailchimp is an email marketing platform that helps individuals and businesses create, send, and manage email campaigns. With Mailchimp, users can create and design professional-looking emails using a range of templates and design tools, and they can easily manage their email lists and segment their audiences based on various criteria.

Mailchimp provides a range of features to help users improve their email marketing performance, including analytics and reporting tools, the ability to automate email campaigns, and integrations with other platforms and tools, such as e-commerce platforms and social media networks.

Mailchimp is widely used by digital marketers, small business owners, and individuals who want to reach and engage with their audience through email. The platform is known for its ease of use, and it offers a range of pricing options to suit different needs and budgets.

Getting certified in Mailchimp demonstrates a deep understanding of the platform and its features, and it can help individuals stand out in a competitive job market. The certification covers a range of topics, including how to create and manage email campaigns, how to use Mailchimp's design and automation tools, and how to use analytics and reporting to measure and improve email marketing performance.

❖ Buffer

Buffer is a social media management platform that helps individuals and businesses manage their social media presence across multiple networks, including Twitter, Facebook, Instagram, and LinkedIn. With Buffer, users can schedule and publish posts, monitor their social media accounts for engagement, and analyze their social media performance. Buffer provides a range of features that make it easier for businesses and individuals to manage their social media presence, including the ability to manage multiple profiles from a single dashboard, a content library for storing and organizing assets, and a range of analytics and reporting tools.

Buffer is widely used by digital marketers, social media managers, and businesses of all sizes to improve their social media performance and build stronger relationships with their customers and followers. The platform is known for its simplicity and ease of use, and it offers a range of pricing options to suit different needs and budgets. Getting certified in Buffer demonstrates a deep understanding of the platform and its features, and it can help individuals stand out in a competitive job market. The certification covers a range of topics, including how to use Buffer to manage and schedule social media posts, how to use the platform to monitor and engage with followers, and how to use Buffer's analytics and reporting tools to measure and improve social media performance.

❖ SEMrush

SEMrush is a digital marketing platform that provides tools and insights for search engine optimization (SEO), pay-per-click (PPC) advertising, content marketing, and social media. It is designed to help digital marketers, SEO professionals, and businesses improve their online presence and visibility.

SEMrush provides a range of features to help users improve their digital marketing performance, including keyword research and analysis, site audit and backlink analysis, competitor analysis, and advertising research. It also provides tools for tracking and analyzing rankings, traffic, and conversions, as well as for tracking and analyzing the performance of PPC campaigns.

SEMrush is widely used by digital marketers, SEO professionals, and businesses of all sizes who want to improve their online visibility and reach. The platform is known for its comprehensive suite of tools and its wealth of data, making it a valuable resource for those looking to improve their digital marketing performance.

Getting certified in SEMrush demonstrates a deep understanding of the platform and its features, and it can help individuals stand out in a competitive job market. The certification covers a range of topics, including how to use SEMrush for keyword research and analysis, site audit and backlink analysis, competitor analysis, and advertising research, as well as how to use the platform to track and analyze rankings, traffic, and conversions.

❖ **Moz**

Moz provides a suite of SEO tools that help businesses and individuals monitor their website's ranking and visibility in search engine results. The tools allow users to track keyword rankings, monitor backlinks, and conduct keyword research, among other things. The company's backlink analysis tool, Moz Link Explorer, provides insights into a website's link profile and helps users understand the quality and quantity of links pointing to their site, which is a crucial factor in how search engines determine the relevance and authority of a website. Moz's tools and resources are designed to help users improve their website's SEO performance and visibility in search engine results.

❖ **Bitly**

Bitly is a link management and URL-shortening platform. It allows users to shorten long links into short, memorable, and shareable links that are easier to use, manage, and track. Bitly provides a suite of tools for managing and tracking links, including link analytics and metrics, custom domains, and integrations with social media and other marketing platforms. The platform is widely used by individuals and businesses to share links on social media, in email campaigns, and on websites. Bitly's link analytics and metrics provide insights into how users interact with shared links, including click-through rates, referral sources, and geographic information. Bitly's custom domains feature allows users to create and use custom, branded domains for their links, which can enhance the visibility and recognition of their brand.

❖ **Ahrefs**

Ahrefs is a digital marketing and SEO toolset that provides a wide range of features for analyzing, tracking, and improving a website's search engine optimization and overall digital performance. The platform provides in-depth backlink analysis, keyword research and tracking, and competitor analysis, among other things. Ahrefs helps website owners, marketers, and SEO professionals understand their own website's performance as well as that of their competitors. The toolset is widely used in the SEO community for its accuracy and depth of data, making it a valuable resource for improving website visibility in search engines, driving traffic, and, ultimately, boosting conversion rates and revenue. Additionally, Ahrefs provides a large database of organic search keywords, helping users discover new opportunities for growth and optimization.

Note: While these tools are free, some of them may have paid plans for additional features and capabilities.

The future of digital marketing and social media

The world of digital marketing and social media is constantly changing and evolving, with new trends and technologies emerging regularly. Artificial Intelligence and Machine Learning are expected to be at the forefront of these changes, as these technologies allow for more targeted and personalized marketing efforts. With the help of AI and ML, businesses can gather more accurate data on their target audiences and create more effective marketing campaigns.

As voice assistants like Amazon Alexa and Google Home continue to gain popularity, Voice Search Optimization is expected to become increasingly important in digital marketing. Brands will need to optimize their content to ensure that it is easily discoverable through voice search. Interactive content is also expected to be a major trend in the future of digital marketing and social media. Interactive content such as quizzes, polls, and augmented reality provides a more engaging and immersive user experience, which can help to increase brand engagement and loyalty.

In the age of short attention spans, capturing consumers' attention in the "micro-moments" when they are searching for information or making a decision is critical. Micro-moments will be a key focus for digital marketers, who will need to provide targeted and relevant information to consumers in these brief windows of time. Video Marketing will continue to grow in popularity, with brands using videos for product demonstrations, tutorials, and storytelling. The increasing use of mobile devices and social media platforms makes video an ideal format for capturing the attention of consumers and delivering engaging content. Social Media E-commerce is another trend that is expected to shape the future of digital marketing. Social media platforms will increasingly become a primary source of e-commerce transactions, with features such as shoppable posts and in-platform purchasing making it easier for consumers to make purchases directly from social media.

Influencer Marketing is expected to continue to grow, with brands collaborating with social media influencers to reach new audiences and build brand trust. Influencers have a significant impact on consumer purchasing decisions, and their endorsement of a brand can help to build trust and credibility among their followers. The future of digital marketing and social media is full of exciting possibilities, with new technologies and trends constantly emerging. Brands that can stay ahead of these trends and adapt to changing consumer behaviours and preferences will be well-positioned to succeed in the ever-evolving world of digital marketing.

13
E-LEARNING EXPERTS

Learning technology encompasses the use of various tools and methods to enhance the process of learning and education. This can include online learning platforms, educational software, learning management systems, virtual and augmented reality, gamification, and artificial intelligence. It has revolutionized the way people access and process information, providing new opportunities for personalized and interactive learning experiences. However, it's important to consider the potential drawbacks, such as unequal access to technology, privacy concerns, and the need for critical evaluation of online resources. The effective use of learning technology requires a balanced approach that considers both its benefits and challenges.

E-Learning Systems refer to computer-based systems designed to support the delivery of educational content. They provide a platform for delivering instructional content, assessment, and collaboration. Some common features of e-learning systems include the following:

- Course management: Enables instructors to create, manage and deliver course content.

- Assessment: Includes tools for creating and grading assignments, tests, and quizzes.

- Collaboration: Facilitates communication and collaboration between instructors and students through discussion forums, group projects, and virtual classrooms.

- Multimedia support: Supports the use of various media formats, including text, audio, video, and images, to enhance the learning experience.

- Accessibility: Allows students to access the course material from anywhere, at any time, and on any device.

E-Learning systems have become increasingly popular due to their accessibility and flexibility, allowing students to study at their own pace. However, they also have their limitations, such as the need for reliable internet access and the potential for students to feel isolated without face-to-face interaction. E-Learning systems should be evaluated in terms of their instructional design, multimedia support, assessment features, and their ability to meet the needs of both instructors and students

Current e-learning Technologies

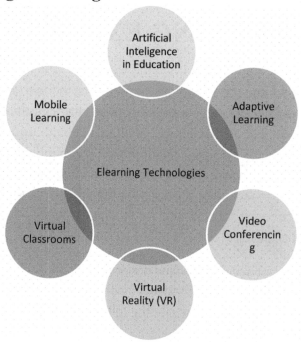

Figure 24:Trending e-Learning Technologies

In recent years, e-learning technologies have revolutionized the field of education by offering a wide range of tools and resources to enhance the learning experience. Learning Management Systems (LMS) are one such technology that has gained immense popularity among students and educators alike. LMS platforms provide a centralized hub where students can access course materials, engage in online discussions, and track their progress. They also provide instructors with tools to create and manage course content, monitor student progress, and provide feedback.

Artificial Intelligence (AI) is another technology that has had a significant impact on education. AI algorithms can be used to personalize learning and provide real-time feedback to students, helping them to understand complex concepts and identify areas where they need improvement. AI can also be used to automate certain aspects of the learning process, such as grading, allowing instructors to focus on other aspects of teaching.

Virtual Reality (VR) and Augmented Reality (AR) are technologies that create immersive learning environments, enabling students to explore subjects in ways that would not be possible in a traditional classroom. For example, VR and AR can be used to simulate historical events, scientific experiments, or language immersion experiences. These technologies can help students to better understand and retain information while also promoting engagement and motivation. **Gamification** is another e-learning technology that has gained popularity in recent years. By using game elements such as points, badges, and leaderboards, gamification can help to engage and motivate learners. It can also be used to promote collaboration and competition among students, enhancing the learning experience.

Adaptive Learning is a technology that uses algorithms to adapt to the learning pace and abilities of individual students. This allows for personalized feedback and content recommendations, helping students to stay engaged and motivated. Adaptive learning can also help to identify areas where students may be struggling, allowing instructors to provide targeted support. **Video Conferencing** and **Virtual Classrooms** are technologies that have become increasingly important in recent years due to the COVID-19 pandemic. These technologies allow students and instructors to connect and collaborate in real-time, even when they are not in the same physical location. They provide a platform for online discussions, group projects, and live lectures, enabling students to stay connected and engaged.

Mobile Learning is a technology that allows students to access course content and resources using their mobile devices. This provides flexibility and convenience, allowing students to learn on the go and outside of the traditional classroom setting. Mobile learning can also help to promote engagement and motivation, as students can access learning materials at their own pace and convenience.

E-learning technologies have transformed the way we learn and teach, providing a wide range of tools and resources to enhance the learning experience. From Learning Management Systems to Mobile Learning, these technologies have the potential to revolutionize the field of education and make learning more accessible, engaging, and effective for students of all ages and backgrounds

Different roles in e-learning and education technology

In the field of e-learning and education technology, there are several roles that individuals may occupy.

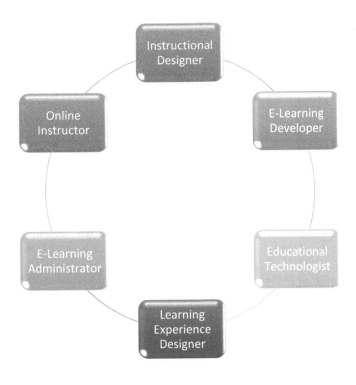

Figure 25:Different roles in e-learning and education technology

❖ Instructional Designer.

An instructional designer is a professional who designs and develops educational and training materials and programs. They use a variety of media, including multimedia, text, and graphics, to create engaging and effective learning experiences. The goal of an instructional designer is to create instructional materials that are both effective in transmitting knowledge and skills and enjoyable for the learner. Instructional designers work in a variety of settings, including corporate training, higher education, government, and non-profit organizations. They may work independently or as part of a team and collaborate with subject matter experts, trainers, and other stakeholders to ensure that the instructional materials meet the needs of the target audience.

Instructional designers use a systematic and iterative process to design and develop instructional materials. This process typically includes needs analysis, design, development, implementation, and evaluation. Instructional designers use a variety of learning theories, instructional design models, and instructional technologies to create materials that support different learning styles and meet the needs of diverse learners.

❖ E-Learning Developer

An e-Learning developer is a professional who specializes in creating online learning experiences using digital technologies. They work in a variety of settings, including corporate training, higher education, government, and non-profit organizations. Their goal is to create engaging and effective online courses and training programs that are accessible to a wide range of learners. E-Learning developers use a variety of tools and technologies to create interactive and multimedia-rich learning experiences. This may include authoring tools, learning management systems, multimedia software, and programming languages. They also use instructional design principles and learning theories to create effective and engaging learning experiences.

E-Learning developers work closely with subject matter experts, instructional designers, and other stakeholders to create online courses and training programs that meet the needs of the target audience. They may also be involved in the development of assessments and interactive learning activities that help learners apply what they have learned. E-Learning developers play a key role in creating online learning experiences that are accessible, effective, and enjoyable for learners. Their work helps organizations and individuals to develop new skills and knowledge and advance their careers.

❖ Educational Technologist

An educational technologist is a professional who uses technology to enhance the process of teaching and learning. They work in a variety of settings, including K-12 schools, higher education, government, and non-profit organizations. Their goal is to improve the quality and effectiveness of education and training programs by leveraging technology. Educational technologists use a variety of tools and technologies to support the process of teaching and learning. This may include learning management systems, multimedia software, educational games and simulations, and mobile technologies. They also use principles of instructional design and learning theories to create effective and engaging learning experiences.

Educational technologists collaborate with teachers, instructional designers, and other stakeholders to integrate technology into the curriculum and instructional materials. They may also provide professional development and training for teachers and other staff on the use of technology in the classroom. In addition to their work in the classroom, educational technologists may also conduct research and development in the field of educational technology. They use this research to inform their work and to improve the quality and effectiveness of technology-enhanced education and training programs. Educational technologists play a critical role in leveraging technology to enhance the process of teaching and learning. Their work helps organizations and individuals to develop new skills and knowledge and advance their careers.

❖ Learning Experience Designer

A learning experience designer is a professional who focuses on creating engaging and effective learning experiences for learners. They work in a variety of settings, including K-12 schools, higher education, corporate training, government, and non-profit organizations. Their goal is to design learning experiences that are relevant, meaningful, and impactful for learners. Learning experience designers use a variety of tools and technologies to create learning experiences, including multimedia software, learning management systems, and educational games and simulations.

They also use principles of instructional design and learning theories to create learning experiences that are aligned with the needs and preferences of learners. Learning experience designers work closely with teachers, instructional designers, subject matter experts, and other stakeholders to create learning experiences that are relevant and engaging for learners. They may also use data and feedback from learners to continually refine and improve their designs. In addition to designing learning experiences, learning experience designers may also be involved in creating assessments and evaluating the impact of their designs. They use this information to identify areas for improvement and to ensure that their designs meet the needs of learners.

Learning experience designers play a critical role in creating learning experiences that are engaging, effective, and impactful for learners. Their work helps organizations and individuals to develop new skills and knowledge and advance their careers.

❖ E-Learning Administrator

An e-Learning administrator is a professional who manages and oversees the implementation and delivery of online learning programs and systems. They work in a variety of settings, including K-12 schools, higher education, corporate training, government, and non-profit organizations. Their goal is to ensure that online learning programs and systems are effective, efficient, and accessible to learners. E-Learning administrators are responsible for managing the technical infrastructure and systems that support online learning, including learning management systems, multimedia software, and virtual classrooms. They may also manage the development and implementation of online courses and programs, working with instructional designers, subject matter experts, and other stakeholders to create engaging and effective online learning experiences.

E-Learning administrators are responsible for ensuring that online learning programs and systems are secure, accessible, and up-to-date. They may also provide training and support for teachers, students, and other users and ensure that online learning programs and systems comply with relevant regulations and standards. In addition to their technical and operational responsibilities, e-Learning administrators may also play a strategic role in the development of online learning initiatives. They may participate in the development of new programs and services and work with stakeholders to identify opportunities for improvement and innovation.

E-Learning administrators play a critical role in ensuring the success of online learning programs and systems. Their work helps organizations and individuals to develop new skills and knowledge and advance their careers.

❖ Online Instructor

An online instructor is a teacher or trainer who delivers educational content and facilitates learning over the Internet. They work in a variety of settings, including K-12 schools, higher education, corporate training, and non-profit organizations. Their goal is to provide students with engaging and effective learning experiences that are accessible from anywhere with an internet connection. Online instructors use a variety of tools and technologies to deliver their content, including learning management systems, multimedia software, and virtual classrooms. They also use instructional design principles and learning theories to create effective and engaging online learning experiences.

Online instructors may teach a wide range of subjects, including basic skills such as reading and math, as well as more specialized topics such as business, technology, and the arts. They work with students in a virtual environment, using a variety of methods to facilitate learning and provide support, including asynchronous discussion forums, live chat, and virtual office hours. Online instructors are responsible for creating and delivering instructional materials, assessing student learning, providing feedback and support, and promoting student engagement. They may also be involved in the design and development of assessments and other learning activities that help students apply what they have learned.

Online instructors play a critical role in providing students with access to quality education and training, regardless of their location or schedule. Their work helps individuals and organizations to develop new skills and knowledge and advance their careers.

These roles can overlap, and individuals may have multiple responsibilities depending on the size and complexity of the organization. Effective e-learning and education technology requires a team approach, with individuals from different roles working together to achieve common goals

Technical knowledge and skills required by e-learning experts

E-learning experts are required to possess a combination of technical and instructional design skills to succeed in their roles. Knowledge of Learning Management Systems (LMS) and authoring tools such as Articulate Storyline, Captivate, and others is a must-have. These tools are used to create interactive and engaging e-learning content that meets the needs of the learner. Multimedia production skills such as video, audio, and graphic design are also necessary for creating high-quality e-learning content that is engaging and effective. In addition to technical skills, e-learning experts should also possess knowledge of HTML, CSS, and JavaScript for web-based course development. They should be familiar with mobile learning and responsive design principles to ensure that e-learning content is accessible across all devices. E-learning experts must also have a good understanding of instructional design principles and the ability to apply them in creating effective e-learning content.

E-learning experts should also have an understanding of e-learning standards such as SCORM, AICC, and Tin Can API. These standards ensure that e-learning content can be easily shared and reused across different systems. Project management skills are also important for e-learning experts as they are often responsible for managing multiple projects simultaneously. Good communication skills are also necessary to collaborate effectively with instructional designers, subject matter experts, and other stakeholders.

E-learning experts must stay up-to-date with current e-learning trends and possess the ability to apply them to course design and development. They should be adaptable to changes in technology and learning styles and be able to create innovative e-learning solutions that meet the needs of modern learners.

Available certification on e-learning technologies

There are several certifications available for e-learning technologies, including:

◎ **Articulate 360 Certified**

Autodesk Articulate 360 is a suite of tools that enables content creators to build engaging e-learning courses, presentations, and other types of content. The Articulate 360 certification program is a way for individuals to demonstrate their knowledge and skills in using the Articulate 360 suite of tools. To become an Articulate 360 certified professional, you will need to take an exam that covers a range of topics, including creating interactive content with Articulate Storyline, designing responsive e-learning courses with Articulate Rise, and using the Articulate 360 Review and Articulate 360 Assets features.

The certification exam is designed to test your knowledge of the Articulate 360 tools and your ability to create high-quality e-learning content. Once you pass the exam, you will receive an Articulate 360 certification and be listed as a certified professional on the Articulate website. Having an Articulate 360 certification can demonstrate your expertise to potential employers and clients and can help you stand out in a competitive job market. Additionally, it can be a valuable professional development opportunity, allowing you to improve your skills and stay up-to-date with the latest developments in e-learning technology.

◎ Certified Tin Can API Developer

The Tin Can API, also known as the Experience API or xAPI, is a widely adopted standard for tracking and reporting on learning experiences outside of a traditional learning management system (LMS). A "Certified Tin Can API Developer" would typically be someone who has demonstrated a certain level of knowledge and competency in developing software and applications that use the Tin Can API. However, there is no official certification program for Tin Can API developers at this time.

Some organizations may offer training and certification programs, but these are not universally recognized or endorsed. The best way to demonstrate expertise in Tin Can API development is to build a portfolio of projects that use the API and to actively participate in the learning technology community by contributing to open-source projects, attending events, and engaging with others on forums and social media.

◎ Adobe Certified Expert (ACE)

Adobe Certified Expert (ACE) is a certification program offered by Adobe Systems Incorporated to demonstrate a high level of proficiency and expertise in using Adobe Creative Cloud applications such as Photoshop, Illustrator, InDesign, and others. To become an Adobe Certified Expert, individuals must pass a certification exam that tests their knowledge and skills in using a specific Adobe application. The certification is valid for two years and can be renewed by taking the latest version of the certification exam.

Holding an Adobe Certified Expert certification can demonstrate to employers, clients, and peers that an individual has a high level of proficiency in using Adobe Creative Cloud applications, which can help in career advancement and increase credibility. The certification can also provide access to exclusive resources, such as the Adobe Certified Expert community and discounts on Adobe products and services.

◎ Certified SCORM Developer

SCORM (Shareable Content Object Reference Model) is a set of technical standards for e-learning software products that allow for interoperability, reusability, and tracking of online learning content. A "Certified SCORM Developer" is someone who has demonstrated a high level of proficiency and expertise in developing e-learning content and applications that comply with the SCORM standards. However, there is no official certification program for SCORM developers.

Some organizations may offer training and certification programs, but these are not universally recognized or endorsed. The best way to demonstrate expertise in SCORM development is to build a portfolio of projects that use the standards and to actively participate in the e-learning technology community by contributing to open-source projects, attending events, and engaging with others on forums and social media.

◉ Certified eLearning Professional (CeLP)

The Certified eLearning Professional (CeLP) is a certification program offered by the International Association for Continuing Education and Training (IACET) to recognize individuals who have demonstrated a high level of expertise and knowledge in the design, development, and delivery of e-learning programs. To become a Certified eLearning Professional, individuals must complete the IACET Continuing Education Unit (CEU) program and pass the CeLP certification exam, which tests their knowledge of e-learning design and development principles, instructional design theories, and e-learning technologies.

Holding a CeLP certification demonstrates to employers, clients, and peers that an individual has a strong understanding of e-learning best practices and a commitment to continuing education and professional development. It can also provide access to a network of other certified professionals and opportunities for continued growth and learning.

◉ Learning Management System (LMS) Administrator Certification

A Learning Management System (LMS) Administrator Certification is a certification program that recognizes individuals who have demonstrated a high level of expertise and knowledge in managing and administering an LMS. An LMS is a software application that is used to plan, deliver, manage, and evaluate a training or education program. There is no single, widely recognized LMS Administrator Certification program, and the requirements for obtaining such a certification can vary depending on the organization offering the program. In general, however, LMS Administrator Certification programs will require individuals to demonstrate their knowledge and skills in areas such as setting up and configuring an LMS, managing users and content, running reports and analytics, and troubleshooting technical issues.

Holding an LMS Administrator Certification can demonstrate to employers, clients, and peers that an individual has the skills and knowledge needed to effectively manage and administer an LMS, and it can help in career advancement and increase credibility. The certification can also provide access to exclusive resources, such as the LMS Administrator community and ongoing professional development opportunities.

◉ Certified E-Learning Instructional Designer (CEID)

The Certified E-Learning Instructional Designer (CEID) is a certification program offered by the International Society for Technology in Education (ISTE) to recognize individuals who have demonstrated a high level of expertise and knowledge in designing and developing effective e-learning programs. To become a Certified E-Learning Instructional Designer, individuals must complete ISTE's CEID program, which includes completing a course on e-learning instructional design and passing a certification exam that tests their knowledge of instructional design theories and practices, as well as their ability to apply these principles to the design of e-learning programs.

Holding a CEID certification demonstrates to employers, clients, and peers that an individual has a strong understanding of instructional design principles and a commitment to designing effective e-learning programs. It can also provide access to a network of other certified professionals and opportunities for continued growth and learning.

These certifications can demonstrate the knowledge and skills required for e-learning technologies and can help individuals advance in their careers.

Areas where e-learning experts are required

E-learning experts are in high demand in various areas, including instructional design, learning management systems (LMS), EdTech startups, corporate training, higher education, educational technology consulting, digital marketing, e-learning content creation, and learning analytics. Instructional designers are responsible for designing and developing effective online learning content and materials that engage and educate learners. LMS experts implement, administer, and customize LMSs for delivering e-learning. In the EdTech industry, e-learning experts are needed to build and launch innovative e-learning products and services.

Corporate training also relies heavily on e-learning experts to design and deliver online training programs for employees in organizations. In higher education, e-learning experts are involved in developing and delivering online courses and programs in colleges and universities. Educational technology consultants advise clients on e-learning strategies, technology, and best practices.

Digital marketing experts promote and market e-learning products and services through various digital channels. E-learning content creators are responsible for creating multimedia-rich, interactive, and engaging e-learning content. Finally, learning analytics experts analyze and use data to improve e-learning programs and outcomes, making their skills highly sought after.

Salaries for e-learning experts

The field of e-learning has seen significant growth in recent years, leading to an increase in specialized professionals. The salary of an e-learning expert varies based on several factors, such as their level of experience, location, and industry. In the United States, common job titles for e-learning professionals include instructional designers, e-learning developers, LMS administrators, corporate trainers, online course developers, EdTech startup founders, digital marketing managers, and learning analytics specialists. The salary ranges for these roles in the US vary from $60,000 to $150,000 per year.

The e-learning industry provides a wide range of job opportunities with competitive salaries. Professionals can pursue careers in instructional design, course development, educational technology consulting, and more. The industry's growth indicates that e-learning will continue to be an essential part of education, training, and professional development, creating more opportunities for those interested in the field.

Available free online course for e-learning professionals

There are several free online courses available for e-learning professionals to enhance their skills and knowledge. Some popular platforms offering free courses include:

Table 13:Free online courses for e-learning Professionals

SN	Institution	Course Name	Level	Duration	Link
1	Coursera	Introduction to Learning Technologies	Beginner	4 weeks	https://www.coursera.org/learn/learning-technologies-introduction
2	edX	Leading Ambitious Teaching and Learning	Intermediate	8 weeks	https://www.edx.org/course/leading-ambitious-teaching-and-learning
3	edX	Digital Transformation of Education	Intermediate	8 weeks	https://www.edx.org/course/digital-transformation-of-education
4	Khan Academy	Education and Digital Media	Beginner	Self-paced	https://www.khanacademy.org/partner-content/pixar/education-and-digital-media/

These are just a few examples of the many free online courses available to e-learning professionals. It is important to evaluate the quality of the course and the credentials of the instructor before enrolling in a free course.

Free resources and tools for e-learning experts

There are many free resources and tools available to e-learning experts to create, deliver, and evaluate e-learning programs. Some of these include:

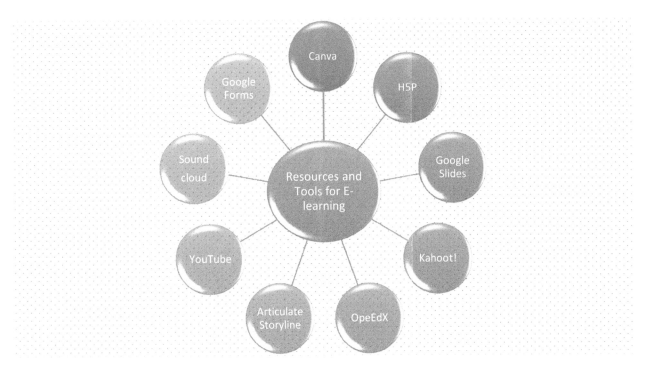

Figure 26:Free resources and tools for e-learning experts

❖ Canva

Canva is a graphic design platform that provides an easy-to-use, drag-and-drop interface for creating a wide range of visual content, including graphics, presentations, posters, social media posts, and more. Canva is available in both free and paid versions, with the paid version offering additional features and capabilities.

One of Canva's main strengths is its large library of templates, pre-made designs, and elements, including images, icons, shapes, and text styles, which can be easily customized to fit your needs. It also offers a variety of design tools and features, such as the ability to add and edit images, create charts and graphs, and add text and annotations to your designs.

Canva is widely used by individuals, businesses, and organizations for creating visually appealing and effective designs for various purposes, including marketing and advertising, social media, and branding. Whether you're a beginner or an experienced graphic designer, Canva provides a user-friendly and accessible platform for creating professional-looking designs.

H5P

H5P is a free, open-source software platform for creating and sharing interactive content, such as interactive videos, quizzes, presentations, and more. The platform is based on HTML5 and is designed to be used within a learning management system (LMS) or as a standalone tool.

H5P content can be created using a simple drag-and-drop interface and can be easily shared and reused. This makes it an effective tool for creating engaging, interactive learning experiences that can be accessed and used by others in a variety of settings.

There is no formal certification program for H5P, but individuals can demonstrate their expertise in using the platform by building a portfolio of H5P content and by actively participating in the H5P community by contributing to open-source projects, attending events, and engaging with others on forums and social media.

❖ Google Slides

Google Slides is a web-based presentation software developed by Google. It is part of the Google Workspace (formerly known as G Suite) productivity suite and is similar to Microsoft PowerPoint and Apple Keynote. Google Slides allows users to create, edit, and collaborate on presentations with others in real-time. It offers a range of tools and features for creating professional-looking presentations, including templates, themes, and the ability to add multimedia elements such as images, videos, and audio.

Google does not offer a certification program for Google Slides, but individuals can demonstrate their proficiency in using the software by creating a portfolio of presentations and by actively participating in the Google Workspace community by attending events, engaging with others on forums and social media, and seeking out training and resources.

❖ Kahoot!

Kahoot! is a gamified learning platform that allows educators and trainers to create interactive quizzes, surveys, and discussions. It is widely used in classrooms, corporate training programs, and other educational settings. With Kahoot!, users can create quizzes and surveys using a variety of question types, including multiple-choice, true/false, and open-ended questions. The platform also allows users to add images, videos, and audio to questions to create engaging and interactive learning experiences.

Kahoot! does not currently offer any certifications, but individuals can demonstrate their expertise in using the platform by creating a portfolio of quizzes and surveys and by actively participating in Kahoot! Community by attending events, engaging with others on forums and social media and seeking out training and resources. Additionally, Kahoot! offers a range of resources and support for educators, including best practices, tips, and tutorials.

❖ OpenEdX

OpenEdX is an open-source learning management system (LMS) platform for delivering online courses, educational programs, and training initiatives. It was originally developed by edX, a non-profit organization founded by Harvard University and MIT. OpenEdX provides a comprehensive and flexible platform for delivering online courses, including features for managing course content, assessing student progress, and facilitating collaboration and communication between students and instructors. It also includes a range of tools and features for analytics and reporting, making it an effective tool for tracking and evaluating the success of online learning initiatives.

There is no formal certification program for OpenEdX, but individuals can demonstrate their expertise in using the platform by building a portfolio of online courses and by actively participating in the OpenEdX community by contributing to open-source projects, attending events, and engaging with others on forums and social media. Additionally, organizations and individuals may offer training and support services for OpenEdX, which can provide individuals with an opportunity to further develop their skills and knowledge.

❖ Articulate Storyline

Articulate Storyline is a widely used authoring tool for creating interactive e-learning content and presentations. It is part of the Articulate 360 suite of e-learning tools and is known for its intuitive drag-and-drop interface and its wide range of features and capabilities. With Articulate Storyline, users can create a wide range of interactive e-learning content, including courses, simulations, and assessments. The software also includes a range of built-in templates and themes, making it easy to create professional-looking e-learning content with minimal design experience.

Articulate does not offer a certification program specifically for Articulate Storyline, but individuals can demonstrate their expertise in using the software by building a portfolio of e-learning content and by actively participating in the Articulate community by attending events, engaging with others on forums and social media, and seeking out training and resources. Additionally, organizations and individuals may offer training and support services for Articulate Storyline, which can provide individuals with an opportunity to further develop their skills and knowledge.

❖ YouTube

YouTube is a popular video hosting platform that is widely used to host and share video content, including e-learning videos. It provides a free and accessible platform for delivering video content, making it a popular choice for educators, trainers, and organizations looking to create and deliver e-learning content. With YouTube, users can upload and share videos, embed videos on websites and other platforms, and monetize their content through advertising and sponsorship. The platform also provides tools and features for organizing and categorizing videos, as well as for tracking views, engagement, and feedback from users.

YouTube does not offer a certification program specifically for e-learning, but individuals can demonstrate their expertise in using the platform for e-learning by creating a portfolio of e-learning videos and by actively participating in the YouTube community by attending events, engaging with others on forums and social media, and seeking out training and resources.

❖ Soundcloud

SoundCloud is a popular online audio distribution platform that enables users to upload, share, and promote their original audio content. It is used by a wide range of users, including musicians, podcasters, and sound artists, to showcase their work and connect with audiences around the world.SoundCloud provides a range of features for audio hosting and distribution, including the ability to upload and share audio tracks, add comments and annotations to tracks, and embed audio tracks on websites and other platforms. The platform also includes tools for organizing and categorizing audio content, as well as for tracking plays, likes, and reposts.

SoundCloud does not offer a certification program, but individuals can demonstrate their expertise in using the platform by building a portfolio of audio content and by actively participating in the SoundCloud community by attending events, engaging with others on forums and social media, and seeking out training and resources. Additionally, organizations and individuals may offer training and support services for SoundCloud, which can provide individuals with an opportunity to further develop their skills and knowledge.

❖ Google Forms

Google Forms is a free and accessible form-building tool that is part of the Google Drive suite of productivity tools. It is widely used for creating and delivering assessments, quizzes, and surveys for e-learning programs, as well as for a wide range of other purposes.

Google Forms provides a simple and intuitive drag-and-drop interface for creating forms and includes a range of built-in templates and question types, making it easy to create professional-looking forms with minimal design experience. The platform also provides tools for organizing and analyzing form responses, as well as for sharing and embedding forms on websites and other platforms.

Google does not offer a certification program specifically for Google Forms, but individuals can demonstrate their expertise in using the tool by building a portfolio of forms and by actively participating in the Google community by attending events, engaging with others on forums and social media, and seeking out training and resources. Additionally, organizations and individuals may offer training and support services for Google Forms, which can provide individuals with an opportunity to further develop their skills and knowledge.

These are just a few examples of the many free resources and tools available to e-learning experts. It is important to evaluate the quality and reliability of these resources and tools before using them in e-learning programs.

The future of e-learning technology

The future of e-learning technology is expected to bring significant changes to online education. With the advancements in technology, e-learning is becoming more personalized, interactive, and accessible. Artificial Intelligence and Machine Learning are expected to play a significant role in the future of e-learning by delivering personalized and adaptive learning experiences. With AI, learners can receive tailored content and feedback, leading to an enhanced learning experience. Machine learning algorithms can help track learners' progress and suggest learning paths to achieve their goals. Virtual and Augmented Reality technologies are another exciting development in e-learning that is expected to be widely used in the future. These technologies provide immersive and interactive learning experiences that are more engaging than traditional methods. With virtual and augmented reality, learners can visualize complex concepts and interact with them, making learning more memorable and effective.

Cloud computing is another technology that is expected to play a significant role in the future of e-learning. Cloud computing enables easy access to e-learning resources and courses from anywhere in the world. This technology provides flexibility, scalability, and cost-effectiveness, making it a popular choice for e-learning providers. With cloud computing, learners can access learning materials from their devices without worrying about storage limitations.

The future of e-learning technology is promising, with exciting advancements and trends that are expected to shape the future of online education. E-learning is becoming more personalized, interactive, and accessible thanks to technologies such as AI and machine learning, virtual and augmented reality, cloud computing, mobile learning, gamification, microlearning, and social learning. These technologies will provide learners with engaging and effective learning experiences, leading to improved outcomes and increased satisfaction.

14

WEB AND MOBILE DEVELOPMENT CAREERS

Web and mobile development are two of the most in-demand and rapidly growing careers in the tech industry. As businesses and individuals continue to rely on digital platforms and mobile devices, the need for skilled developers who can create and maintain these systems is only increasing.

Web development is the process of creating websites, web applications, and other online platforms. It involves designing and coding the user interface, creating and managing databases, and ensuring that the site or application is functional and responsive. Web developers work with a variety of programming languages, including HTML, CSS, JavaScript, and PHP, among others.

Mobile development, on the other hand, is the process of creating mobile applications for smartphones, tablets, and other mobile devices. Mobile developers work with specific programming languages, such as Java for Android and Swift for iOS, to create apps that are optimized for the smaller screen sizes and touch-based interfaces of mobile devices.

Both web and mobile development careers offer a variety of opportunities for individuals interested in technology and programming. Some developers work as part of larger teams, while others may work independently or as part of a smaller startup. Some may specialize in front-end development, focusing on the user interface and experience, while others may focus on back-end development, dealing with server-side programming and database management.

One of the advantages of pursuing a career in web or mobile development is the flexibility and potential for remote work. Many companies allow their developers to work from home, and freelance opportunities are also widely available. Additionally, developers often have the opportunity to work on a variety of projects, from e-commerce websites to mobile games to enterprise-level software applications.

However, the field of web and mobile development is constantly evolving, and developers must stay up to date with the latest trends, tools, and technologies to remain competitive. This requires a commitment to ongoing learning and professional development, as well as a willingness to adapt to new challenges and opportunities as they arise.

A career in web or mobile development can offer a challenging and rewarding opportunity for individuals with a passion for technology and programming. Whether working as part of a team or as an independent freelancer, web and mobile developers play a critical role in the creation and maintenance of digital platforms and applications that are increasingly essential to our daily lives.

Web and mobile development are two closely related fields that are essential in the modern era of technology. The internet and mobile devices have revolutionized the way people interact with information, products, and services, and web and mobile developers play a crucial role in creating the digital experiences that power these interactions.

The evolution of web and mobile development

The field of web and mobile development has undergone significant evolution in recent years, driven by advances in technology, changing user preferences, and the increasing demand for digital solutions in a wide range of industries. This evolution has been marked by the emergence of new programming languages, frameworks, and tools, as well as shifts in best practices and design principles.

In the early days of web development, HTML and CSS were the primary programming languages used to create websites. These languages were limited in their functionality and flexibility, and developers often had to rely on tables and other hacks to achieve the desired layout and design. However, the introduction of JavaScript and its integration with HTML and CSS opened up new possibilities for creating interactive and dynamic web experiences.

Over time, new frameworks and libraries emerged to streamline web development and make it more efficient. These include jQuery, a popular JavaScript library for front-end development, and Bootstrap, a front-end framework that allows developers to create responsive and mobile-friendly websites. In addition, server-side programming languages such as PHP, Python, and Ruby on Rails have become increasingly popular for back-end development, providing developers with powerful tools for building and managing databases, server-side scripting, and other functionality.

In the mobile development space, the emergence of iOS and Android platforms has led to the development of new programming languages and frameworks. Objective-C and Swift are the primary programming languages used for iOS development, while Java and Kotlin are used for Android development. In addition, hybrid app development frameworks such as React Native and Ionic have gained popularity in recent years, allowing developers to create apps that can run on both iOS and Android platforms.

One of the most significant recent developments in web and mobile development is the emergence of cloud computing and serverless architecture. This has enabled developers to build and deploy applications more quickly and easily without the need for complex server setups and management. Cloud-based platforms such as Amazon Web Services (AWS) and Google Cloud Platform (GCP) have become increasingly popular for web and mobile application hosting, and serverless frameworks such as AWS Lambda and Google Cloud Functions have made it easier for developers to build and deploy serverless applications.

Essential skills for web and mobile developers

Web and mobile development are among the most in-demand skills in today's job market. To excel in these fields, it's essential to possess certain skills and knowledge that can help you build efficient, scalable, and high-quality web and mobile applications. Here we will discuss some of the essential skills for web and mobile developers, including coding languages, database management, and version control.

Coding Languages

Web and mobile developers should have expertise in coding languages such as HTML, CSS, and JavaScript. These languages are used to build the front end of web applications and mobile apps. HTML is used to create the structure of web pages, CSS is used for styling, and JavaScript is used for creating dynamic user interfaces and enhancing interactivity.

For mobile app development, it's important to know programming languages such as Java, Kotlin, and Swift. Java is the most commonly used language for developing Android apps, while Kotlin is the newer and preferred option. Swift is used for developing iOS apps, and it's a powerful language that allows for efficient app development.

Database Management

Web and mobile applications store and retrieve data from databases. As a developer, it's essential to know about database management systems (DBMS) such as MySQL, MongoDB, and PostgreSQL. These systems allow you to store, organize, and retrieve data efficiently.

It's important to know how to design and implement database schemas, create queries, and optimize database performance. Additionally, developers should know how to integrate databases with web and mobile applications.

Version Control

Version control systems allow developers to manage changes made to code, collaborate with other developers, and maintain code quality. Git is the most widely used version control system, and web and mobile developers need to know Git and its commands.

Developers should know how to create and manage repositories, commit changes, and resolve conflicts. It's also important to understand branching and merging, which allow developers to work on different features simultaneously without disrupting each other's work.

In addition to these essential skills, web and mobile developers should know other technologies such as APIs, web servers, and front-end frameworks. It's also important to stay up-to-date with the latest industry trends and technologies to maintain a competitive edge. By honing these skills, web and mobile developers can build high-quality, efficient, and scalable applications that meet the needs of users and businesses.

The differences between web and mobile development

Web and mobile development are two distinct fields of software development, each with its unique set of challenges and requirements. While there are some similarities between the two, there are also several significant differences that developers should be aware of. Here we will discuss the differences between web and mobile development.

User Experience

One of the most significant differences between web and mobile development is the user experience. Web applications are accessed through browsers and are designed to work on desktops and laptops. In contrast, mobile applications are designed to be used on smartphones and tablets and have different interfaces.

Mobile apps are designed to be more intuitive and user-friendly, with a focus on touch-based interactions, while web applications are optimized for keyboard and mouse-based interactions. Additionally, mobile apps have access to hardware-specific features such as GPS, cameras, and accelerometers that are not available on web applications.

Development Environment

Another difference between web and mobile development is the development environment. Web applications are developed using web technologies such as HTML, CSS, and JavaScript and can be tested on a desktop or laptop computer using a web browser.

In contrast, mobile apps require a mobile development environment, which typically includes an emulator or simulator for testing on various devices. Developers must also consider different screen sizes, resolutions, and device capabilities when developing mobile applications.

Performance

Web and mobile applications have different performance requirements. Web applications are accessed over the Internet, and their performance can be affected by factors such as internet speed, server load, and client-side processing power.

Mobile apps, on the other hand, must be designed to work efficiently on limited resources, including battery life and network connectivity. Developers must optimize mobile apps for performance to ensure that they can run smoothly and efficiently on a wide range of devices.

Distribution

Finally, web and mobile applications have different distribution methods. Web applications are typically hosted on servers and accessed through URLs. They can be easily updated, and users do not need to download any software to use them.

In contrast, mobile apps must be distributed through app stores such as the Apple App Store or Google Play Store. App stores have strict guidelines for app approval, and developers must comply with these guidelines to ensure that their apps are approved for distribution.

Web and mobile development are two distinct fields of software development that require different skills, tools, and approaches. While there are some similarities between the two, developers must understand the differences between web and mobile development to create successful applications.

Developing different mobile platforms

When developing mobile applications, developers need to consider the different mobile platforms that their applications will run on. The two most widely used mobile platforms are iOS and Android, and developers must be familiar with both platforms to create successful applications. Here we will discuss some of the key considerations when developing for iOS and Android.

Development Languages

Developing for iOS and Android requires knowledge of different programming languages. For iOS development, developers typically use Swift or Objective-C. Swift is the newer and preferred language for iOS development, while Objective-C is an older language that is still used in some legacy applications.

For Android development, developers typically use Java or Kotlin. Java is the most commonly used language for Android development, while Kotlin is a newer and preferred option that offers many benefits, including better readability and fewer errors.

User Interface Design

Both iOS and Android have different user interface design guidelines that developers must follow. iOS has a more standardized user interface design, with specific guidelines for elements such as icons, buttons, and navigation. Android, on the other hand, allows for more flexibility in design, but developers still need to follow the Material Design guidelines for consistency.

Developers need to consider the differences in screen sizes, resolutions, and aspect ratios between iOS and Android devices when designing their applications.

App Store Distribution

iOS and Android have different app store distribution processes that developers must follow. The Apple App Store has strict guidelines for app approval, and developers must comply with these guidelines to ensure that their apps are approved for distribution.

Google Play Store has fewer restrictions, but developers must still follow certain guidelines to ensure that their apps are approved. Additionally, Android allows for the distribution of apps through other channels, such as direct downloads from a website or third-party app stores.

Device Fragmentation

Another key consideration when developing for iOS and Android is device fragmentation. Android devices come in a wide variety of screen sizes, resolutions, and processing power, which can make it challenging to ensure that an application runs smoothly on all devices.

iOS, on the other hand, has a more standardized set of devices, but developers must still consider the differences in screen sizes and resolutions between iPhones and iPads.

Developing for different mobile platforms requires developers to consider different programming languages, user interface design guidelines, app store distribution processes, and device fragmentation. By understanding these differences, developers can create successful applications that run smoothly on both iOS and Android devices.

Creating responsive web designs

Creating a responsive web design is crucial in today's world, where people access the internet using various devices, such as smartphones, tablets, laptops, and desktops. Responsive design ensures that your website looks great and functions well on all screen sizes, providing a seamless user experience regardless of the device.

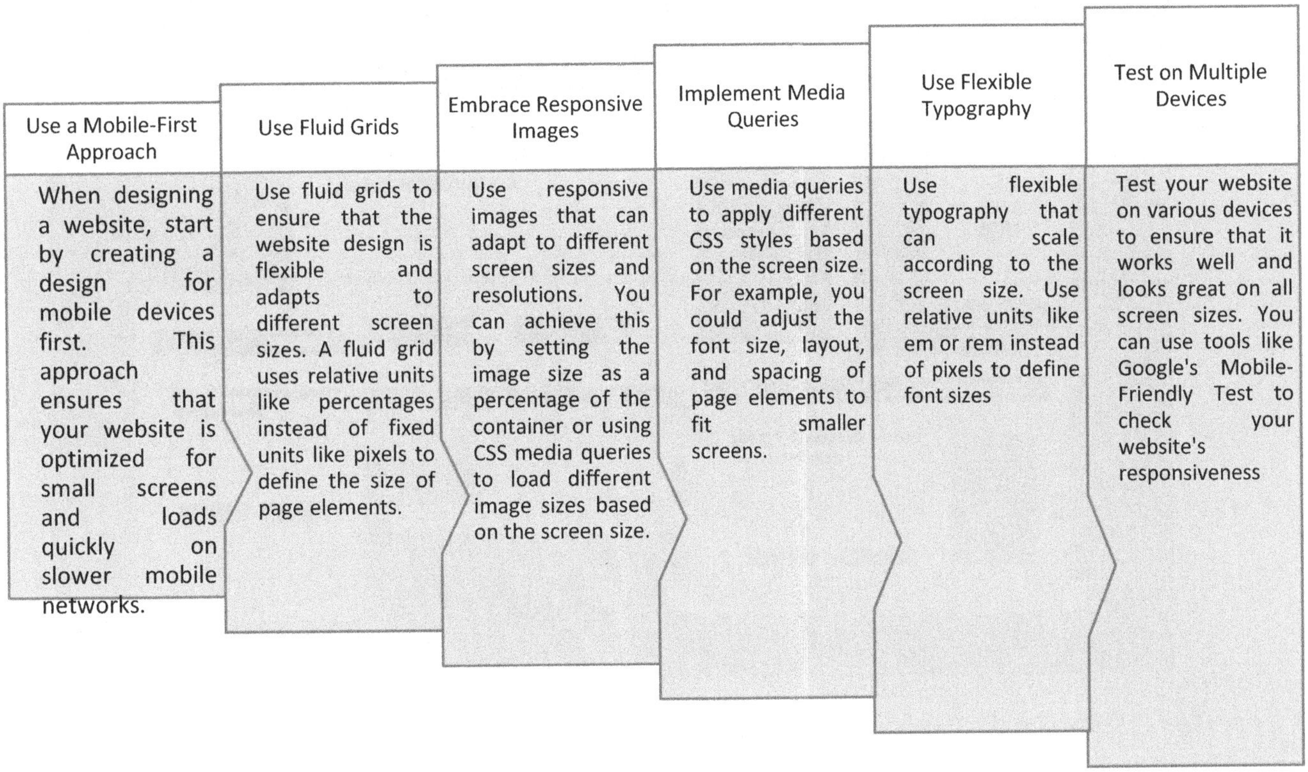

Use a Mobile-First Approach	Use Fluid Grids	Embrace Responsive Images	Implement Media Queries	Use Flexible Typography	Test on Multiple Devices
When designing a website, start by creating a design for mobile devices first. This approach ensures that your website is optimized for small screens and loads quickly on slower mobile networks.	Use fluid grids to ensure that the website design is flexible and adapts to different screen sizes. A fluid grid uses relative units like percentages instead of fixed units like pixels to define the size of page elements.	Use responsive images that can adapt to different screen sizes and resolutions. You can achieve this by setting the image size as a percentage of the container or using CSS media queries to load different image sizes based on the screen size.	Use media queries to apply different CSS styles based on the screen size. For example, you could adjust the font size, layout, and spacing of page elements to fit smaller screens.	Use flexible typography that can scale according to the screen size. Use relative units like em or rem instead of pixels to define font sizes	Test your website on various devices to ensure that it works well and looks great on all screen sizes. You can use tools like Google's Mobile-Friendly Test to check your website's responsiveness

Figure 27:some tips for creating responsive web designs for different screen sizes and devices

Creating a responsive web design is essential for providing a great user experience on all devices. By using a mobile-first approach, fluid grids, responsive images, media queries, flexible typography, and testing on multiple devices, you can create a website that looks great and functions well on any screen size or device.

Figure 28:Responsive web design

The Role of APIs and web services in Web and mobile development

In web and mobile development, APIs (Application Programming Interfaces) and web services play a critical role in enabling different software applications to communicate and share data. APIs and web services are essential tools for building scalable and dynamic web and mobile applications that can deliver a seamless user experience.

Key roles of APIs and web services in web and mobile development

Enabling Integration: APIs and web services enable software applications to communicate and share data, allowing developers to integrate different systems and services seamlessly. For example, an e-commerce website can integrate with a payment gateway API to enable online payments.

Enhancing Functionality: APIs and web services provide access to pre-built functionality and features that can be easily integrated into an application. This allows developers to enhance the functionality of their applications without having to build everything from scratch.

Improving Performance: APIs and web services can improve the performance of web and mobile applications by reducing the load on the server and improving data transfer times. For example, an application can use a caching API to store data locally, reducing the need for server requests.

Enabling Cross-Platform Development: APIs and web services enable developers to build applications that can run on different platforms, such as mobile devices, web browsers, and desktop computers. This allows developers to reach a wider audience and create a consistent user experience across different platforms.

Enabling Third-Party Integration: APIs and web services allow developers to integrate third-party services and applications.

User authentication and security in web and mobile development

User authentication and security are essential components of web and mobile development. They help ensure that users' data and privacy are protected and that unauthorized access to sensitive information is prevented. Here we will discuss user authentication and security in web and mobile development.

User Authentication:

User authentication is the process of verifying the identity of a user who wants to access a system, application, or website. It involves the use of credentials, such as a username and password, to verify the user's identity. User authentication is crucial in preventing unauthorized access to sensitive information. There are various methods of user authentication, including:

Password-based authentication:

This is the most common method of user authentication. Users are required to provide a unique combination of a username and password to gain access to a system or website. Passwords should be complex and should be changed frequently to ensure the security of the user's account.

Two-factor authentication:

Two-factor authentication (2FA) is a more secure form of user authentication that requires two types of identification to access an account. It involves the use of a password and a second factor, such as a fingerprint or a one-time code sent to the user's mobile device.

Biometric authentication

Biometric authentication involves the use of unique physical characteristics, such as a fingerprint or facial recognition, to verify a user's identity. This method is more secure than traditional password-based authentication and is becoming more popular on mobile devices.

Security

Security is essential in web and mobile development to ensure that users' data and privacy are protected. Various security measures can be implemented to prevent unauthorized access and protect user data, including:

Encryption

Encryption involves the use of algorithms to convert data into a secure format that can only be decrypted with a specific key. This method is commonly used to protect sensitive information such as passwords, credit card numbers, and personal information.

HTTPS

HTTPS is a secure version of HTTP that encrypts data in transit between the user's device and the server. HTTPS is essential for websites that handle sensitive data, such as online banking, e-commerce, and healthcare.

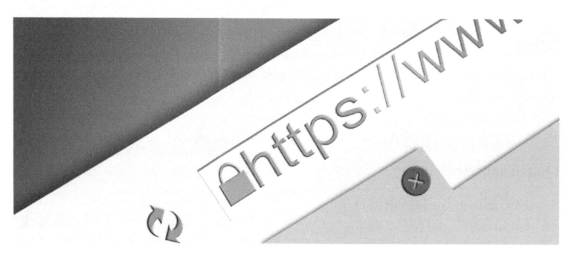

Figure 29:HTTPS on the web address

Access control

Access control involves restricting access to sensitive information to authorized users only. This can be achieved by implementing user roles and permissions, where users are only granted access to the information they need to perform their tasks.

User authentication and security are crucial in web and mobile development. They help protect users' data and privacy and prevent unauthorized access to sensitive information. Developers should implement secure user authentication methods and security measures to ensure that their applications and websites are secure. By doing so, users can have confidence that their information is protected and secure.

Cross-browser compatibility and performance optimization

Cross-browser compatibility and performance optimization are essential aspects of web development.

They help ensure that web applications and websites function correctly across different browsers and devices and provide a good user experience. Here we will discuss cross-browser compatibility and performance optimization in web development.

Cross-browser compatibility: This is the ability of a web application or website to function correctly on different web browsers and devices. Since different browsers interpret HTML, CSS, and JavaScript differently, it is crucial to test web applications and websites on multiple browsers and devices to ensure cross-browser compatibility. Developers can ensure cross-browser compatibility by following best practices such as:

Using standards-compliant HTML, CSS, and JavaScript: This ensures that the code is written in a way that adheres to industry standards, making it more likely to function correctly across different browsers and devices.

Testing on different browsers and devices: Developers should test their applications and websites on multiple browsers, including Internet Explorer, Firefox, Safari, and Chrome. They should also test on different devices, including desktops, laptops, tablets, and mobile devices

Using browser-specific code: If a particular browser requires specific code, developers should use conditional statements or browser detection techniques to serve the correct code to that browser.

Performance optimization: involves optimizing the speed and efficiency of a web application or website. This is crucial in providing a good user experience and can also impact search engine rankings. There are various techniques that developers can use to optimize performance, including:

Minimizing HTTP requests: This involves reducing the number of HTTP requests that the web application or website makes. Developers can do this by combining CSS and JavaScript files, using image sprites, and minimizing the use of external resources.

Optimizing images: Images can significantly impact the performance of a web application or website. Developers should optimize images by compressing them, using the correct file format, and using appropriate image sizes.

Caching: Caching involves storing frequently used resources, such as CSS and JavaScript files, on the user's device. This can significantly improve the speed and performance of the web application or website.

Using Content Delivery Networks (CDNs): CDNs can significantly improve the speed and performance of a web application or website by delivering content from servers that are geographically closer to the user.

Cross-browser compatibility and performance optimization are essential aspects of web development. Developers should follow best practices to ensure that web applications and websites function correctly across different browsers and devices and provide a good user experience. By doing so, they can improve user satisfaction and engagement, increase conversions, and improve search engine rankings.

Deploying web and mobile applications to production environments

Deploying web and mobile applications to production environments is a critical aspect of software development. It involves taking the code that was developed in a testing environment and making it available to users in a live production environment. This process requires careful planning and execution to ensure that the application is stable, secure, and performs as expected. Here we will discuss the steps involved in deploying web and mobile applications to production environments.

Step 1: Prepare for Deployment

Before deploying the application to a production environment, developers should ensure that the code is ready for deployment. This includes performing quality assurance testing to ensure that the application is stable and functional. The application should also be optimized for performance and security, and any necessary documentation should be prepared.

Step 2: Choose a Hosting Platform

The next step in deploying an application to a production environment is to choose a hosting platform. This can include a dedicated server, cloud hosting, or a third-party hosting service. The hosting platform should be chosen based on the requirements of the application, including scalability, security, and cost.

Step 3: Configure the Production Environment

The production environment should be configured to meet the requirements of the application. This includes setting up the necessary infrastructure, such as servers, databases, and other resources. Developers should also configure the necessary security settings, including firewalls and access controls.

Step 4: Deploy the Application

Once the production environment is configured, the application can be deployed. This involves uploading the code to the production server and configuring any necessary settings. This step requires careful attention to detail, as any mistakes can result in the application not functioning correctly.

Step 5: Perform Testing

After the application is deployed, developers should perform testing to ensure that it is functioning correctly. This includes functional testing, performance testing, and security testing. Any issues should be addressed before making the application available to users.

Step 6: Monitor the Application

Once the application is live, it is essential to monitor it for performance and security issues. This includes monitoring server logs, tracking user activity, and using monitoring tools to identify and address any issues that arise.

Deploying web and mobile applications to production environments requires careful planning and execution. Developers should ensure that the application is stable and secure and performs as expected before deploying it to a production environment. They should also choose an appropriate hosting platform, configure the production environment, and perform testing before making the application available to users. By following best practices for deploying applications, developers can ensure that the application is reliable and meets the needs of users.

Working with content management systems (CMS) and e-commerce platforms

Content management systems (CMS) and e-commerce platforms are essential tools for businesses to manage their online content and conduct e-commerce transactions. These platforms provide an easy-to-use interface that allows businesses to create and manage content and products without requiring extensive technical knowledge. Here we will discuss the benefits of working with CMS and e-commerce platforms and provide tips for choosing the right platform for your business.

Benefits of Using CMS:

CMS platforms provide a range of benefits for businesses, including:

- Ease of Use: CMS platforms offer a user-friendly interface that allows businesses to manage their content without requiring extensive technical knowledge.

- Customizability: CMS platforms offer a range of customization options, allowing businesses to tailor their website to their specific needs and branding.

- Scalability: CMS platforms are designed to handle a high volume of content, making them ideal for businesses with large websites or those with growth plans.

- SEO Optimization: Many CMS platforms come with built-in SEO optimization features that can help improve search engine rankings.

Benefits of Using E-Commerce Platforms:

E-commerce platforms provide a range of benefits for businesses, including:

- Ease of Use: E-commerce platforms offer a user-friendly interface that allows businesses to manage their online store without requiring extensive technical knowledge.

- Customizability: E-commerce platforms offer a range of customization options, allowing businesses to tailor their online store to their specific needs and branding.

- ◉ Payment Integration: E-commerce platforms integrate with popular payment gateways, allowing businesses to accept payments from customers easily.

- ◉ Inventory Management: E-commerce platforms offer inventory management features, allowing businesses to keep track of their stock levels and avoid overselling products.

Choosing the Right Platform:

When choosing a CMS or e-commerce platform, it is essential to consider several factors, including:

- ❖ Features: The platform should offer the necessary features and functionality for your business.

- ❖ Customizability: The platform should offer customization options that allow you to tailor your website or online store to your specific needs and branding.

- ❖ Scalability: The platform should be scalable, allowing your website or online store to grow with your business.

- ❖ Security: The platform should have robust security features to protect your website or online store from cyber threats.

- ❖ Support: The platform should offer reliable customer support to assist with any technical issues that may arise.

CMS and e-commerce platforms are essential tools for businesses looking to manage their online content and conduct e-commerce transactions. These platforms offer a range of benefits, including ease of use, customizability, and scalability. When choosing a platform, businesses should consider factors such as features, customizability, scalability, security, and support. By choosing the right platform for their needs, businesses can create a reliable and secure online presence that meets the needs of

Collaborating with designers and stakeholders in the development process

Collaborating with designers and stakeholders is an essential part of the development process. It helps to ensure that the end product meets the needs of all parties involved and is of high quality. Here are some tips for effectively collaborating with designers and stakeholders in the development process:

Define the scope and objectives: Before starting the development process, it's important to define the scope and objectives of the project. This will help to ensure that everyone involved is on the same page and has a clear understanding of what needs to be accomplished.

Involve designers early: Designers play a critical role in the development process, and it's important to involve them early on. This will help to ensure that the design is aligned with the project's objectives and requirements. Designers can provide valuable insights into the design process and help to identify potential issues that may arise.

Communicate regularly: Communication is key when collaborating with designers and stakeholders. Regular updates and meetings can help to keep everyone informed of the project's progress and any changes that may occur. Clear and concise communication can help to avoid misunderstandings and ensure that everyone is working towards the same goals.

Embrace feedback: Feedback is a crucial part of the development process. Designers and stakeholders may have different perspectives on the project, and their feedback can help to improve the end product. It's important to listen to feedback and make changes where necessary.

Use collaboration tools: Collaboration tools can help to streamline the development process and make it easier to work with designers and stakeholders. Tools like project management software, communication platforms, and design collaboration tools can help to keep everyone on the same page and ensure that the project stays on track.

Test and iterate: Testing and iteration are important parts of the development process. Testing can help to identify any issues or bugs in the product, while iteration can help to refine the design and make improvements. It's important to involve designers and stakeholders in the testing and iteration process to ensure that the end product meets their needs and expectations.

Collaborating with designers and stakeholders is a critical part of the development process. By defining the scope and objectives, involving designers early, communicating regularly, embracing feedback, using collaboration tools, and testing and iterating, you can ensure that the end product meets the needs of all parties involved and is of high quality.

Quality assurance and testing techniques for web and mobile applications

Quality assurance and testing are critical aspects of developing web and mobile applications. They help to ensure that the application meets the desired level of quality and performs as expected. Below are some of the quality assurance and testing techniques used for web and mobile applications.

Functional testing: Functional testing is a type of testing that checks whether the application's functions are working correctly. It involves testing individual functions of the application to ensure that they are performing as expected. Functional testing can be automated or manual.

Usability testing: Usability testing is a type of testing that checks the user-friendliness of the application. It involves testing the application's ease of use, navigation, and overall user experience. Usability testing can be done through surveys, focus groups, or usability testing software.

Performance testing: Performance testing checks how well the application performs under different conditions. It involves testing the application's speed, stability, and scalability. Performance testing can be automated or manual.

Security testing: Security testing checks the application's vulnerability to security threats. It involves testing the application's ability to protect user data and prevent unauthorized access. Security testing can be done using automated security testing tools or manual penetration testing.

Cross-platform testing: Cross-platform testing involves testing the application on different platforms, such as different web browsers or mobile devices. It ensures that the application is compatible with different platforms and performs consistently across them.

Regression testing: Regression testing checks whether changes to the application have affected existing functionality. It involves retesting previously tested features to ensure that they still work as expected after changes have been made.

A/B testing: A/B testing involves testing two versions of the same application or webpage to determine which one performs better. It can be used to test different features, designs, or user interfaces.

Quality assurance and testing are critical components of developing web and mobile applications. Using techniques such as functional testing, usability testing, performance testing, security testing, cross-platform testing, regression testing, and A/B testing can help ensure that the application meets the desired level of quality and performs as expected.

Best practices for web and mobile application development

Developing high-quality web and mobile applications requires a combination of technical skills, creativity, and attention to detail. Here we will discuss some best practices for web and mobile application development that can help you create applications that are reliable, user-friendly, and scalable.

Plan and design the application thoroughly: Before starting development, it's essential to have a clear understanding of the application's purpose, target audience, and features. Creating wireframes, mockups, and prototypes can help to identify potential issues early on and ensure that the design is aligned with the project's objectives.

Follow coding standards and best practices: Adhering to coding standards and best practices can help ensure that the code is readable, maintainable, and scalable. It can also help prevent security vulnerabilities and other issues.

Use responsive design: With the increasing use of mobile devices, it's crucial to ensure that the application is optimized for different screen sizes and resolutions. Using responsive design can help ensure that the application displays correctly on different devices and provides a consistent user experience.

Optimize for performance: Application performance can significantly impact user experience and retention. Optimizing the application's performance can involve techniques such as minimizing page load times, reducing server response times, and using caching.

Test and iterate: Testing and iteration are critical aspects of developing web and mobile applications. Testing should be done throughout the development process to identify issues early on and ensure that the application meets the desired level of quality. Iteration involves refining the application based on feedback and test results.

Use version control: Version control software such as Git can help manage changes to the application's codebase and collaborate with other developers. It can also help to track and revert changes if necessary.

Prioritize security: Security is a critical aspect of web and mobile application development. Implementing security best practices such as using secure authentication and encryption, performing regular security testing, and staying up to date with security patches can help protect the application and user data.

Web and mobile application development requires a combination of technical skills and attention to detail. By planning and designing thoroughly, following coding standards and best practices, using responsive design, optimizing for performance, testing and iterating, using version control, and prioritizing security, you can create high-quality applications that meet the needs of users and stakeholders.

Figure 30:Mobile Applications

Future outlook and emerging trends in web and mobile development.

Web and mobile development are constantly evolving industries, and keeping up with emerging trends and future outlooks is essential for developers to remain competitive. Below are some of the emerging trends and future outlooks in web and mobile development.

i. Artificial Intelligence and Machine Learning: Artificial Intelligence (AI) and Machine Learning (ML) are rapidly evolving technologies that are being integrated into web and mobile applications. AI and ML can enable applications to make intelligent decisions, provide personalized recommendations, and improve user experience.

ii. Progressive Web Applications: Progressive Web Applications (PWAs) are web applications that provide a native app-like experience on mobile devices. PWAs use modern web technologies to provide features such as offline capabilities, push notifications, and home screen installation.

iii. Voice User Interface: Voice User Interface (VUI) is an emerging trend in mobile development that enables users to interact with applications using voice commands. VUI can provide a more natural and intuitive user experience and can be integrated with AI and ML technologies.

iv. Internet of Things: The Internet of Things (IoT) is a network of physical devices that are connected to the Internet and can exchange data. Mobile applications can be developed to control and monitor IoT devices, enabling users to control their homes, cars, and other connected devices from their mobile devices.

v. Virtual and Augmented Reality: Virtual Reality (VR) and Augmented Reality (AR) technologies are becoming more prevalent in web and mobile development. VR and AR can provide immersive and interactive experiences for users, such as virtual tours, training simulations, and gaming.

vi. Low-code and No-code Development: Low-code and no-code development platforms are emerging trends in web and mobile development that allow developers to create applications using visual interfaces and pre-built components. This approach can enable faster development and reduce the need for specialized technical skills.

vii. Blockchain: Blockchain technology is becoming more widely used in web and mobile development for applications such as secure data storage, digital identity verification, and cryptocurrency transactions.

viii. Cross-Platform Development: Cross-platform development allows developers to create applications that can run on multiple platforms, such as iOS, Android, and web browsers. This approach can reduce development time and costs and enable a wider user base.

ix. Mobile Payments: Mobile payments are an emerging trend in mobile development, enabling users to make transactions using their mobile devices. Mobile payment technologies can include QR codes, NFC, and mobile wallets.

x. 5G Technology: The rollout of 5G technology is expected to have a significant impact on web and mobile development, enabling faster download and upload speeds, lower latency, and more reliable connectivity.

Web and mobile development are rapidly evolving industries, and keeping up with emerging trends and future outlooks is essential for developers to remain competitive. Technologies such as AI and ML, PWAs, VUI, IoT, VR/AR, low-code/no-code development, blockchain, cross-platform development, mobile payments, and 5G technology are expected to shape the future of web and mobile development in the coming years.

15
STARTUPS AND ENTREPRENEURSHIP IN ICT

The ICT industry has emerged as one of the fastest-growing industries globally. The sector is characterized by constant innovation and technological advancements, and this has led to the emergence of numerous startups in the industry. Startups are businesses that are in their early stages of development, usually with limited resources and a small team of founders. These startups are essential to the growth and development of the ICT industry and play a critical role in driving innovation.

Entrepreneurship in the ICT industry involves identifying a business opportunity in the industry and taking the necessary steps to establish a business that meets that need. Entrepreneurs in the ICT industry must have a solid understanding of the industry, the market, and the technological trends shaping the industry's future. They must also be adept at identifying opportunities for innovation and be willing to take risks.

The ICT industry provides a conducive environment for startups and entrepreneurship. The sector is characterized by a low barrier to entry, meaning that anyone with a great idea can start a business in the industry. Moreover, there is a vast pool of talent and resources available in the industry, making it easy for entrepreneurs to access the necessary skills and resources to grow their businesses.

The startup ecosystem in the ICT industry is also supported by various incubators, accelerators, and venture capitalists that provide funding, mentorship, and other resources to startups. These resources help startups overcome the challenges they face in their early stages of development, such as funding, talent acquisition, and market penetration.

One of the critical advantages of startups in the ICT industry is their ability to innovate and disrupt established markets. Startups can develop new products and services that can transform the industry and create new market opportunities. Moreover, startups can respond quickly to changes in the market and adapt their business models accordingly, making them more agile and flexible than established players in the industry.

However, startups in the ICT industry face several challenges, such as intense competition, rapid technological changes, and regulatory issues. These challenges require entrepreneurs to be creative, innovative, and agile in their approach to business. Successful entrepreneurs in the ICT industry must be able to pivot their business models quickly, anticipate changes in the market, and identify growth opportunities.

Startups and entrepreneurship are critical to the growth and development of the ICT industry. The sector provides a conducive environment for startups to thrive, with a low barrier to entry, a vast pool of talent and resources, and a supportive ecosystem. Successful entrepreneurs in the industry must be creative, innovative, and agile to overcome the challenges they face and take advantage of the opportunities presented by the industry.

Advantages and challenges of starting an ICT business

ICT has transformed the business landscape, allowing companies to operate more efficiently, communicate better, and reach new customers. Starting an ICT business can be an exciting venture with many advantages, but it also comes with its own set of challenges. Here we will discuss the advantages and challenges of starting an ICT business.

Advantages of starting an ICT business:

1. High demand: With the increasing reliance on technology, there is a high demand for ICT products and services. Businesses, organizations, and individuals require ICT solutions to optimize their operations, and this presents an opportunity for entrepreneurs to fill the gap in the market.

2. Scalability: ICT businesses are highly scalable, allowing entrepreneurs to grow their businesses without the need for significant infrastructure investments. With the right skills and knowledge, an ICT business can grow rapidly and reach a global audience.

3. Flexibility: The ICT industry is constantly evolving, with new technologies and trends emerging all the time. This presents an opportunity for entrepreneurs to be creative and flexible in their approach and to adapt to changes quickly.

4. Potential for high profits: Due to the high demand for ICT products and services, there is potential for high profits in this industry. Entrepreneurs who can develop innovative and effective solutions can command premium prices for their offerings.

Challenges of starting an ICT business:

1. High competition: The ICT industry is highly competitive, with many established players and new entrants vying for market share. Entrepreneurs need to have a unique value proposition and competitive advantage to succeed in this industry.

2. Rapid technological change: The pace of technological change in the ICT industry can be challenging to keep up with. Entrepreneurs need to be constantly learning and adapting to new technologies to remain relevant and competitive.

3. High startup costs: Starting an ICT business can require significant investment in hardware, software, and infrastructure. Entrepreneurs need to have access to sufficient capital to start and grow their businesses.

4. Security and privacy concerns: As an ICT business, it is critical to protect the security and privacy of your client's data. Entrepreneurs need to be aware of the latest security threats and implement appropriate measures to protect their clients' data.

Starting an ICT business presents many opportunities for entrepreneurs, but it also comes with its own set of challenges. Entrepreneurs need to have a unique value proposition, be adaptable to changes in the industry, and have access to sufficient capital to succeed in this competitive field. With the right approach and execution, starting an ICT business can be a rewarding and profitable venture.

Ideation and brainstorming techniques for ICT startups

When starting an ICT startup, it's essential to have a solid idea that can lead to a viable business. However, coming up with an innovative and feasible idea can be challenging, and that's where ideation and brainstorming techniques come in. Here we will discuss ideation and brainstorming techniques for ICT startups.

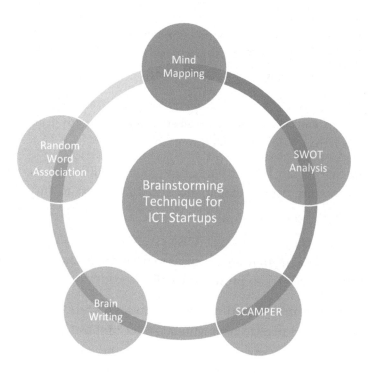

Figure 31:Ideation and brainstorming techniques for ICT startups

- Mind Mapping: This is a technique that involves generating ideas by creating a visual representation of your thoughts. Start by writing down your central idea in the middle of a sheet of paper and then branch out into related concepts, drawing connections and adding details as you go. Mind mapping allows you to explore different ideas and make connections between them.

- SWOT Analysis: A SWOT analysis is a structured method of evaluating the strengths, weaknesses, opportunities, and threats of a potential business idea. Start by listing the strengths and weaknesses of your idea and then identify the opportunities and threats in the market. This technique helps you identify the strengths and weaknesses of your idea and how to leverage opportunities and mitigate threats.

- SCAMPER: SCAMPER stands for Substitute, Combine, Adapt, Modify, Put to another use, Eliminate, and Reverse. This technique involves taking an existing idea and applying different modifications to it. For example, you can substitute a feature of an existing product with a new one, combine two products to create a new one or reverse the function of a product to create a new user.

- Brainwriting: Brainwriting is a technique that involves generating ideas in a group setting. Instead of verbalizing ideas, each team member writes down their ideas on a piece of paper, and then they are passed around for feedback and refinement. This technique allows everyone to contribute their ideas without fear of criticism or interruption.

- Random Word Association: This technique involves generating ideas by associating random words with your business idea. Start by selecting a random word, and then associate it with your idea, and keep going until you have several ideas to work with. This technique can lead to unexpected connections and creative solutions.

Ideation and brainstorming techniques are essential tools for generating innovative and feasible ideas for your ICT startup. These techniques allow you to explore different perspectives, identify potential opportunities and threats, and generate new ideas. Try out different techniques and find the ones that work best for you and your team. With the right approach, ideation and brainstorming can be powerful tools for developing a successful ICT startup.

Developing a business plan for an ICT startup

Developing a business plan is an essential step for any startup, and an ICT startup is no exception. A business plan outlines the key elements of your business, including your target market, value proposition, revenue streams, and financial projections. Here we will discuss the steps involved in developing a business plan for an ICT startup.

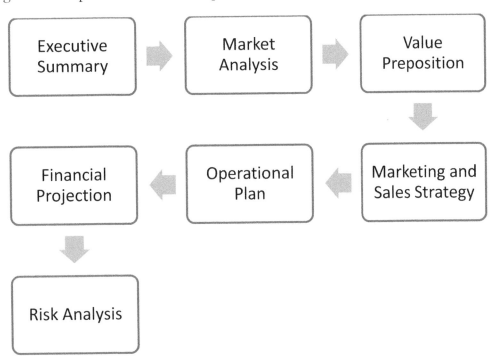

Figure 32:Developing a business plan for an ICT startup

- Executive Summary: The executive summary provides an overview of your business plan, including your mission statement, value proposition, and key objectives. It should be concise and compelling to grab the reader's attention.

- Market Analysis: The market analysis section of your business plan should provide a comprehensive overview of the industry and market you are entering. This includes analyzing the size of the market, the competition, and any potential opportunities or threats.

- Value Proposition: Your value proposition should clearly articulate the unique benefits your product or service provides to your target market. It should differentiate your offering from competitors and demonstrate how it solves a problem for your target market.

- Marketing and Sales Strategy: Your marketing and sales strategy should outline how you plan to reach and acquire customers. This includes identifying your target audience, developing a marketing plan, and outlining your sales process.

- Operations Plan: The operations plan should describe how you plan to run your business, including the processes and systems you will use. This includes everything from hiring and managing employees to managing your supply chain and logistics.

- Financial Projections: The financial projections section should outline your revenue streams, cost structure, and cash flow projections. This includes creating a budget, forecasting your revenue and expenses, and developing a cash flow statement.

- Risk Analysis: The risk analysis section should identify potential risks to your business and outline how you plan to mitigate them. This includes everything from market risks to operational risks to legal risks.

Developing a business plan is a critical step for any ICT startup. A well-crafted business plan can help you secure funding, attract investors, and guide your business operations. By following the steps outlined above, you can create a comprehensive and effective business plan that sets your ICT startup up for success.

Funding options for ICT startups

Funding is a critical aspect of starting and growing an ICT startup. It's important to have a solid understanding of the different funding options available to determine which ones align with your goals, resources, and growth potential. Here we will discuss three common funding options for ICT startups: angel investment, venture capital, and crowdfunding.

Angel Investment: Angel investors are high-net-worth individuals who invest their own money in startups in exchange for equity. They often invest in early-stage companies with high growth potential and are willing to take on higher risks in exchange for potentially high returns. Angel investors can provide funding, industry expertise, and valuable connections to help your ICT startup succeed.

Venture Capital: Venture capital firms invest in startups in exchange for equity. They typically invest in companies with high growth potential and a proven track record of success. Venture capital firms provide funding, industry expertise, and strategic support to help ICT startups scale their operations, expand their market reach, and achieve their growth objectives.

Crowdfunding: Crowdfunding is a method of raising capital by collecting small contributions from a large number of individuals. There are different types of crowdfunding, including donation-based crowdfunding, rewards-based crowdfunding, and equity crowdfunding. Equity crowdfunding allows startups to raise capital by offering equity to investors who contribute to their campaigns. This type of crowdfunding allows startups to raise capital from a large pool of investors without giving up control of their company.

Other funding options for ICT startups include bank loans, government grants, and incubator programs. It's important to research and evaluate each option to determine which one aligns with your goals and resources. Factors to consider when selecting a funding option include the amount of funding required, the level of control you are willing to give up, and the potential for future growth and success.

Funding is an essential aspect of starting and growing an ICT startup. Angel investment, venture capital, and crowdfunding are three common funding options for ICT startups. Each option has its benefits and risks, and it's important to research and evaluates each one to determine which one aligns with your goals and resources. With the right funding, ICT startups can achieve their growth objectives, expand their market reach, and bring their innovative ideas to life.

Building a team for an ICT startup

Building a team is a critical step in starting and growing an ICT startup. As a startup founder, you need to assemble a team of talented, dedicated, and passionate individuals who share your vision and can help you achieve your goals. Essential steps for building a team for an ICT startup.

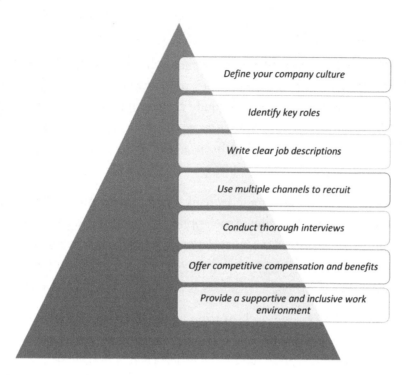

Figure 33: Building a team for an ICT startup

Define your company culture: Before you start recruiting, you need to define your company culture. This includes your values, mission, and vision for your ICT startup. Defining your company culture will help you attract and retain employees who share your values and can contribute to your company's success.

Identify key roles: The next step is to identify the key roles you need to fill to launch and grow your ICT startup. This includes identifying the technical roles, such as software developers, data scientists, and engineers, as well as the non-technical roles, such as marketing, sales, and customer support.

Write clear job descriptions: Once you've identified the key roles, you need to write clear and compelling job descriptions that attract the right candidates. Your job descriptions should outline the job responsibilities, required qualifications, and desired skills and experience.

Use multiple channels to recruit: To attract the best candidates, you need to use multiple channels to recruit. This includes posting job ads on job boards, social media, and professional networking sites. You can also leverage your personal and professional networks and attend industry events to connect with potential candidates.

Conduct thorough interviews: When you've identified potential candidates, it's important to conduct thorough interviews to assess their skills, experience, and fit with your company culture. You can use different interview formats, such as phone interviews, video interviews, and in-person interviews, to assess different aspects of their candidacy.

Offer competitive compensation and benefits: To attract and retain top talent, you need to offer competitive compensation and benefits. This includes salary, equity, health insurance, retirement benefits, and professional development opportunities.

Provide a supportive and inclusive work environment: Finally, you need to provide a supportive and inclusive work environment that promotes collaboration, innovation, and growth. This includes providing opportunities for professional development, recognizing and rewarding employee contributions, and fostering a culture of open communication and feedback.

Building a team is a critical step in starting and growing an ICT startup. By defining your company culture, identifying key roles, writing clear job descriptions, using multiple channels to recruit, conducting thorough interviews, offering competitive compensation and benefits, and providing a supportive and inclusive work environment, you can assemble a talented and dedicated team that helps you achieve your goals and drive your ICT startup's success.

Figure 34:Gathering Ideas from Startup Team

Intellectual property protection for ICT startups

Intellectual property (IP) protection is critical for ICT startups to safeguard their innovative ideas and products from unauthorized use and exploitation. In the digital age, IP protection has become more important than ever as technology advancements have made it easier for others to copy, steal or infringe on someone else's intellectual property. Here are some essential steps that ICT startups can take to protect their IP.

1. Identify and protect your IP: The first step in IP protection is to identify and protect your IP assets. This includes trademarks, patents, copyrights, and trade secrets. You should conduct a comprehensive audit of your IP assets to determine what needs to be protected and take appropriate steps to secure your IP rights.

2. File for patents: Patents are a key way to protect the technology and products developed by ICT startups. Patents give inventors the exclusive right to prevent others from making, using, or selling their inventions for a certain period. It is important to file for patents early to prevent others from patenting similar technology or products.

3. Register trademarks: Trademarks are another important form of IP protection that ICT startups should consider. Trademarks protect your brand and distinguish your products and services from those of your competitors. Registering a trademark can help you prevent others from using similar names or logos that may confuse customers.

4. Protect copyrights: Copyrights protect original works of authorship, such as software code, music, videos, and written content. Copyright protection is automatic when a work is created, but it is important to register your copyrights to have legal proof of ownership.

5. Use non-disclosure agreements: Non-disclosure agreements (NDAs) are legal contracts that prohibit individuals or entities from sharing confidential information with others. NDAs can help protect trade secrets and confidential information that may be essential to your ICT startup's success.

6. Conduct regular IP audits: Conducting regular IP audits can help you identify and protect any new IP assets that may have been developed since the last audit. This also helps you to identify any potential IP infringement issues, take corrective action, and safeguard your IP.

7. Enforce your IP rights: If you discover that someone has infringed on your IP rights, you should take immediate legal action to protect your IP. This may include sending cease-and-desist letters, filing lawsuits, and seeking damages.

IP protection is a critical factor in the success of an ICT startup. By identifying and protecting your IP assets, filing for patents, registering trademarks, protecting copyrights, using non-disclosure agreements, conducting regular IP audits, and enforcing your IP rights, you can safeguard your innovative ideas and products from unauthorized use and exploitation. These steps can also help you attract investors and customers who value the protection of IP rights and can ultimately contribute to the growth and success of your ICT startup.

Creating a minimum viable product (MVP) for ICT startups

For ICT startups, creating a minimum viable product (MVP) is an essential step in the early stages of the product development process. An MVP is a prototype version of a product that is designed to test the core functionalities of the product and gather feedback from potential customers. Here are some steps to creating a successful MVP for ICT startups.

Identify the core functionalities: The first step in creating an MVP is to identify the core functionalities of your product. These are the features that are essential to your product and that your customers will value the most. It's important to focus on these features and prioritize them in your MVP.

Develop a prototype: Once you have identified the core functionalities, you can start developing a prototype of your product. This can be a basic version of your product with limited features. The prototype should be functional and able to demonstrate the core functionalities of your product.

Test your MVP: Once you have a prototype of your product, it's time to test it. You can start by sharing it with a small group of potential customers to get their feedback. This feedback will help you understand what works and what doesn't work with your product.

Refine your MVP: Based on the feedback you receive, you can refine your MVP to improve its functionality and usability. This could involve adding new features, improving existing features, or removing features that are not necessary.

Launch your MVP: Once you have refined your MVP, it's time to launch it. This could involve releasing it to a wider audience or making it available for purchase. The goal of launching your MVP is to get it into the hands of your customers and start generating feedback and data.

Analyze feedback and iterate: After launching your MVP, it's important to analyze the feedback and data you receive from your customers. This feedback can help you identify areas for improvement and guide your product development process. You can then iterate on your MVP by refining and improving it based on the feedback you receive.

Creating an MVP is a critical step in the product development process for ICT startups. By identifying the core functionalities of your product, developing a prototype, testing and refining your MVP, and launching it to your customers, you can gather valuable feedback and data that will help you improve your product and grow your business.

Scaling and growing an ICT startup

Starting an ICT startup can be an exciting venture. However, the real challenge comes with scaling and growing the business. Below are some tips and strategies for scaling and growing an ICT startup.

Build a solid foundation

To scale and grow an ICT startup, it is essential to have a solid foundation. This includes having a clear vision and mission, a well-defined business model, a talented team, and a reliable technology stack. It is also important to have a strong company culture and values that align with your business goals.

Focus on customer acquisition

One of the biggest challenges for ICT startups is acquiring customers. To overcome this challenge, you should focus on building a solid customer acquisition strategy. This may involve building partnerships with other businesses, leveraging social media platforms, or creating a referral program.

Invest in marketing

Marketing is key to growing any business, and ICT startups are no exception. You need to create a brand identity and invest in digital marketing strategies such as search engine optimization (SEO), pay-per-click (PPC) advertising, and content marketing to reach your target audience.

Leverage technology

As an ICT startup, you have the advantage of being able to leverage technology to your advantage. This may involve using automation tools to streamline your operations, adopting cloud-based solutions to improve scalability, or investing in artificial intelligence (AI) and machine learning (ML) technologies to enhance your products or services.

Focus on customer retention

Acquiring new customers is important, but retaining existing customers is just as crucial. To ensure customer loyalty, you should focus on providing exceptional customer service and continuously improving your products or services based on customer feedback.

Hire the right talent

As you scale and grow your ICT startup, you will need to hire the right talent to support your business goals. This includes hiring individuals with the right skills and experience, as well as individuals who align with your company's culture and values.

Seek funding

To scale and grow your ICT startup, you may need to seek funding from investors or venture capitalists. It is important to have a solid business plan and financial projections to demonstrate your potential for growth and profitability.

In essence, scaling and growing an ICT startup requires a solid foundation, a focus on customer acquisition and retention, leveraging technology, hiring the right talent, and seeking funding. By following these tips and strategies, you can position your ICT startup for success and sustainable growth.

Exiting an ICT startup, including mergers and acquisitions

Exiting an ICT startup can be a complex process, with several options available to the founders, including mergers and acquisitions. Below are the different methods of exiting an ICT startup and a guide on how to choose the best option for your business.

1. **Selling the Company:** One of the most common ways to exit an ICT startup is by selling the company. This can be done in several ways, including:

a. Acquisition by a larger company In this scenario, a larger company buys the ICT startup to integrate its products or services into its offerings. This can be an attractive option for the ICT startup, as it provides a quick exit with a lump sum payment.

b. Sale to a competitor This option involves selling the company to a direct competitor, who may be looking to expand its market share or acquire new technology or talent. This option can also provide a quick exit and a lump sum payment.

c. Private equity or venture capital investment Private equity or venture capital firms may also be interested in investing in an ICT startup to grow the company and eventually sell it for a profit. This can provide an opportunity for the founders to retain some ownership and control of the company while still realizing some financial gain.

2. **Going Public:** Another option for exiting an ICT startup is to take the company public through an initial public offering (IPO). This involves selling shares of the company to the public through a stock exchange. Going public can provide the founders with a significant windfall, as well as provide the company with access to public capital markets.

3. **Liquidation:** If the ICT startup is unable to find a buyer or go public, the last option may be to liquidate the company. This involves selling off all of the company's assets and paying off any remaining debts or obligations. While this may not provide the founders with a significant financial gain, it can help them to avoid any further financial losses.

Mergers and Acquisitions Mergers and acquisitions (M&A) can be a particularly attractive option for ICT startups, as they can provide a quick exit with a substantial payout. In an acquisition, a larger company buys the ICT startup outright, while in a merger, the two companies combine to form a single entity. M&A can provide several benefits, including access to new markets, technologies, and talent. However, it is essential to carefully consider the terms of any M&A deal, as well as the cultural fit between the two companies.

Exiting an ICT startup can be a complex process, and the best option will depend on a variety of factors, including the company's financial situation, growth potential, and the founders' personal goals. By carefully considering each option and seeking professional advice where necessary, founders can ensure they make the best decision for their business and themselves.

Success Stories and case studies of ICT Startups

ICT startups have been at the forefront of technological innovation and disruption, transforming industries and creating new ones. Below are some success stories and case studies of ICT startups that have made a significant impact in their respective industries.

1. Zoom is a video conferencing software company founded in 2011. The company experienced explosive growth during the COVID-19 pandemic as remote work and virtual meetings became the norm. As of 2021, Zoom has over 300 million daily meeting participants and a market capitalization of over $100 billion.

2. Slack is a communication and collaboration platform for teams. The company was founded in 2013 and has grown to over 12 million daily active users as of 2021. In 2019, Slack went public with a direct listing and had a market capitalization of $20 billion on its first day of trading.

3. Airbnb is an online marketplace for short-term vacation rentals. The company was founded in 2008 and has disrupted the traditional hotel industry. As of 2021, Airbnb has over 7 million listings worldwide and a market capitalization of over $100 billion.

4. Stripe is a payment processing platform for online businesses. The company was founded in 2010 and has grown rapidly, processing billions of dollars in transactions annually. As of 2021, Stripe has a valuation of over $95 billion and has expanded its offerings to include fraud prevention and business management tools.

5. Uber is a ride-hailing platform that has revolutionized the transportation industry. The company was founded in 2009 and has expanded to over 900 metropolitan areas worldwide. Uber's disruptive business model has led to controversy and regulatory challenges, but the company has still achieved a market capitalization of over $100 billion.

6. Pinterest is a social media platform for visual discovery and bookmarking. The company was founded in 2009 and had over 450 million, monthly active users. In 2019, Pinterest went public with a market capitalization of over $12 billion.

7. Dropbox is a cloud storage and file-sharing platform. The company was founded in 2007 and has grown to over 700 million registered users. Dropbox went public in 2018 with a market capitalization of over $8 billion.

These success stories and case studies of ICT startups demonstrate the transformative power of technology and entrepreneurship. By identifying and addressing unmet needs in their respective industries, these startups have created significant value for their users and investors. While not every startup will achieve the same level of success, these examples provide inspiration and guidance for those seeking to create the next big thing in the world of technology.

Incubators and accelerators for ICT startups

Incubators and accelerators are programs that provide support and resources to early-stage ICT startups. These programs can be instrumental in helping startups to succeed by providing mentorship, networking opportunities, funding, and other resources. Below are the differences between incubators and accelerators, and they highlight some of the top programs for ICT startups.

Incubators vs Accelerators While the terms "incubator" and "accelerator" are often used interchangeably, they have distinct differences. Incubators are programs designed to support startups in the early stages of development. They typically provide office space, mentorship, and access to resources such as legal and financial advice. Incubators tend to be longer-term programs, with startups staying for up to two years or more.

Accelerators, on the other hand, are designed to provide a shorter-term, more intensive experience. They typically offer mentorship, networking opportunities, and funding in exchange for equity in the company. Accelerators often have a specific focus, such as technology or social impact, and have a set timeline, usually ranging from three to six months.

Top Incubators and Accelerators for ICT Startups

SN	INCUBATOR	DUTIES
1	Y Combinator	Y Combinator is one of the most well-known accelerators in the world. The program provides funding, mentorship, and resources to early-stage startups. Y Combinator has backed companies such as Dropbox, Airbnb, and Reddit, among others.
2	Techstars	Techstars is another well-respected accelerator that provides mentorship and funding to early-stage startups. The program has a global network of mentors and investors and has backed companies such as SendGrid, DigitalOcean, and ClassPass.
3	500 Startups	500 Startups is a seed fund and accelerator that provides mentorship and funding to early-stage startups. The program has a global network of mentors and investors and has backed companies such as Udemy, Canva, and Talkdesk.
4	Seedcamp	Seedcamp is a European-based accelerator that provides mentorship, funding, and resources to early-stage startups. The program has a focus on technology and has backed companies such as TransferWise, Revolut, and UiPath.

Incubators and accelerators can be instrumental in helping early-stage ICT startups to succeed. By providing mentorship, networking opportunities, funding, and other resources, these programs can help startups to grow and reach their full potential. While there are many different incubators and accelerators available, those listed above are some of the most well-respected and successful programs in the world.

Community and networking resources for ICT startups

Community and networking resources can be essential for ICT startups, as they provide opportunities to connect with other entrepreneurs, industry experts, and potential investors. Below are some of the top community and networking resources available for ICT startups.

SN	Name	Community & Networking Resource
1	Startup Grind	Startup Grind is a global community of entrepreneurs that hosts events and provides resources and support for startups. The community has chapters in over 600 cities worldwide and features interviews with successful entrepreneurs, investor panels, and networking opportunities.
2	Techstars Community	Techstars Community is a global network of entrepreneurs, mentors, and investors that provides resources and support for startups. The community offers events, online resources, and opportunities to connect with mentors and investors.
2	AngelList	AngelList is an online platform that connects startups with investors. The platform provides a database of investors, syndicates, and startup jobs, as well as a fundraising platform for startups.
3	Founder Institute	Founder Institute is a startup accelerator program that provides mentorship, training, and resources for early-stage startups. The program is global, with chapters in over 200 cities worldwide, and features mentorship from successful entrepreneurs and investors.
4	LinkedIn	LinkedIn is a social networking platform for professionals that can be a valuable resource for startups. The platform provides opportunities to connect with other entrepreneurs, industry experts, and potential investors, as well as access to job listings and industry insights.
5	Meetup	Meetup is a platform that connects people with similar interests, including entrepreneurs and startups. The platform provides opportunities to join or start groups focused on entrepreneurship, technology, and innovation, as well as attend events and networking opportunities.

Community and networking resources can be essential for ICT startups to succeed. By connecting with other entrepreneurs, industry experts, and potential investors, startups can gain valuable insights, resources, and support. While there are many different community and networking resources available, those listed above are some of the most well-respected and successful resources in the world of entrepreneurship and startups.

Future Outlook and emerging trends in ICT Entrepreneurship

ICT entrepreneurship is a dynamic and rapidly evolving field, with new trends and innovations emerging every day. Below are some of the key emerging trends and future outlooks for ICT entrepreneurship.

Artificial Intelligence (AI) AI is a rapidly growing field that is poised to transform many aspects of ICT entrepreneurship. Startups are increasingly using AI to develop innovative solutions for a range of industries, from healthcare and finance to marketing and customer service. AI is also enabling startups to automate and streamline many business processes, reducing costs and increasing efficiency.

Blockchain technology has the potential to transform many industries by enabling secure and transparent transactions. Startups are increasingly using blockchain to develop solutions for industries such as finance, healthcare, and supply chain management. As blockchain technology continues to evolve, it is likely to play an increasingly important role in the world of ICT entrepreneurship.

Internet of Things (IoT) The IoT refers to the network of interconnected devices that are becoming increasingly common in our homes, offices, and communities. Startups are developing innovative solutions that leverage IoT technology to improve efficiency, reduce costs, and enhance the user experience. As the IoT continues to grow and evolve, it is likely to play an increasingly important role in the world of ICT entrepreneurship.

Cybersecurity As more and more businesses and individuals rely on technology to store sensitive data and conduct transactions, cybersecurity is becoming increasingly important. Startups are developing innovative solutions to address cybersecurity threats and protect businesses and individuals from cyberattacks. As the threat of cyberattacks continues to grow, cybersecurity is likely to remain a key area of focus for ICT entrepreneurship.

Virtual and Augmented Reality Virtual and augmented reality technologies have the potential to transform a range of industries, from gaming and entertainment to education and healthcare. Startups are developing innovative solutions that leverage virtual and augmented reality technology to create immersive experiences and enhance learning and training. As technology continues to evolve, it is likely to play an increasingly important role in the world of ICT entrepreneurship.

Cloud Computing Cloud computing technology has transformed the way businesses store, manage, and access data. Startups are developing innovative solutions that leverage cloud computing to improve efficiency, reduce costs, and enhance the user experience. As more and more businesses adopt cloud computing technology, startups are likely to continue to play a key role in the development and evolution of technology.

ICT entrepreneurship is a dynamic and rapidly evolving field, with new trends and innovations emerging every day. As technologies such as AI, blockchain, IoT, cybersecurity, virtual and augmented reality, and cloud computing continue to evolve, startups will be at the forefront of innovation, developing new solutions to address the challenges and opportunities presented by these technologies.

While the future of ICT entrepreneurship is uncertain, one thing is clear: the pace of innovation is unlikely to slow down anytime soon, and startups will continue to play a key role in shaping the future of the industry.

16

THE FUTURE OF ICT CAREERS AND INDUSTRY TRENDS

The ICT industry has been rapidly growing and changing in recent years, and this trend is expected to continue. As technology continues to evolve, so too will the careers and job opportunities in the ICT industry. Below are some of the emerging industry trends and the future of ICT careers.

1. Increased Demand for Cybersecurity Professionals As more and more businesses rely on technology to store sensitive data and conduct transactions, cybersecurity has become an increasingly important issue. The demand for cybersecurity professionals is expected to continue to grow as businesses seek to protect themselves from cyberattacks and data breaches.

2. Emphasis on Data Analytics and Artificial Intelligence Data analytics and artificial intelligence (AI) are becoming increasingly important in a range of industries, from healthcare and finance to marketing and customer service. As more businesses seek to leverage data and AI to improve efficiency and gain a competitive advantage, there will be an increased demand for professionals with expertise in these areas.

3. Greater Emphasis on Remote Work The COVID-19 pandemic has accelerated the trend towards remote work, and many businesses are now embracing remote work as a permanent solution. This trend is expected to continue, creating new opportunities for professionals who can work remotely.

4. Focus on Cloud Computing Cloud computing has transformed the way businesses store, manage, and access data. As more and more businesses adopt cloud computing technology, there will be an increased demand for professionals with expertise in this area.

5. Emphasis on Soft Skills While technical expertise will always be important in the ICT industry, there is also an increasing emphasis on soft skills such as communication, collaboration, and problem-solving. As businesses seek to build diverse and inclusive teams, professionals with strong, soft skills will be in high demand.

6. Greater Emphasis on Sustainability is becoming an increasingly important issue in the ICT industry, and businesses are beginning to recognize the importance of reducing their carbon footprint and operating in an environmentally responsible manner. Professionals with expertise in sustainable ICT practices will be in high demand in the coming years.

The future of ICT careers is bright, with many exciting opportunities emerging as technology continues to evolve. As businesses seek to leverage new technologies to gain a competitive advantage, professionals with expertise in areas such as cybersecurity, data analytics, and cloud computing will be in high demand. Additionally, professionals with strong, soft skills and expertise in sustainable ICT practices will be well-positioned to succeed in the changing ICT industry. By staying up-to-date with emerging industry trends and developing expertise in these key areas, ICT professionals can ensure that they remain competitive and in demand in the years to come.

17

SAMPLE INTERVIEW QUESTIONS AND ANSWERS

Sample interview questions for Database Experts

1. What are the key considerations when designing a database schema?

When designing a database schema, it is important to consider the requirements of the system, including the types of data to be stored, the relationships between the data, and the expected usage patterns. It is also important to consider performance and scalability, as well as security and access control. A well-designed database schema should be efficient, flexible, and easy to maintain.

2. How do you ensure data integrity and consistency in a database?

Data integrity and consistency are essential aspects of database design. To ensure data integrity, designers can use constraints and rules to enforce data validation and prevent data corruption. Consistency can be ensured through the use of transactions and concurrency control mechanisms, which ensure that data is updated atomically and consistently across multiple concurrent transactions.

3. What are some common database performance issues, and how can they be addressed?

Common database performance issues include slow query response times, inefficient indexing, and excessive disk I/O. These issues can be addressed by optimizing queries, creating appropriate indexes, and configuring database caching and buffering settings. Additionally, database administrators can monitor system performance and tune database settings to optimize performance.

4. How do you ensure database security and privacy?

Database security and privacy are critical considerations in database design. This involves implementing appropriate access controls and authentication mechanisms, encrypting sensitive data, and monitoring and auditing database activity to detect and respond to security breaches. Additionally, designers should ensure compliance with relevant regulations and standards, such as the General Data Protection Regulation (GDPR) or the Health Insurance Portability and Accountability Act (HIPAA).

5. What are some strategies for scaling a database to handle large volumes of data and high levels of traffic?

To scale a database to handle large volumes of data and high levels of traffic, designers can use strategies such as horizontal partitioning, sharding, and replication. These techniques involve distributing data across multiple servers or partitions, which can increase throughput and availability. Additionally, designers can use caching and load balancing to optimize performance and handle bursts of traffic.

6. How do you ensure database backup and disaster recovery?

Database backup and disaster recovery are essential aspects of database management. To ensure backup and recovery, designers can implement a backup and restore strategy that includes regular backups, offsite storage, and testing of backup and recovery procedures. Additionally, designers should develop a disaster recovery plan that outlines procedures for restoring the database in the event of a catastrophic failure or data loss.

7. What is a database? Answer: A database is an organized collection of data stored and accessed electronically.

8. What is your experience with SQL? Answer: I have extensive experience working with SQL and related technologies.

9. What is normalization in database design? Answer: Normalization is the process of organizing data in a database so that it is consistent and minimizes redundancy.

10. What is indexing in a database? Answer: Indexing is the process of creating an index on a database table to improve performance.

11. What is a primary key in a database? Answer: A primary key is a unique identifier for a database table.

12. What is a foreign key in a database? Answer: A foreign key is a field in a database table that links to the primary key of another table.

13. What is a clustered index? Answer: A clustered index is an index that determines the physical order of the data in a database table.

14. What is a non-clustered index? Answer: A non-clustered index is an index that does not determine the physical order of the data in a database table.

15. What is the difference between a view and a table in a database? Answer: A view is a virtual table based on the result of a SQL statement, whereas a table is a physical structure that stores data.

16. What is a stored procedure in a database? Answer: A stored procedure is a pre-compiled SQL statement that can be called multiple times with different parameters.

17. How do you optimize database performance? Answer: Database performance can be optimized by ensuring proper indexing, minimizing redundant data, and optimizing SQL queries.

18. What is the difference between a backup and a restore in a database? Answer: A backup is a copy of a database taken at a specific point in time, whereas a restore is a process of using that backup to restore the database to its original state.

19. How do you secure a database? Answer: A database can be secured by using proper access controls, encrypting sensitive data, and monitoring access logs for suspicious activity.

20. What is database replication? Answer: Database replication is the process of copying a database to one or more additional servers.

21. What is a data warehouse? Answer: A data warehouse is a large, centralized repository of data used for business intelligence and analytics.

22. What is data mining? Answer: Data mining is the process of analyzing large datasets to discover patterns, trends, and insights.

23. What is data modelling? Answer: Data modelling is the process of creating a conceptual, logical, and physical model of a database.

24. What is big data? Answer: Big data refers to extremely large datasets that require specialized tools and technologies to manage and analyze.

25. What is NoSQL? Answer: NoSQL is a category of databases that do not use SQL as their primary query language.

26. What is cloud computing? Answer: Cloud computing is the delivery of computing services, including databases, over the internet on a pay-per-use basis.

27. ten database essay questions with answers

28. What are the different types of databases, and how do they differ from one another?

29. Answer: The four main types of databases are relational, NoSQL, object-oriented, and hierarchical. Relational databases are the most common and are organized into tables with rows and columns. NoSQL databases are designed for large and complex data sets, while object-oriented databases are designed to store complex objects. Hierarchical databases are organized into a tree-like structure.

30. What is data normalization, and why is it important?

31. Answer: Data normalization is the process of organizing data in a database so that it is consistent and minimizes redundancy. It is important because it helps to eliminate data inconsistencies, making it easier to maintain and update the database.

32. What is database indexing, and how does it improve database performance?

33. Answer: Database indexing is the process of creating an index on a database table to improve performance. Indexes help to speed up database queries by allowing the database to quickly locate the relevant data.

34. What is database replication, and why is it useful?

35. Answer: Database replication is the process of copying a database to one or more additional servers. Replication is useful because it provides redundancy and increases availability, allowing multiple users to access the database simultaneously without overloading the server.

36. What is the difference between a backup and a restore in a database?

37. Answer: A backup is a copy of a database taken at a specific point in time, while a restore is a process of using that backup to restore the database to its original state. Backups are important because they provide a way to recover from data loss or corruption.

38. How do you secure a database, and what are some best practices for database security?

39. Answer: To secure a database, access controls should be put in place, sensitive data should be encrypted, and access logs should be monitored for suspicious activity. Best practices for database security include using strong passwords, limiting access to sensitive data, and keeping software up-to-date.

40. What is big data, and how is it changing the way we manage and analyze data?

41. Answer: Big data refers to extremely large datasets that require specialized tools and technologies to manage and analyze. Big data is changing the way we manage and analyze data by allowing us to analyze large data sets in real time and make better-informed decisions.

42. What is data mining, and how is it used in database management?

43. Answer: Data mining is the process of analyzing large datasets to discover patterns, trends, and insights. It is used in database management to help identify potential problems, optimize database performance, and discover new business opportunities.

44. What are some common challenges in database management, and how can they be overcome?

45. Answer: Common challenges in database management include data consistency, security, and scalability. These challenges can be overcome by implementing best practices for database design, using proper access controls, and using specialized tools and technologies to manage large and complex data sets.

46. What is cloud computing, and how is it changing the way we manage and store data?

Sample Interview Questions for Networking Experts

1. What are the key considerations when designing a network architecture?

When designing a network architecture, it is important to consider the requirements of the system, including the types of devices and applications to be supported, the expected usage patterns, and the security and privacy needs of the network. Additionally, designers should consider performance and scalability, as well as the physical layout and connectivity of the network. A well-designed network architecture should be flexible, secure, and easy to maintain.

2. What are some common network security threats, and how can they be addressed?

Common network security threats include malware, phishing attacks, and unauthorized access to sensitive data. These threats can be addressed through the use of firewalls, intrusion detection and prevention systems, and encryption technologies. Additionally, designers should implement strong authentication and access control mechanisms, and ensure that all devices and software are up-to-date with the latest security patches.

3. How do you ensure network performance and scalability?

To ensure network performance and scalability, designers can use techniques such as load balancing, traffic shaping, and Quality of Service (QoS) controls. These techniques can help to distribute traffic across multiple network resources, prioritize important traffic, and optimize bandwidth usage. Additionally, designers should consider the physical infrastructure of the network, such as the number and placement of switches and routers, and ensure that the network is designed with sufficient capacity to handle future growth.

4. What are some strategies for managing network traffic and congestion?

To manage network traffic and congestion, designers can implement traffic shaping and QoS controls to prioritize traffic and ensure that critical applications and services receive sufficient bandwidth. Additionally, designers can use caching and content distribution technologies to reduce the amount of traffic on the network and implement load balancing to distribute traffic across multiple servers or resources.

5. How do you ensure network availability and reliability?

Network availability and reliability are essential aspects of network design. This involves using redundant network components, such as backup servers and power supplies, to ensure that the network remains operational even in the event of a failure. Additionally, designers should implement monitoring and alerting systems to detect and respond to network issues and implement failover and disaster recovery procedures to minimize downtime in the event of a catastrophic failure.

6. What are some best practices for network documentation and management?

To ensure effective network documentation and management, designers should maintain accurate and up-to-date documentation of network components, configurations, and policies. This can include network diagrams, inventory lists, and user manuals. Additionally, designers should implement network management tools and processes to automate network administration tasks and monitor network performance and availability. Finally, designers should regularly review and update network documentation and management processes to ensure that they remain effective and relevant.

7. What is computer networking, and how does it work?

Answer: Computer networking is the process of connecting multiple devices to communicate with each other. It works by using protocols, such as TCP/IP, to transmit data across a network of devices.

8. What are the different types of network topologies, and how do they differ from one another?

Answer: The four main types of network topologies are bus, star, ring, and mesh. A bus topology connects devices in a linear sequence, while a star topology connects devices to a central hub. A ring topology connects devices in a circular pattern, and a mesh topology connects devices in a more complex, interconnected manner.

9. What is the difference between a LAN and a WAN?

Answer: A LAN (Local Area Network) is a network that connects devices within a small geographic area, such as a building or campus. A WAN (Wide Area Network) is a network that connects devices over a large geographic area, such as a city, state, or country.

10. What is the OSI model, and how is it used in networking?

Answer: The OSI (Open Systems Interconnection) model is a seven-layer model that describes how data is transmitted over a network. It is used in networking to standardize communication protocols and ensure compatibility between different types of devices.

11. What is DNS, and how does it work?

Answer: DNS (Domain Name System) is a protocol that translates domain names into IP addresses. When a user types a domain name into a browser, the DNS server looks up the corresponding IP address and sends it back to the user's computer, allowing the user to access the website.

12. What is NAT, and how is it used in networking?

Answer: NAT (Network Address Translation) is a process that allows multiple devices on a LAN to share a single IP address. It is used in networking to conserve IP addresses and improve security by hiding the internal network from the public internet.

13. What is a firewall, and how does it work?

Answer: A firewall is a network security system that monitors and controls incoming and outgoing network traffic. It works by examining the data packets sent and received by a network and blocking or allowing them based on a set of predefined rules.

14. What is a VPN, and how is it used in networking?

Answer: A VPN (Virtual Private Network) is a secure, encrypted connection between two networks over the public internet. It is used in networking to provide remote access to a private network, such as a corporate network, and to secure communications between different networks.

15. What is load balancing, and how is it used in networking?
Answer: Load balancing is the process of distributing network traffic across multiple servers or devices. It is used in networking to improve performance and availability by ensuring that network traffic is evenly distributed across available resources.

16. What is QoS, and how is it used in networking?
Answer: QoS (Quality of Service) is a set of techniques used to prioritize network traffic based on its importance. It is used in networking to ensure that critical applications, such as video conferencing and VoIP, receive priority over less important applications, such as email and web browsing.

17. What is multicast, and how is it used in networking?
Answer: Multicast is a network communication method that allows a single data packet to be sent to multiple recipients simultaneously. It is used in networking to reduce network traffic and improve performance by minimizing the number of data packets that need to be transmitted.

18. What is the difference between TCP and UDP?
Answer: TCP (Transmission Control Protocol) is a connection-oriented protocol that ensures reliable delivery of data by establishing a connection between two devices before transmitting data. UDP (User Datagram Protocol) is a connectionless protocol that does not establish a

19. What is a LAN, and how is it different from a WAN?
Answer: A LAN (Local Area Network) is a network that connects devices within a small geographic area, such as a home or office building. A WAN (Wide Area Network), on the other hand, is a network that connects devices across a larger geographic area, such as across different cities or even countries.

20. What is a firewall, and what is its purpose?
Answer: A firewall is a network security device that monitors and controls the incoming and outgoing network traffic based on a set of rules. Its purpose is to protect a network from unauthorized access and malicious activity.

21. What is a router, and how does it work?
Answer: A router is a networking device that connects multiple networks and routes data between them. It works by analyzing the data packets it receives and determining the best path for them to take to reach its destination.

22. What is a switch, and how is it different from a router?
Answer: A switch is a networking device that connects devices within a network together and facilitates communication between them. It is different from a router in that it only operates within a single network, while a router connects multiple networks.

23. What is DNS, and what is its role in networking?
Answer: DNS (Domain Name System) is a system that translates domain names into IP addresses. Its role in networking is to help computers communicate with each other by resolving domain names to their associated IP addresses.

24. What is a VLAN, and how is it used in networking?

Answer: A VLAN (Virtual Local Area Network) is a logical grouping of devices within a single physical network. It is used in networking to improve security, performance, and manageability by segmenting network traffic into different VLANs based on their function or location.

25. What is a VPN, and what is its purpose?

Answer: A VPN (Virtual Private Network) is a secure network connection that allows users to access a private network over a public network, such as the internet. Its purpose is to provide secure and private access to network resources from remote locations.

26. What is NAT, and how is it used in networking?

Answer: NAT (Network Address Translation) is a process that allows multiple devices on a private network to share a single public IP address. It is used in networking to conserve IP addresses and improve network security by hiding the private IP addresses of devices on a network from the public internet.

27. What is QoS, and what is its role in networking?

Answer: QoS (Quality of Service) is a set of techniques used to manage network traffic and ensure that certain types of traffic, such as voice or video, receive higher priority than others. Its role in networking is to improve the performance and reliability of critical network services.

28. What is Wi-Fi, and how does it work?

Answer: Wi-Fi is a wireless networking technology that allows devices to connect to a network without the need for cables or wires. It works by using radio waves to transmit data between devices and an access point, which is connected to a wired network.

29. What is a MAC address, and how is it used in networking?

Answer: A MAC (Media Access Control) address is a unique identifier assigned to a network interface controller (NIC) by its manufacturer. It is used in networking to identify devices on a network and facilitate communication between them.

Sample Interview Questions for Computer Security Experts

1. What are some of the most common cybersecurity threats facing organizations today?

Answer: There are many different cybersecurity threats that organizations face today, but some of the most common include phishing attacks, ransomware, malware, and DDoS attacks. Phishing attacks are typically carried out via email and aim to trick individuals into revealing sensitive information or clicking on malicious links. Ransomware is a type of malware that locks down a user's computer or data until a ransom is paid. Malware refers to any type of malicious software that can be used to steal data, take control of systems, or cause other harm. DDoS attacks are aimed at overwhelming a network with traffic to make it unusable. All of these threats are constantly evolving, and organizations must take steps to protect themselves against them.

2. How can organizations ensure that their employees are properly trained on cybersecurity best practices?

Answer: Organizations can ensure that their employees are properly trained on cybersecurity best practices by providing regular training sessions and resources. This can include online courses, workshops, and seminars that cover topics such as how to identify phishing emails, how to create strong passwords, and how to avoid common cybersecurity pitfalls. Additionally, organizations can develop clear policies and procedures for handling sensitive information and ensure that employees are aware of these policies. Regular reminders and updates can also be sent to employees to help keep cybersecurity practices top of mind.

3. How important is encryption in cybersecurity, and how can organizations ensure that their data is properly encrypted?

Answer: Encryption is a critical component of cybersecurity, as it can help to protect sensitive data from being intercepted and read by unauthorized individuals. Organizations can ensure that their data is properly encrypted by implementing encryption protocols for all sensitive data both at rest and in transit. This can include using encryption tools such as HTTPS, SSL, and TLS for web traffic, and implementing data encryption standards such as AES for stored data. Additionally, organizations can use encryption software to protect sensitive files and data, and ensure that encryption keys are properly managed and secured.

4. How can organizations protect against insider threats?

Answer: Protecting against insider threats requires a multi-layered approach that includes both technical controls and employee training. Technical controls can include limiting access to sensitive data and systems, monitoring user activity, and implementing user behaviour analytics (UBA) software to identify unusual behaviour. Employee training can help to promote a culture of security awareness and help employees recognize and report suspicious activity. Additionally, organizations can implement strong security policies and procedures, such as mandatory password changes, two-factor authentication, and regular security audits.

5. How can organizations ensure that their third-party vendors are properly securing their data?

Answer: Organizations can ensure that their third-party vendors are properly securing their data by performing due diligence during the vendor selection process and by implementing strict security requirements in their vendor contracts. This can include requiring vendors to undergo security audits and assessments, and to provide regular reports on their security practices. Organizations should also make sure that their vendors are compliant with relevant regulations such as GDPR, HIPAA, and PCI-DSS. Regular monitoring and auditing of vendor practices can also help to ensure that data is being properly secured.

6. What are some emerging cybersecurity threats that organizations should be aware of, and how can they protect against them?

Answer: Emerging cybersecurity threats that organizations should be aware of include AI-powered attacks, IoT-based attacks, and supply chain attacks. AI-powered attacks can use machine learning algorithms to target vulnerabilities in an organization's systems, while IoT-based attacks can exploit vulnerabilities in connected devices such as smart home appliances and industrial control systems. Supply chain attacks can occur when attackers target third-party vendors and suppliers to gain access to an organization's data or systems. To protect against these threats, organizations should implement strong security controls and monitoring practices, as well as regularly assess and update

7. What is computer security, and why is it important?
Answer: Computer security refers to the protection of computer systems and networks from unauthorized access, theft, damage, or other malicious attacks. It is important because it helps to ensure the confidentiality, integrity, and availability of sensitive data and critical systems.

8. What are the main threats to computer security?
Answer: The main threats to computer security include malware (such as viruses, worms, and Trojan horses), phishing and social engineering attacks, ransomware, denial-of-service attacks, and insider threats.

9. What is encryption, and how does it help improve computer security?

Answer: Encryption is the process of converting plain text into an unreadable form, known as ciphertext, using a mathematical algorithm and a key. It helps improve computer security by protecting data from unauthorized access, theft, or modification.

10. What is a firewall, and how does it help improve computer security?

Answer: A firewall is a network security device that monitors and controls the incoming and outgoing network traffic based on a set of rules. It helps improve computer security by blocking unauthorized access, preventing malware infections, and filtering out potentially harmful traffic.

11. What is two-factor authentication, and how does it help improve computer security?

Answer: Two-factor authentication is a security process that requires users to provide two different forms of authentication, such as a password and a security token before being granted access to a system or network. It helps improve computer security by making it more difficult for unauthorized users to gain access to sensitive data or systems.

12. What is a vulnerability assessment, and why is it important for computer security?

Answer: A vulnerability assessment is a process of identifying and evaluating potential vulnerabilities in computer systems and networks. It is important for computer security because it helps organizations proactively identify and remediate vulnerabilities before they can be exploited by attackers.

13. What is penetration testing, and why is it important for computer security?

Answer: Penetration testing is a process of simulating a cyber attack on a computer system or network to identify vulnerabilities and weaknesses. It is important for computer security because it helps organizations identify and address security gaps before they can be exploited by attackers.

14. What is a security incident, and how should it be handled?

Answer: A security incident is an event that compromises the confidentiality, integrity, or availability of computer systems or data. It should be handled by following a predefined incident response plan, which outlines the steps to be taken in the event of a security incident, such as containment, investigation, and remediation.

15. What is malware, and how can it be prevented or removed?

Answer: Malware is a type of software that is designed to cause harm to computer systems or networks. It can be prevented or removed by using antivirus software, keeping software up to date, avoiding suspicious links or downloads, and practising good cyber hygiene.

16. What is social engineering, and how can it be prevented?

Answer: Social engineering is a type of attack that relies on manipulating people into divulging sensitive information or performing actions that are not in their best interest. It can be prevented by raising awareness among employees about the risks of social engineering, providing security training, and implementing security policies and procedures.

17. What is ransomware, and how can it be prevented or mitigated?

Answer: Ransomware is a type of malware that encrypts data on a computer system or network and demands a ransom in exchange for the decryption key. It can be prevented or mitigated by using antivirus software, keeping software up to date, backing up data regularly, and implementing security policies and procedures.

18. What is a denial-of-service attack, and how can it be prevented in computer security?

Answer: A denial-of-service (DoS) attack is a type of cyberattack that floods a network or system with traffic, causing it to become unavailable. It can be prevented in computer security by using firewalls, intrusion detection systems, and other security measures to block or filter malicious traffic.

19. What is phishing, and how can it be prevented in computer security?

Answer: Phishing is a type of cyberattack that uses fake emails or websites to trick users into revealing sensitive information, such as passwords or credit card numbers. It can be prevented in computer security by using spam filters, educating users about phishing scams, and implementing multi-factor authentication.

20. What is patch management, and why is it important for computer security?

Answer: Patch management is the process of applying software updates or patches to computer systems and networks to fix known vulnerabilities and security flaws. It is important for computer security because unpatched systems can be exploited by attackers to gain unauthorized access or cause damage.

21. What is a security audit, and how can it improve computer security?

Answer: A security audit is a process of evaluating the security of a computer system or network to identify vulnerabilities and assess the effectiveness of security measures. It can improve computer security by identifying and addressing weaknesses before they can be exploited by attackers.

22. What is an intrusion detection system, and how can it be used in computer security?

Answer: An intrusion detection system (IDS) is a network security device that monitors network traffic for signs of unauthorized access or malicious activity. It can be used in computer security to detect and

Sample Interview Questions for Computer Programmers

1. What is the difference between compiled and interpreted languages?

Answer: Compiled languages are those in which the source code is compiled into machine code or executable code before the program is run. This means that the code is translated into a language that the computer can understand directly, which can result in faster and more efficient execution. Interpreted languages, on the other hand, are those in which the source code is interpreted by the computer at runtime. This means that the code is translated into machine code on the fly, which can result in slower performance but can also make the code more flexible and easier to debug.

2. What is object-oriented programming, and what are some of its advantages?

Answer: Object-oriented programming (OOP) is a programming paradigm that focuses on creating objects that encapsulate data and behaviour. OOP is based on the concept of classes, which are blueprints for objects that define their attributes and methods. Some of the advantages of OOP include code reuse, encapsulation, and modularity. By creating reusable classes and objects, OOP can help to simplify code and make it easier to maintain. Encapsulation can help to protect data and methods from being modified or accessed by unauthorized code, while modularity can help to make code more scalable and easier to test.

3. What are some best practices for writing maintainable code?

Answer: Some best practices for writing maintainable code include using descriptive and meaningful variable and function names, writing clear and concise comments, and organizing code into logical modules or classes. Additionally, writing code that follows established style guidelines can help to make it more consistent and easier to read. Other best practices include avoiding complex or nested control structures, minimizing the use of global variables, and using exception handling to handle errors and edge cases.

4. What is version control, and how can it help developers manage their code?

Answer: Version control is a system for managing changes to code and other digital assets over time. It allows developers to track changes to their code, collaborate with other developers, and revert changes if necessary. Version control can also help to keep a history of changes to the code, which can be useful for debugging or troubleshooting. Some popular version control systems include Git, SVN, and Mercurial.

5. What is a design pattern, and how can it help improve the quality of code?

Answer: A design pattern is a reusable solution to a common programming problem or challenge. Design patterns can help to improve the quality of code by promoting good coding practices and providing a common vocabulary for developers to use when discussing code. By using design patterns, developers can create code that is more flexible, maintainable, and scalable. Some common design patterns include the Singleton pattern, the Factory pattern, and the Observer pattern.

6. What are some best practices for debugging code?

Answer: Some best practices for debugging code include using logging and debugging tools to help identify and isolate issues, writing clear and informative error messages, and using a systematic approach to isolate and fix bugs. Additionally, developers should always test their code thoroughly before deploying it and should use automated testing tools to catch issues before they become problems. Finally, it is important to maintain a positive attitude and remain patient and persistent when debugging code, as finding and fixing issues can sometimes be a complex and time-consuming process.

7. What inspired you to become a computer programmer?
Answer: I have always had an interest in technology and how it can be used to solve problems. When I learned about computer programming and how it could be used to create software, automate tasks, and build applications, I was immediately hooked.

8. How do you stay up-to-date with the latest trends and developments in computer programming?

Answer: I stay up-to-date with the latest trends and developments in computer programming by reading industry blogs, attending conferences, and participating in online communities. I also like to experiment with new technologies and try out different programming languages to stay current.

9. What programming languages are you proficient in?

Answer: I am proficient in a variety of programming languages, including Java, Python, JavaScript, and C++. I also have experience with HTML, CSS, and SQL.

10. What is your approach to debugging complex code?

Answer: My approach to debugging complex code is to break the problem down into smaller parts and isolate the issue. I like to use debugging tools and step through the code to identify the root cause of the problem. Once I have identified the issue, I work to find a solution and test it thoroughly.

11. What is your experience with agile software development?

Answer: I have extensive experience with agile software development methodologies, including Scrum and Kanban. I have worked on multiple agile teams and understand the importance of collaboration, communication, and iteration in delivering high-quality software.

12. How do you approach testing your code?

Answer: I approach testing my code by writing automated unit tests and integration tests. I also like to perform manual testing to ensure that the software meets the user's requirements and expectations.

13. Can you describe a project that you worked on and what you learned from it?

Answer: One project that I worked on involved developing a mobile app that integrated with an existing web-based platform. During the project, I learned a lot about mobile development, including the unique challenges of building software for small screens and touch-based interfaces. I also learned a lot about integrating different systems and APIs.

14. What is your experience with version control systems like Git?

Answer: I have extensive experience using Git for version control. I understand how to create branches, merge changes, and resolve conflicts. I also have experience with GitHub and GitLab for collaboration and code review.

15. Can you explain the difference between functional programming and object-oriented programming?

Answer: Functional programming is a programming paradigm that focuses on writing code that is composed of pure functions. These functions do not have any side effects and always return the same output given the same input. Object-oriented programming, on the other hand, focuses on creating objects that encapsulate data and behaviour. Objects can interact with each other to solve problems.

16. How do you ensure that your code is maintainable and scalable?

Answer: I ensure that my code is maintainable and scalable by following best practices like writing clean and readable code, using design patterns, and separating concerns. I also like to document my code and use comments to explain complex logic or algorithms.

17. What is your experience with cloud computing and serverless architecture?

Answer: I have experience with cloud computing platforms like AWS, Google Cloud Platform, and Microsoft Azure. I have also worked with serverless architecture using technologies like AWS Lambda and Google Cloud Functions.

18. Can you explain how HTTP works?

Answer: HTTP, or Hypertext Transfer Protocol, is a protocol used to transfer data over the internet. It uses a client-server model, where the client sends a request to the server and the server responds with a response. HTTP requests and responses are composed of headers and a message body.

Sample Interview Questions for Computer Engineers

1. What inspired you to pursue a career in computer engineering?

Answer: My passion for technology and problem-solving led me to pursue a career in computer engineering. I have always been fascinated by the way computers work and how they can be used to solve complex problems.

2. What programming languages are you proficient in?

Answer: I am proficient in several programming languages, including C, C++, Java, Python, and Assembly Language. I am also experienced in web development technologies like HTML, CSS, and JavaScript.

3. Can you explain the difference between hardware and software?

Answer: Hardware refers to the physical components of a computer system, such as the CPU, RAM, and hard drive. Software, on the other hand, refers to the programs and instructions that run on the hardware.

4. What is your experience with circuit design and analysis?

Answer: I have experience with circuit design and analysis, including using software tools like LTSpice and Multisim. I also have experience with analogue and digital circuit design.

5. How do you approach troubleshooting hardware issues?

Answer: When troubleshooting hardware issues, I first try to isolate the problem and determine whether it is a hardware or software issue. If it is a hardware issue, I will use diagnostic tools and techniques like multimeters and oscilloscopes to identify the root cause of the problem.

6. Can you explain the difference between digital and analogue signals?

Answer: Digital signals are discrete signals that can only have two possible states, typically represented as 0 and 1. Analog signals, on the other hand, are continuous signals that can have an infinite number of possible values.

7. What is your experience with microcontrollers and embedded systems?

Answer: I have experience with microcontrollers like Arduino and Raspberry Pi, as well as embedded systems development. I have worked on projects that involved designing and programming custom hardware to solve specific problems.

8. Can you explain the difference between synchronous and asynchronous communication protocols?

Answer: Synchronous communication protocols involve transmitting data in real time and require both the sender and receiver to operate on the same clock. Asynchronous communication protocols, on the other hand, involve transmitting data at irregular intervals and do not require a shared clock.

9. What is your experience with digital signal processing?

Answer: I have experience with digital signal processing techniques like Fourier analysis and filtering. I have also worked on projects that involved implementing real-time signal-processing algorithms on microcontrollers.

10. Can you explain the difference between sequential and combinational logic circuits?

Answer: Sequential logic circuits contain memory elements like flip-flops and registers and can store information from previous inputs. Combinational logic circuits, on the other hand, do not have memory elements and produce outputs based solely on the current input.

11. What is your experience with operating systems like Windows and Linux?

Answer: I have experience with operating systems like Windows and Linux and understand how they manage system resources and provide a platform for software development.

12. Can you explain the difference between RAM and ROM?

Answer: RAM (Random Access Memory) is a type of memory that is used for the temporary storage of data and program code while a computer is running. ROM (Read-Only Memory), on the other hand, is a type of memory that contains permanent data and program code that cannot be modified.

13. What is your experience with network protocols like TCP/IP and UDP?

Answer: I have experience with network protocols like TCP/IP and UDP and understand how they enable communication between devices on a network. I have also worked with network programming APIs like sockets in languages like C and Python.

Sample Interview Questions for Data Analysis experts

1. What inspired you to pursue a career in data analysis?

Answer: My passion for working with data and finding insights from it inspired me to pursue a career in data analysis. I enjoy the challenge of turning complex data into actionable insights that can drive business decisions.

2. Can you describe your experience with data analysis software like Excel and SQL?

Answer: I have extensive experience working with data analysis software like Excel and SQL. I am comfortable using Excel to manipulate and analyze large data sets, and I have experience using SQL to query databases and extract relevant data.

3. Can you walk me through your data analysis process?

Answer: My data analysis process involves gathering and cleaning data, exploring and visualizing data to identify patterns and trends, and then using statistical techniques to draw insights and make recommendations.

4. What is your experience with data visualization tools like Tableau or Power BI?

Answer: I have experience using data visualization tools like Tableau and Power BI to create interactive dashboards and visualizations that allow stakeholders to explore data and gain insights quickly.

5. How do you ensure data accuracy and integrity in your analysis?

Answer: I ensure data accuracy and integrity by carefully validating and cleaning data before beginning analysis, using appropriate statistical techniques, and constantly reviewing my work to ensure that it aligns with business objectives.

6. Can you give an example of a time when you identified a significant insight from a data analysis project?

Answer: One example of a significant insight I uncovered was identifying a correlation between customer satisfaction scores and the amount of time spent on hold when calling customer service. This insight led to changes in the customer service process that resulted in improved customer satisfaction and a reduction in customer complaints.

7. What is your experience with machine learning algorithms and predictive modelling?

Answer: I have experience using machine learning algorithms and predictive modelling techniques to build predictive models and identify trends and patterns in large datasets.

8. Can you describe your experience with database management systems?

Answer: I have experience working with database management systems like Oracle and SQL

Server, including designing and implementing database structures, creating queries and stored procedures, and optimizing database performance.

9. How do you communicate data analysis findings to non-technical stakeholders?

Answer: I use visualizations, data storytelling techniques, and clear, concise language to communicate data analysis findings to non-technical stakeholders. I focus on providing actionable insights that align with business objectives and can be easily understood by a broad audience.

10. What is your experience with data privacy and security regulations like GDPR and CCPA?

Answer: I have experience working with data privacy and security regulations like GDPR and CCPA, including understanding their requirements and implementing appropriate measures to ensure compliance.

11. Can you describe a time when you had to collaborate with other departments or stakeholders to complete a data analysis project?

Answer: I have collaborated with other departments and stakeholders on several data analysis projects. One example is a project where I worked closely with the marketing department to analyze customer data and identify trends in customer behaviour that could inform marketing strategies.

12. What is your experience with big data technologies like Hadoop and Spark?

Answer: I have experience working with big data technologies like Hadoop and Spark, including setting up clusters, configuring data pipelines, and optimizing performance.

13. Can you explain how you stay up-to-date with the latest trends and developments in the field of data analysis?

Answer: I stay up-to-date with the latest trends and developments in the field of data analysis by attending conferences, reading industry publications, and participating in online communities and forums. I also regularly participate in training and certification programs to expand my knowledge and skill set.

Sample Interview Questions for Digital Media and Graphics experts

1. What inspired you to pursue a career in digital media and graphics?

Answer: I have always been fascinated by the intersection of art and technology. Digital media and graphics allow me to use my creativity and technical skills to create visual experiences that can communicate complex ideas and emotions.

2. Can you describe your experience with graphic design software like Adobe Creative Suite?

Answer: I have extensive experience working with graphic design software like Adobe Creative Suite, including Photoshop, Illustrator, and InDesign. I am comfortable using these tools to create designs for both print and digital media.

3. Can you walk me through your graphic design process?

Answer: My graphic design process involves researching the project's requirements and audience, creating sketches and rough drafts, refining the design, and delivering a final product that meets the client's needs.

4. What is your experience with video editing software like Premiere Pro and Final Cut Pro?

Answer: I have experience using video editing software like Premiere Pro and Final Cut Pro to edit and create video content. I am comfortable working with timelines, transitions, and effects to create visually engaging videos.

5. Can you give an example of a time when you used digital media and graphics to solve a complex problem?

Answer: One example of using digital media and graphics to solve a complex problem was creating an infographic for a client that clearly explained a complicated medical process. The infographic used visual elements to simplify the process and make it easier for patients to understand.

6. Can you describe your experience with web design and development?

Answer: I have experience designing and developing websites using HTML, CSS, and JavaScript. I am comfortable using content management systems like WordPress and Drupal and have experience creating responsive designs that work across multiple devices.

7. What is your experience with user experience design?

Answer: I have experience creating user experience designs that prioritize user needs and make it easy for users to complete tasks. I am comfortable using user research and user testing to inform design decisions and create intuitive interfaces.

8. Can you give an example of a time when you used data analysis to inform your digital media and graphics work?

Answer: One example of using data analysis to inform digital media and graphics work was analyzing website traffic data to inform design decisions for a client's website. The data showed that users were having trouble finding key information, which led to changes in the site's navigation and content organization.

9. Can you describe a time when you had to collaborate with other departments or stakeholders to complete a digital media and graphics project?

Answer: I have collaborated with other departments and stakeholders on several digital media and graphics projects. One example is a project where I worked with the marketing department to create a series of social media graphics that aligned with the company's branding and marketing objectives.

10. Can you describe your experience with motion graphics and animation software like After Effects?

Answer: I have experience using motion graphics and animation software like After Effects to create visually engaging animations and videos. I am comfortable using keyframes, animation presets, and other tools to create dynamic visuals.

11. Can you explain your approach to creating a brand identity?

Answer: My approach to creating a brand identity involves researching the company's values, mission, and target audience, creating a visual style that aligns with these elements, and refining the design based on feedback and testing.

12. Can you describe your experience with 3D modelling and rendering software like Maya or Blender?

Answer: I have experience using 3D modellings and rendering software like Maya and Blender to create 3D models and animations. I am comfortable using modelling tools, materials, lighting, and rendering settings to create realistic and visually appealing 3D visuals.

Sample Interview Questions for Artificial Intelligence and Robotics Experts

1. What inspired you to pursue a career in AI and Robotics?

Answer: I have always been fascinated by the intersection of technology and human behaviour. AI and robotics allow me to use my technical skills to create intelligent systems that can interact with humans and solve complex problems.

2. Can you describe your experience with programming languages commonly used in AI and robotics, such as Python and C++?

Answer: I have extensive experience programming in languages commonly used in AI and robotics, including Python and C++. I am comfortable using these languages to create algorithms and models that power intelligent systems.

3. Can you walk me through your process for developing an AI or robotics system?

Answer: My process for developing an AI or robotics system involves identifying the problem or opportunity, gathering data and defining the requirements, creating a model or algorithm that meets those requirements, testing and refining the system, and deploying it in the real world.

4. Can you give an example of a time when you used AI or robotics to solve a complex problem?

Answer: One example of using AI to solve a complex problem was creating a natural language processing model that could accurately classify and respond to customer support inquiries. The system used machine learning to improve its accuracy over time, resulting in faster response times and higher customer satisfaction.

5. Can you describe your experience with machine learning and deep learning algorithms?

Answer: I have extensive experience working with machine learning and deep learning algorithms, including supervised and unsupervised learning, neural networks, and reinforcement learning. I am comfortable using these techniques to create models that can classify, predict, or optimize outcomes.

6. Can you give an example of a project where you used computer vision to create an AI or robotics system?

Answer: One example of using computer vision to create an AI or robotics system was developing an autonomous drone that could navigate through complex environments using visual cues. The drone used a combination of cameras, machine learning algorithms, and motion planning to navigate through tight spaces and avoid obstacles.

7. Can you describe your experience with natural language processing and chatbot development?

Answer: I have experience developing chatbots that use natural language processing to understand and respond to user inquiries. I am comfortable working with tools like Dialogflow and creating custom chatbot models using machine learning algorithms.

8. Can you give an example of a time when you used robotics to solve a real-world problem?

Answer: One example of using robotics to solve a real-world problem was developing a robotic arm that could assist with surgical procedures. The arm used sensors and machine learning algorithms to precisely control its movements, reducing the risk of human error and improving surgical outcomes.

9. Can you describe your experience with reinforcement learning and how you have used it in AI and robotics projects?

Answer: I have experience using reinforcement learning to create AI and robotics systems that can learn from experience and optimize their behaviour over time. One example is developing a self-driving car that uses reinforcement learning to improve its driving behaviour based on feedback from its environment.

10. Can you explain your approach to creating a humanoid robot?

Answer: My approach to creating a humanoid robot involves designing a physical form that is both functional and aesthetically pleasing, programming the robot with intelligent algorithms that can interpret and respond to sensory input, and training the robot through interactions with humans and its environment.

11. Can you give an example of a project where you used AI and robotics to address an environmental or social issue?

One example of using AI and robotics to address an environmental issue is the use of autonomous drones to monitor and protect endangered species. In this project, we developed a system that uses drones equipped with cameras and machine-learning algorithms to identify and track animals in their natural habitats. The system can detect changes in behaviour or habitat and alert conservationists to potential threats, allowing them to take action to protect the animals.

Another example of using AI and robotics to address a social issue is developing robotic prosthetics that can be controlled using neural signals from the user's brain. These prosthetics can help people with disabilities regain mobility and independence, improving their quality of life and reducing the social stigma associated with disability. The use of AI algorithms and machine learning can help improve the accuracy and precision of prosthetics, making them more effective and user-friendly.

Sample Interview Questions for System Analysis experts

1. Can you describe your experience with system analysis and design?

Answer: I have extensive experience with system analysis and design, including requirements gathering, system modelling, and creating technical specifications. I have worked on projects ranging from small software systems to large-scale enterprise applications.

2. Can you walk me through your process for conducting a system analysis?

Answer: My process for conducting a system analysis involves understanding the problem or opportunity, gathering and analyzing user requirements, creating system models to visualize and validate the solution, and creating a technical specification that outlines the system architecture, components, and interfaces.

3. Can you describe your experience with software development life cycles, such as Agile or Waterfall?

Answer: I have experience working with various software development life cycles, including Agile and Waterfall. I am comfortable using Agile methodologies like Scrum and Kanban to manage development processes and ensure the timely delivery of quality software.

4. Can you give an example of a time when you identified a gap in a system and developed a solution to fill that gap?

Answer: One example of identifying a gap in a system and developing a solution was when I worked on a project to automate a manual data entry process. I identified that the manual process was prone to errors and was time-consuming, so I proposed a solution that used optical character recognition (OCR) technology to automatically extract data from scanned documents, reducing errors and improving efficiency.

5. Can you describe your experience with system modelling tools such as UML?

Answer: I have experience using system modelling tools like UML to create visual representations of systems and their components. I am comfortable using UML to create use case diagrams, class diagrams, and activity diagrams.

6. Can you give an example of a project where you used system analysis and design to improve a business process?

Answer: One example of using system analysis and design to improve a business process was developing a customer relationship management system for a retail company. The system included features like customer profiles, purchase histories, and targeted marketing campaigns, resulting in improved customer engagement and sales.

7. Can you describe your experience with creating technical specifications for software systems?

Answer: I have experience creating technical specifications for software systems that outline the system architecture, components, interfaces, and dependencies. These specifications help ensure that the software meets the functional and non-functional requirements and can be used as a guide for developers during the implementation phase.

8. Can you give an example of a time when you had to make trade-offs between system requirements and constraints?

Answer: One example of making trade-offs between system requirements and constraints was when I worked on a project to develop a mobile application for a client. The client had a strict deadline and limited budget, so we had to prioritize features and optimize the system architecture to meet the requirements within the constraints.

9. Can you describe your experience with database design and management?

Answer: I have experience designing and managing databases for software systems using technologies like MySQL, Oracle, and MongoDB. I am comfortable designing database schemas, writing queries, and optimizing database performance.

10. Can you give an example of a project where you used system analysis and design to integrate multiple systems?

Answer: One example of using system analysis and design to integrate multiple systems was developing an enterprise resource planning system for a manufacturing company. The system integrated data from multiple sources, including inventory, production, and finance systems, providing a unified view of the company's operations and enabling better decision-making.

11. Can you describe your experience with software testing and quality assurance?

Answer: I have experience designing and executing software tests to ensure that software systems meet functional and non-functional requirements. I am comfortable using tools like Selenium and JUnit for automated testing and have experience with manual testing as well.

12. Can you give an example of a project where you used system analysis and design to improve user experience
One example of a project where I used system analysis and design to improve user experience was when I worked on a website redesign project for a client. The client had received feedback from users that the existing website was difficult to navigate and confusing to use, leading to a high bounce rate and low engagement.

To address these issues, I conducted a system analysis to understand the user needs and requirements for the website. I used techniques like user interviews, user surveys, and usability testing to gather feedback and insights from users. Based on the feedback, I created a user persona and user journey map to visualize the user experience and identify pain points and areas for improvement.

Using this information, I worked with the design team to create a new user interface design that was intuitive, easy to navigate, and visually appealing. We also restructured the website content and navigation to better align with user needs and expectations.

During the implementation phase, I worked closely with the development team to ensure that the new design was implemented accurately and that the website was optimized for performance and usability.

After the website redesign, we conducted user testing to evaluate the effectiveness of the changes. The results showed a significant improvement in user engagement, with a lower bounce rate and higher conversion rate. Overall, the system analysis and design process helped us to improve the user experience and meet the client's goals for the project.

Sample Interview Questions for Digita Marketing and Social Networking experts

1. What is your approach to creating a successful digital marketing strategy?

A successful digital marketing strategy requires a deep understanding of the target audience, market trends, and competitive landscape. My approach starts with researching to identify the target audience's needs, pain points, and behaviour. This information helps to create buyer personas that represent the ideal customer and guide the development of messaging and content.

Next, I evaluate the competitive landscape to identify opportunities and gaps in the market. This analysis helps to identify unique value propositions and messaging that differentiate the brand from competitors. Based on this information, I develop a comprehensive marketing plan that includes a mix of tactics such as search engine optimization (SEO), content marketing, social media marketing, email marketing, and advertising.

I regularly evaluate the effectiveness of the strategy through analytics and adjust tactics as needed to improve performance and meet business objectives.

2. How do you measure the success of a social media campaign?

The success of a social media campaign can be measured through various metrics such as engagement, reach, impressions, conversions, and brand sentiment. Engagement metrics such as likes, comments, and shares indicate how well the content resonates with the target audience. Reach and impressions metrics indicate how many people were exposed to the content. Conversions metrics such as clicks, leads, and sales indicate how well the campaign is achieving its objectives.

Brand sentiment metrics such as the tone of mentions and comments can provide insights into how the campaign is affecting the brand's reputation. Other metrics to consider are the cost per click (CPC) and cost per acquisition (CPA), which indicate the effectiveness of the campaign in generating revenue.

It is essential to regularly monitor these metrics and adjust the campaign strategy as needed to improve performance and achieve business objectives.

3. Can you describe a successful digital marketing campaign you've led in the past?
Answer: One successful digital marketing campaign I led in the past was for a consumer goods company launching a new product line. Our goal was to increase brand awareness, generate leads, and drive sales through digital channels. We developed a multi-channel campaign that included social media, email marketing, influencer marketing, and search advertising.

We started by creating a social media strategy that focused on engaging with our target audience through user-generated content and influencer partnerships. We identified and reached out to relevant influencers in our industry, offering them free products in exchange for promoting our brand on their social media channels. This generated a lot of buzz and social media engagement, leading to an increase in brand awareness.

We also created a targeted email marketing campaign that segmented our audience based on their interests and past purchase behaviour. This allowed us to deliver personalized and relevant messaging to each segment, resulting in a higher open rate and click-through rate.

In addition, we ran search advertising campaigns targeting relevant keywords and landing pages optimized for conversions. This drove high-quality traffic to our website and increased our lead generation and sales numbers.

Overall, the campaign was a huge success, exceeding our goals for brand awareness, lead generation, and sales. It was a great example of the power of a multi-channel digital marketing approach.

4.   How do you measure the effectiveness of a social media campaign?
Answer: Measuring the effectiveness of a social media campaign is essential to understanding its impact and making informed decisions for future campaigns. There are several key metrics to consider when evaluating a social media campaign's effectiveness.

First, reach and impressions are important indicators of how many people were exposed to your content. This can be measured through social media analytics tools like Facebook Insights, Twitter Analytics, or Instagram Insights.

Engagement metrics, such as likes, comments, shares, and retweets, can also provide insights into the level of audience engagement and how well your content resonated with your target audience.

Conversion metrics, such as click-through rates and conversion rates, can help you understand how many people took action as a result of your social media content. This can include website visits, form submissions, or product purchases.

Finally, it's important to track the overall return on investment (ROI) of your social media campaign. This can include metrics such as cost per click, cost per conversion, and revenue generated from the campaign.

By analyzing these metrics, you can gain a better understanding of the effectiveness of your social media campaign and make data-driven decisions for future campaigns.

Sample Interview Questions for E-Learning experts

1. How do you decide on the appropriate e-learning strategies and instructional methods for a given learning objective?

When designing e-learning, it is important to first understand the learning objectives and then choose strategies and methods that align with those objectives. This involves identifying the target audience and their preferred learning styles, as well as considering factors such as the level of interactivity and multimedia elements that will engage learners. Additionally, it is essential to evaluate the effectiveness of different strategies and methods through user testing and assessment data.

2. How do you ensure that e-learning courses are accessible to learners with disabilities?

To ensure accessibility for learners with disabilities, e-learning designers need to follow accessibility guidelines such as the Web Content Accessibility Guidelines (WCAG). This involves making sure that e-learning courses are compatible with assistive technologies such as screen readers, providing alternative text for images and videos, and ensuring that the course is navigable using a keyboard. Additionally, designers can seek input from users with disabilities during the design and development process to identify and address any accessibility issues.

3. How do you incorporate feedback from learners into the design process of e-learning courses?

Incorporating feedback from learners is crucial to ensuring that e-learning courses meet their needs and are effective in achieving the intended learning outcomes. This can involve using surveys, focus groups, and user testing to gather feedback from learners at different stages of the design process. Designers should take feedback seriously and make changes based on the input received, while also considering the feasibility and impact of proposed changes.

4. How do you ensure that e-learning courses are engaging and interactive?

To make e-learning courses engaging and interactive, designers can incorporate a variety of multimedia elements such as videos, animations, and interactive simulations. Additionally, they can use gamification techniques such as leaderboards, badges, and rewards to motivate learners and increase engagement. Designers should also consider the pace of the course, ensuring that learners are not overloaded with information and that the course is broken up into digestible sections with frequent opportunities for learners to apply their knowledge.

5. How do you evaluate the effectiveness of e-learning courses?

To evaluate the effectiveness of e-learning courses, designers can use a variety of methods such as pre-and post-assessment tests, surveys, and feedback from learners and instructors. Additionally, designers should analyze data on learner performance and behaviour, such as completion rates and time spent on different sections of the course. By evaluating the effectiveness of e-learning courses, designers can identify areas for improvement and make changes to enhance the learning experience.

6. How do you ensure that e-learning courses are culturally appropriate and sensitive?

To ensure that e-learning courses are culturally appropriate and sensitive, designers should take into account the cultural backgrounds and diversity of the target audience. This can involve incorporating diverse perspectives and examples into the course content, using inclusive language, and avoiding stereotypes and cultural biases. Additionally, designers can seek input from members of the target audience to identify and address any cultural concerns or issues.

INDEX

BIBLIOGRAPHY

Bates, A. W., & Poole, G. (2003). Effective teaching with technology in higher education: Foundations for success. Jossey-Bass.

Blank, S. G., & Dorf, B. (2012). The startup owner's manual: The step-by-step guide for building a great company. K&S Ranch.

Boyd, D., & Ellison, N. B. (2007). Social network sites: Definition, history, and scholarship. Journal of Computer-Mediated Communication, 13(1), 210-230.

Brynjolfsson, E., & McAfee, A. (2014). The second machine age: Work, progress, and prosperity in a time of brilliant technologies. WW Norton & Company.

Bureau of Labor Statistics. (2021). Occupational outlook handbook: Computer and information technology occupations. U.S. Department of Labor.

Castells, M. (2000). The rise of the network society. Blackwell Publishers.

Davis, G. B., & Olson, M. H. (1985). Management information systems: conceptual foundations, structure, and development. McGraw-Hill.

Dice. (2021). Tech salary report. Retrieved from https://www.dice.com/salary-calculator

Feld, B. (2012). Startup communities: Building an entrepreneurial ecosystem in your city. John Wiley & Sons.

Flanagan, D. (2017). JavaScript: The definitive guide. O'Reilly Media, Inc.

Foley, J. D., van Dam, A., Feiner, S. K., & Hughes, J. F. (1990). Computer graphics: principles and practice. Addison-Wesley Professional.

Hennessy, J. L., & Patterson, D. A. (2017). Computer architecture: a quantitative approach. Morgan Kaufmann.

Hockenberry, C. (2017). iOS programming: The Big Nerd Ranch guide. Big Nerd Ranch.

Horton, W. (2014). E-learning by design. John Wiley & Sons.

Kelleher, J. D., & Tierney, B. (2018). Data science: an introduction. CRC Press.

Kernighan, B. W., & Ritchie, D. M. (1988). The C programming language. Prentice Hall.

Kshetri, N. (2018). Blockchain's roles in meeting key supply chain management objectives. International Journal of Information Management, 39, 80-89.

Kurose, J. F., & Ross, K. W. (2017). Computer networking: a top-down approach. Pearson.

Lee, R. B. (2010). The design of CMOS radio-frequency integrated circuits. Cambridge University Press.

Li, C., & Bernoff, J. (2011). Groundswell: Winning in a world transformed by social technologies. Harvard Business Review Press.

Liu, Y., & Li, L. (2018). Digital media and society: transforming economics, politics and social practices. Routledge.

Martin, R. C. (2008). Clean code: a handbook of agile software craftsmanship. Prentice Hall.

Murphy, R. R., & Woods, D. D. (2009). Key issues in robotics. IEEE Robotics & Automation Magazine, 16(3), 33-45.

Provost, F., & Fawcett, T. (2013). Data science for business: what you need to know about data mining and data-analytic thinking. O'Reilly Media, Inc.

Rosenfeld, L., & Morville, P. (2006). Information architecture for the World Wide Web: designing

ABOUT THE AUTHOR

Mniko Simon works as Assistant Lecturer(Informatics) at the Institute of Accountancy Arusha-Dar es salaam Campus. Mniko has an impressive educational background, having obtained a Master's degree in Information and Communication Technology for Development from the College of Business Education Dar es Salaam in 2018 and a Bachelor's degree in Information Systems from The University of Dodoma in 2012.

From 2013 to 2021, he worked full-time as an ICT Officer-Data Management at The Open University of Tanzania, where he played a crucial role in managing and analyzing data for the university. From 2016 to 2021, he worked as a part-time research assistant and data manager at KU-Leuven-The Open University of Tanzania Project, where he honed his skills in data management, analysis, and research. He has also pursued various courses and certifications to enhance his skills and knowledge.

Mniko Simon is a highly skilled and accomplished professional who has significantly contributed to ICT, research, and web development. His passion for learning and development and his advanced skills and qualifications make him knowledgeable in ICT Profession.

Made in the USA
Columbia, SC
31 May 2023

17553420R00154